Prisons and Health in the Age
of Mass Incarceration

Prisons and Health in the Age of Mass Incarceration

Jason Schnittker
University of Pennsylvania

Michael Massoglia
University of Wisconsin

Christopher Uggen
University of Minnesota

OXFORD
UNIVERSITY PRESS

Oxford University Press is a department of the University of Oxford. It furthers the University's objective of excellence in research, scholarship, and education by publishing worldwide. Oxford is a registered trade mark of Oxford University Press in the UK and certain other countries.

Published in the United States of America by Oxford University Press
198 Madison Avenue, New York, NY 10016, United States of America.

© Oxford University Press 2022

Library of Congress Cataloging-in-Publication Data
Names: Schnittker, Jason, author. | Massoglia, Michael, author. |
Uggen, Christopher, author.
Title: Prisons and health in the age of mass incarceration /
Jason Schnittker, Michael Massoglia, Christopher Uggen.
Description: New York, NY : Oxford University Press, 2022. |
Series: Studies crime and public policy series | Includes bibliographical references and index.
Identifiers: LCCN 2022002734 (print) | LCCN 2022002735 (ebook) |
ISBN 9780190603823 (hardback) | ISBN 9780190603847 (epub)
Subjects: LCSH: Imprisonment. | Prisoners—Health and hygiene. |
Ex-convicts—Health aspects. | Ex-convicts—Social conditions.
Classification: LCC HV8705 .S35 2022 (print) | LCC HV8705 (ebook) |
DDC 365—dc23/eng/20220224
LC record available at https://lccn.loc.gov/2022002734
LC ebook record available at https://lccn.loc.gov/2022002735

DOI: 10.1093/oso/9780190603823.001.0001

1 3 5 7 9 8 6 4 2

Printed by Sheridan Books, Inc., United States of America

Contents

Acknowledgments

We would like to thank Sarah Shannon, Suzy Maves McElrath, Michael Vuolo, Naomi Cowan, Anneliese Ward, Melissa Thompson, Sara Wakefield, and Valerio Bacak with help on various parts of this book, including with some of the underlying research. We also thank Felix Elwert, Mike Light, Ted Gerber, Brianna Remster, John Karl Scholz, Carolyn Lesch, Martine Delaney, Mustafa Emirbayer, Glenn Firebaugh, Roger Finke, and Colin Massoglia. James Cook at Oxford was instrumental in formulating the original scope and organization of this book, and Meredith Keffer and Macey Fairchild helped to carry it across the finish line. This research was partially supported by the University of Wisconsin–Madison Office of the Vice Chancellor and Graduate Education, with funding from the Wisconsin Alumni Research Foundation. We are also grateful to the Robert Wood Johnson Foundation for a Health Investigator Award, which provided essential funding in the early stages of this project. This project has been rewarding not least for bringing us together and putting us in a community of scholars who greatly broadened our individual perspectives.

1
The Institutional Setting of Prisons and Health

In *Homeward*, Bruce Western (2018) describes the shock, panic, and bewilderment of people recently released from prison. After the immediate joy of leaving confinement and returning to family and friends, people released from prison soon encounter stress, isolation, depression, and anxiety. Reintegrating is difficult under the best of circumstances, but it is made all the more difficult by a criminal record and poor health. For many people returning from prison, securing adequate medical care is a relief and even an opportunity. In his interviews, Western describes A.J., who served a two-year sentence, much of it spent in solitary confinement, and continued to suffer from severe anxiety and isolation. But seven weeks from release, A.J. was keen to share good news: "I'm on my meds now. I got a doctor. I can go out and be around people" (p. 56). Another person Western interviewed, Carla, received extensive counseling and medical treatment while in prison, including for hepatitis C, a heart problem, and back pain. But months after release her chronic conditions and disability grew worse, preventing her from working, diminishing her enthusiasm, and accelerating her slide into depression (pp. 58–59).

At the heart of the relationship between prisons and health is a paradox. Prisons are charged, at once, with being punitive and therapeutic, with denying freedom and providing care. Common correctional concepts are replete with ironies. Protective custody, for instance, is a type of confinement where the intent is to shield those in prison from harm, especially from other people in prison. But the idea is a contradiction if custody itself is harmful. And, indeed, incarceration is often harmful. The language of protective custody, for instance, is often used synonymously with solitary confinement, which is especially detrimental to well-being.

The paradoxes are apparent in other ways too. In the spring and summer of 2020, over 900 imprisoned Americans died of COVID-19, and thousands more will die of other causes (Carson and Cowhig 2020). Prisons are implicated in the spread of other infectious diseases as well, including, at least historically, human immunodeficiency virus and tuberculosis. Physical and sexual abuse are not uncommon in prison environments, leading to emotional and physical harm. At the same time, though, many people in prison receive urgently needed health care, and they receive care they likely would not have received prior to incarceration. For many people, incarceration increases their access to medical treatment, leading to meaningful improvements in their health and risk profile, from more accurate diagnoses of long-standing problems, to better blood sugar control, to reduced blood pressure. For young Black men, mortality in prison is lower than mortality outside of prison.

The paradox at the heart of prison health care has, if anything, grown sharper over time. While medicine has expanded the range of therapeutic technologies, and concepts of appropriate punishment have evolved, the legal system has failed to provide guidance for what prisons are obligated to provide with respect to health care, making the tension at the heart of the system even more fraught. The tension is heightened further by the seemingly sharp but actually porous boundaries of the prison system's remit. Whatever care prisons are able to provide to those in their custody ends abruptly at their release, even as the health of those previously in prison grows worse and better access to care would aid their rehabilitation.

Understanding the connection between prisons and health requires us to hold both of these ideas at the same time: prisons can undermine health *and* provide meaningful health care services, and they operate in an environment that insists on both. Understanding the connection also requires us to understand the prison system as a complex institution, operating under a varied set of legal, cultural, and political mandates. As an institution, the prison system ostensibly serves the interests of criminal justice. As with many other institutions, however, prisons are increasingly bound up with a variety of coexisting and often incompatible goals. Prisons are required simultaneously to supervise, punish, correct, and maintain the health of those in their care. The same personnel often serve all these functions at once. Given these mandates, there are important distinctions between what prisons are obligated to do, what they are allowed to do, and what they actually do. In addition, prisons intersect with other institutions charged with the care of similar populations, albeit with different responsibilities and operating principles. At present, for instance, the US prison system provides a good deal of care for those who, in an earlier era, might have been treated in a psychiatric hospital. By some accounts, jails can now be regarded as America's largest system of psychiatric hospitals (Ford 2015).

But the legal mandate that undergirds health care in prisons sets prisons apart from other care-providing institutions. At root, prisons are inimical to health. The law stipulates that US prisons must provide health care, in keeping with the Eighth Amendment's prohibition against cruel and unusual punishment. But the constitutional mandate that supports prison health care is far different from the ethic of care that governs normal health care encounters. Unlike hospitals or clinics, prisons are largely defined by punishment. This, of course, is obvious. Punishment is what most people associate with prisons. Prisons involve cells, restraints, supervision, and serving time. And prisons sometimes are involved in state-sanctioned killing, as in the case of capital punishment. Health is the antithesis of punishment. To punish is to harm and wound, whereas to care is to heal and cure. To discipline is to strip away, whereas to treat is to build up. Guards impose passivity, whereas physicians intervene to allow activity. It is difficult to imagine respecting an oath to *first do no harm* when the institutional prerogative is to penalize. When judges sentence people to prison, they do so under the assumption that the experience will be painful. Some judges go a step further: they believe a prison sentence should be not only painful *in itself*—as if the forceful separation from loved ones and severe restrictions on freedom are insufficient— but also *additionally* painful, such that the material and social conditions of prison life should not be at all conducive to well-being. Some prison and jail officials even boast about the pains they inflict, as when they have no air conditioning in the summer heat, no pay for labor, and food costs of pennies per day (Scott 2011).

To be sure, the philosophy behind incarceration has shifted over time (Clear and Frost 2014). Strict punishment was not always the guiding philosophy. It is possible, for instance, to regard a prison sentence as an opportunity to rehabilitate people, as we did much earlier in our nation's history. It is also possible to regard prisons as a place to provide people with the skills necessary for re-entry, as we did until relatively late in the twentieth century. Yet the present era has been defined primarily in terms of a get-tough approach, as well as a reluctance to extend to people in prison anything that might be considered an amenity. Tellingly, even the shared concept of "rehabilitation" is fundamentally different in prisons and hospitals. In corrections, rehabilitation denotes the elimination of offending, whereas in medicine it denotes improving and restoring capacities. In hospitals, rehabilitation is expansive, whereas in prisons it is restrictive. Rehabilitation becomes reducing recidivism or, even more reductively, reducing the cost to society once someone is released.

Yet the fact remains: the correctional system is plainly in the business of providing care. In fact, states spend a great deal on their prison health care systems. Correctional officers are routinely asked to provide diagnoses of a sort. Police, lawyers, judges, and juries are asked to evaluate mental health in deciding whether to arrest, detain, prosecute, or adjudicate individuals. When they leave prison, people often face new burdens of care and are tasked with properly supporting their health. Before describing the complex web of connections that make this equivalence possible, we should take a step back and define the basic elements of the correctional system.

What Are Prisons?

Prisons are a focal point of the US correctional system. Much of our discussion will center on prisons specifically, including how they have grown, how they affect people, and how they address the health problems of those in their custody. In fact, however, there are different kinds of correctional institutions, and each presents its own set of concerns related to health. State prisons, federal prisons, and local jails differ in their size, procedures, and turnover. State prisons house the most people—about 1.9 million at the start of 2019—and are used primarily to hold those convicted of more serious felony-level crimes or those remanded back to prison for violating conditions of their parole. Jails occasionally serve the same function, although they generally house people serving shorter sentences, as well as those awaiting trial. At any one time, more than half of people in jail are not convicted of the crime they are institutionalized for (Minton 2013; Zeng 2020). Conviction often involves a move. Those in jail who are convicted of a felony, for example, are often moved to a state prison facility. In this sense, jails are an important gateway to the prison system, though for many people their involvement with the correctional system is short-lived if they start in a jail. On average, about 60% of the jail population turns over each week. Turnover is even higher at smaller jails, with jails in some regions having weekly turnover rates exceeding 100% (Minton 2013). Overall, US jails reported 10.7 million admissions in 2018 but a cross-sectional population of 738,400 (Zeng 2020). In terms of exposure, this churn reflects a substantial total volume of correctional contact. Federal prisons, meanwhile, resemble state prisons, though they only house about one-tenth as many people, about 180,000 at the end of 2018 (Zeng 2020). In contrast to jails, most people in federal prisons have been convicted of a crime and are serving their sentence.

Although prisons and jails house most of the people in the US correctional system, it is now increasingly important to add another type of facility to the list. In recent years, almost 400,000 individuals were booked into US Immigration and Customs Enforcement (ICE) custody, and the number of people held by ICE officials had risen to over 40,000 in 2018 (Department of Homeland Security 2019). These people are often, though not always, held in special facilities, separate from state or federal prisons. They are also routinely hidden from conventional mechanisms of oversight. Although the number of such detention centers has grown and indefinite detention is common, people in these facilities still represent a relatively small percentage of the total institutionalized population. Furthermore, such facilities involve a fundamentally different dynamic. When people in immigration facilities are released, they are often deported and, therefore, lost to our discussion in this book of the relationship between re-entry (in the United States) and health (Minton 2013).

Most of this book will focus on people currently and formerly in prison as a mechanism for exploring correctional supervision generally. It is important to note that correctional supervision encompasses more than brick-and-mortar facilities. Although prisons have grown over time, the use of community corrections has increased as well. For instance, in 2018 nearly 4.4 million people were under some form of supervision (Kaeble 2020). Community corrections is a broad category, including both people who have served time in prison and those who have avoided a prison sentence through diversion or conditional release. For the most part, though, community corrections reflects those who have had some exposure to jails, prisons, or other detention facilities at some point in their lifetime. In addition, community corrections is often a *conditional* foothold into the community and sets strong conditions for continued release. Indeed, for many people released from prison, community supervision effectively serves as the point of re-entry back into the prison system. A violation of the terms of supervision can result in being remanded back to prison. In some cases, these violations involve new offenses, but in others they involve "technical" violations, such as failing to report for meetings, testing positive for drugs/alcohol, or violating curfew. The percentage of parolees sent back to prison for technical violations has increased over time, paralleling the increase in the size of the prison population (Glaze and Bonczar 2011; Petersilia 2003).

The Rise and Spread of Incarceration over Time

The prison system would not be so consequential for health were it not for its enormous size. For purposes of understanding the relationship between incarceration and health, several features of this growth are especially important. First, it is important to appreciate the scale of the system as it relates to the scope of its responsibilities. Incarceration is now at such a scale that it has potentiated spillovers between the prison system and other systems, including the labor market and the health care system. A large number of people have been to prison themselves, but even more people have had a son, daughter, partner, or parent serve time in prison. Some of the pressures on the prison system would not be so intense were it not for its reach and the size of the population it ultimately comes in contact with. Second, it is important to appreciate not just the number of people *currently* in prison—which, in any case, is easy to enumerate—but also the number of people *formerly* in prison. The presence of many people who were formerly in prison serves as the foundation upon which many of the health effects we will discuss is based. Third, given the relative size of the state and federal prison systems, the bulk of the prison system is a state-level issue and is governed by state-level administration and politics. Discussing the overall increase in incarceration since the 1970s does not meaningfully obscure state-level trends, as incarceration has spread rapidly among virtually all states. Yet there remains important variation in both the level and growth of incarceration between states. Understanding between-state variation of this sort is important for many reasons, not least of which because it points to the role state governments can play in curtailing the negative consequences of incarceration, as well as the role of the state in enhancing some of the health-promoting effects of incarceration. A focus on overall trends in incarceration rightly casts mass incarceration as a systematic issue, but it can also obscure potential intervention points where real change is possible.

In the United States, the incarceration rate was approximately stable from the turn of the century to the early 1970s, leading some to conclude that societies gravitate toward a steady state of offending, arrest, and punishment. Starting around 1973, however, the incarceration rate began an unprecedented increase (Glaze and Heberman 2013; National Research Council 2014). The incarceration rate increased by nearly a factor of five, from 161 incarcerated persons per 100,000 US residents in 1972 to 707 per 100,000 in 2012. After a peak around 2007, this upward trend has abated somewhat, though the US incarceration rate remains the highest in the world. The current US incarceration rate is as anomalous geopolitically as it is historically: the United States accounts for just over 4% of the world's population but holds 23% of the world's incarcerated people (National Research Council 2014, p. 36).

Even if efforts to reduce the size of the prison system gain traction—a point we return to later—the number of people formerly in prison represents the memory of the past. The number of people formerly in prison is considerably larger than the number of people currently in prison. Reforms related to the size of the prison system would not affect the millions of people who have already been released (or are currently incarcerated). The vast majority of people in prison are eventually released and, while many return to prison within a few years, the average prison term is around two years. Estimates of the number of people formerly in prison are, if anything, even more impressive than statistics regarding the number currently so. In 1968 there were just over one million people formerly in prison (including those on parole), but by 2010 this number had swelled to almost five million, corresponding to about 2.1% of the adult population and 3.7% of the adult male population (Uggen, Manza, and Thompson 2006).

Although incarceration affects many people, it does not affect all demographic groups equally. Incarceration is much more common among African Americans, Native Americans, and Hispanics; among the young; among men; and among those with low levels of education. Much has been written about racial discrimination throughout the criminal justice system and, indeed, the disparities are striking. In 2010, approximately a third of adult Black men were either currently (8%) or formerly (25%) under supervision for a felony-level offense, relative to about 13% in 1980 (Shannon et al. 2017). Although racial disparities have declined somewhat since 2000, in part due to explicit efforts to reduce disparities in sentencing, racial differences remain large. In 2018, the Black imprisonment rate was 5.2 times higher than among whites, relative to 6.3 times higher in 2008 (Beck and Blumstein 2012; Carson 2020a; National Research Council 2014).

There are many forms of racial inequality, including in socioeconomic outcomes, though racial inequality in incarceration is striking even in this context. Black-white differences in incarceration exceed, for example, the relative disparities in wealth, employment, and poverty (Western 2006). Educational differences in incarceration are, likewise, very sharp and intersect with racial differences, given the large number of high school dropouts among Black men. Among Black men born in the late 1960s and not college educated, approximately 30% will be incarcerated at some point in their lifetime, whereas among the same men who have at least some college, the risk of incarceration drops to 5% (Pettit 2012; Pettit and Western 2004). Among white men the same percentages are 5% and less than 1%. The vast majority of people in prison are men. The risk of incarceration over a lifetime is much higher among men. It is important to note, though, that incarceration has increased faster over time for women. In 2013, less than 7% of all people in federal and state prisons were female, but the female-male disparity has decreased over time (Carson and Golinelli 2013; National Research Council 2014). Although a substantial sex difference remains, it is smaller than it used to be. In 1972, the incarceration rate was twenty-four times higher among men than women, but in 2010 it was eleven times higher (National Research Council 2014). The sex difference appears to have stabilized. As of 2018, the male imprisonment rate (810 per 100,000 population) was almost thirteen times the rate for women (63 per 100,000) (Carson 2020a).

An often-neglected piece of the incarceration puzzle is variation between states, including recent reductions in incarceration. Although all states have seen an increase in incarceration since the 1970s, the pace has varied, and recently, some states have been proactive in shrinking the size of their prisons. The reasons for such wide state-level variation reflect some of the same reasons for the increase in incarceration over time: trends in incarceration are more closely tied to policy decisions than to crime rates. Between 1972 and 2000, every single state saw an increase in their imprisonment rates (National Research Council 2014, p. 43). Most of the increase was due to changes in criminal justice policy and sentencing, including longer sentences, the war on drugs, and harsher penalties for a wide variety of offenses. No one type of offense is responsible for the entire increase. At the state level, the reasons for the increase are mostly variations on a theme. Many states adopted policies and practices that increased both the length and severity of sentences, as well as the likelihood that a conviction would result in incarceration. In addition, some states effectively removed discretion from sentencing. In 1995, Florida, for instance, abolished credits for time served and required people in prison to serve at least 85% of their sentence (Warren et al. 2008). Many other states adopted so-called three-strikes policies or truth-in-sentencing laws, designed to curb or eliminate early release and, thereby, ensure that people in prison serve more of their actual sentence. For all these reasons, overall time served has increased.

Some of these trends are changing. In recent years, most states have made efforts to reduce the size of their prisons. As of now, thirty-nine states had reduced their prison populations from peak levels (Ghandnoosh 2019). Even among states that have not decreased the size of their prisons, there are signs of change. Of those states that continued to increase imprisonment, virtually all did so at a much slower pace than they had previously. It is important to note that the move to shrink prisons has not always been motivated by justice considerations. The pressure to de-incarcerate has been in no small part a financial matter, and financial pressures have been especially acute in states that incarcerate the most people. Deincarceration has also happened faster in states with the highest incarceration rates. Facing enormous prison costs and a budget shortfall, California, for instance, implemented more diversion programs. In the same vein, Texas expanded drug treatment and diversion programs because of financial considerations. Nonetheless, the outcomes seen in California and Texas reflect a general pattern (Porter 2016). In 2015, at least thirty states adopted changes that could produce reductions in the prison population, including three states that authorized judges to depart from mandatory minimum guidelines under certain conditions. In some instances, health has been central to deincarceration. As COVID-19 swept through the United States in 2020, many judges and correctional institutions tried to slow its progress by releasing certain people from prison. Although these efforts have proven simpler in jails than prisons, where stays are shorter and more discretionary, they are nonetheless consequential and consistent with a general trend. Although the tapestry of prison reform is quite varied, states are generally moving in the same direction. Some states have focused on sentencing reforms, others on alternatives to incarceration, others on more credits for time served, and still others on mitigating the spread of COVID-19, but in all cases reforms have been cast in terms of reducing the size of the prison population (Greene and Mauer 2010).

* * *

This book is about the intersection of prisons and population health, how we got to this point, and the social, legal, cultural, and political forces that have kept the intersection in place. We take a multidimensional approach, tracing connections from the operation of the criminal justice system to the health of populations. Prisons are physically separated from communities, but their actions ripple outward over time and space. Prisons affect the health and well-being of those in prison and those formerly in prison, but prisons are also implicated in the health of the families and communities to which they return. Furthermore, prisons eventually intersect with other institutions, seemingly far removed from criminal justice, including the health care system.

We begin, though, with the legal mandate to provide care in prisons, the cornerstone of this rippling cascade of consequences. Prisons are obligated to provide care to those in their custody, an obligation that some advocates justifiably celebrate as a victory for the rights of people in prison. This legal mandate, though, was a narrow victory, with implications that, at the time, were largely unappreciated. Over time, courts have ruled in ways that have resulted in a standard of care for people in prison that is inconsistent with the standard of care governing doctor-patient interaction in other settings. *Estelle v. Gamble* was a legal victory, to be sure, but settling the right to health care through the framework of avoiding cruel and unusual punishment has resulted in an unusual system, one increasingly ill-suited to the needs of people in prison.

2
The Uncertain Legal Mandate of Prison Health Care

Suicides in prison are deeply unsettling. They are, on the one hand, common. The leading cause of death in jails is suicide, and self-injury short of death is even more prevalent (Noonan, Rohloff, and Ginder 2015). Explanations for suicides in prison are, it would seem, easy to imagine and, for that reason, easy for some people to dismiss. Incarceration is plainly stressful, perhaps especially with the shock of incarceration in a local jail. For some people, incarceration reflects a lifetime of disadvantage and poor mental health, heightening an already elevated risk. For others, incarceration represents a sudden shift, but it is no less consequential for being abrupt. Incarceration can instill a sudden but deep sense of hopelessness. On the other hand, though, suicides in prison would seem to be entirely preventable, to the point that some suicides in prison seem inexplicable. People in prison are monitored routinely and comprehensively. Correctional officers work assiduously to prevent escape and could seemingly extend their vigilance to signs of self-harm. To be sure, suicides are often difficult to predict even among people who are well cared for, but mental health professionals have tools for identifying those who are at risk, and simply identifying those with pre-existing psychiatric disorders can be helpful. Yet prison systems collect little to no data on self-injurious behavior and prisons vary widely in how they manage risk (Appelbaum et al. 2011). This situation partly reflects the ambiguous mandate to care in prisons.

One important cost of prisons is that of providing health care to those in their custody. Although health care is a relatively small part of the overall correctional budget in most states, that part is rapidly growing, consistent with rising costs of health care throughout the economy. Much of this increase simply reflects the rising cost of medical treatment, a cost far outpacing inflation, but part also reflects that some state systems have been remanded to deliver more care than they did in the past. Following a successful lawsuit,

California was directed to spend more on health care staffing, on the treatment of hepatitis C patients in particular, and on improvements to its medical equipment (Pew Charitable Trusts 2017). California now spends more per person in prison than any other state. Understanding the connection between prisons and health requires an understanding of what prisons are required to provide and why. Prisons are required by law to provide health care, and some systems have been successfully sued to provide more. Yet the mandate to care is ultimately thin: a guarantee that prisons will not engage in cruel and unusual punishment by virtue of withholding medical treatment for a serious condition that is known to staff is not the same thing as an entitlement to proactive care and prevention for conditions comprehensively diagnosed or for risks judiciously anticipated.

To many observers, the idea that inmates are guaranteed health care is unusual and perhaps perverse. Americans in general do not enjoy an affirmative right to care. Although the Affordable Care Act requires most Americans to have health insurance, it does not *guarantee* access to health care, let alone (under most conditions) access to free care. What guarantees exist in the US health care system are limited. In its current form, Medicare provides health care to those age sixty-five and over. Most Americans regard Medicare as an appropriate safety net for an especially vulnerable and deserving population. And some advocates would like to expand Medicare eligibility to all Americans. But at present the program remains age based. Similarly, Medicaid provides health insurance to many people, and some states have expanded the program, per the Affordable Care Act's incentives. But Medicaid is a means-tested program, and historically it has provided benefits mostly for the mothers of young children and the disabled.

For the public, people in prison are not as sympathetic as these constituencies, but people in prison nonetheless enjoy certain rights to care. It is important to clarify what the Supreme Court has ruled the Constitution guarantees, as well as how the courts have interpreted some of the remaining legal ambiguities to that right. The crucial decision—*Estelle v. Gamble*—emerged in 1976 under unusual circumstances, and it is not a particularly strong foundation for ensuring adequate care. Moreover, the case is a linchpin for understanding why, at least in prison settings, no discussion of *care* is far removed from a discussion of *punishment*. The two concepts make for strange bedfellows and their conjunction has led to some perverse outcomes.

Health Care in the Context of Punishment

The legal requirement to provide care to people in prison was advanced in 1976 with the Supreme Court's *Estelle v. Gamble* decision. In their decision, the court set a framework for understanding prisons' legal obligations with respect to care. The case hinged on the Eighth Amendment's prohibition against cruel and unusual punishment, a seemingly natural framework for the case. The Eighth Amendment is a cornerstone of prison litigation, but until *Estelle*, the courts rarely applied the amendment to matters of prison *administration*. To the extent that the amendment was used at all, it was almost always with respect to cruel and unusual *punishment*, particularly methods of execution. And to the extent that there was a prevailing legal philosophy regarding prison administration, it was largely one of restraint and deference. For the courts, prisons were viewed almost entirely through the lens of punishment, and prison administrators were allowed to manage the other aspects of prison life as they saw fit. Such deference was premised on the idea that prison administrators were the appropriate experts for all matters relating to custody (Rold 2008). And the task of prison administration was generally viewed sympathetically. The courts regarded prison administration as difficult and fraught, requiring, at times, behavior that might appear cruel to outsiders but would, on closer inspection, be seen as necessary for controlling a difficult population. The courts generally deferred their responsibilities to investigate questions of potential abuse, often on grounds that they lacked the necessary expertise.

In the 1970s, however, it became clear that conditions in many prisons were objectively bad and, no matter the lingering ambiguity of case law, legally intolerable. Although the circumstances of J. W. Gamble, the namesake of the case, have received a lot of attention, his situation provides only one example of the neglect that people in prison faced. Indeed, there were many precursors to the *Estelle* ruling, some involving conditions arguably worse than documented in *Estelle v. Gamble*. In *Newman v. Alabama* (1974a), for instance, the United States Court of Appeals Fifth Circuit denied an appeal regarding conditions in the Alabama state prison system. The most critical problem identified in the court's decision was insufficient medical staffing, but the problems cataloged by the court stretched far beyond having only two physicians serving the system (p. 1322) and no psychiatrists, social workers, or counselors (p. 1324). As the court highlighted, many medical procedures, including surgeries, were administered by unsupervised assistants (p. 1323). In addition, the court highlighted unsanitary and unsafe practices. For instance, linens and dishware from units for tuberculosis and hepatitis patients were cleaned in the same area as those for the general prison population, increasing the risk of contamination (p. 1323). The court also uncovered significant issues with medical supplies. Medications and equipment were outdated and some were obsolete. In one case, an anesthetic delivery system involving drip ether was still being used even though the approach had not been used in general medical practice since 1953 (pp. 1323–1324). As bad as these examples of the material conditions of care were, some specific instances of mistreatment were even worse. One quadriplegic person suffered a twenty-day maggot infestation because of unchanged dressings (p. 1324). In their ruling, the court anticipated the basis for the Supreme Court's decision in *Estelle*: they ruled the quality of medical care for people in prison "transgressed the interdictions of the cruel and unusual punishment clause of the Eighth Amendment" (p. 1325). Of note, some of these conditions remain, almost a half-century later. A 2019 federal investigation described the conditions in Alabama prisons as "gruesome," and the COVID-19 pandemic has once again brought to the fore significant problems in prison understaffing (US Department of Justice, Civil Rights Division 2019).

In this context, the invocation of the Eighth Amendment is hardly a rhetorical flourish. It is easy to see the aforementioned examples as instances of punishment, in the sense that they are not merely occasions of medical malpractice or neglect. Furthermore, it is easy to see these examples as rising above matters of administrative law to violating the guarantees set in our nation's founding document. Yet the invocation of cruel and unusual punishment also highlights the limits of adjudicating access to health care on the basis of a constitutional right, something the Supreme Court struggled with. The inaction prior to *Estelle v. Gamble* is telling: short of gross violations, rising to an obvious constitutional standard of punishment, the court was reluctant to intervene. In *Newman*, the court found intolerable conditions but still found reason to defer to prison administration, stating that courts "must be wary to avoid obtrusively monitoring the conduct of prison officials and thereby encumbering the administration of prison affairs" (p. 1328). The court further noted that it was "sedulously mindful of its circumscribed role" (p. 1328). In support of its reticence, the court cited previous case law, including *Procunier v. Martinez* (1974b), which allowed the court to premise its hands-off approach on an appreciation of the difficult task faced by administrators, combined with what the court appreciated as the broad scope of a prison's responsibilities:

> Prison administrators are responsible for maintaining internal order and discipline, for securing their institutions against unauthorized access or escape, and for rehabilitating, to the extent that human nature and inadequate resources allow, the inmates placed in their custody. The Herculean obstacles to effective discharge of these duties are too apparent to warrant explication. Suffice it to say that the problems of prisons in America are complex and intractable, and, more to the point, they are not readily susceptible of resolution by decree. (*Procunier v. Martinez*, pp. 404–405)

Nonetheless, in *Newman v. Alabama* (1974a), the Fifth Circuit Court noted that the "deference which shields officials engaging in intemperate action and which excuses judicial myopia is incompatible with our role as arbiters of the Constitution and hence cannot be countenanced" (p. 1329). They further acknowledged—again using language implying an imposition on legitimate prerogatives—their responsibility to "fetter prison officials where constraints are constitutionally appropriate," while maintaining deference "only as to these necessary or essential concomitants of incarceration," including the restraint and deprivation inherent to a prison sentence (p. 1329). In a much more expansive vein, the court offered that health care was not unrelated to the goals of incarceration, and that a lack of health care "thwarts the purported goal of rehabilitation" and even "jeopardizes the ability of inmates to assimilate into the population at large when ultimately released" (p. 1333). Such language is strikingly similar to that used in contemporary discussions of prison re-entry and mental health care, as we will discuss later.

Another early court ruling pertained to the death penalty specifically but expanded the meaning of cruel and unusual punishment. In *Gregg v. Georgia* (1976b), the Supreme Court affirmed the use of the death penalty, ruling that it does not violate, under all conditions, the Eighth Amendment. The court also reaffirmed its deference, in this case to both the criminal justice system and legislature. The court noted, "The requirements of the Eighth Amendment must be applied with an awareness of the limited role to be played by the courts" (p. 174) and further that "we may not act as judges as we might as legislators" in striking down extreme "punishment selected by a democratically elected legislature" (pp. 174–175). But in accepting the constitutionality of the death penalty, the court clarified some of the basic parameters of the Eighth Amendment in ways that paved the way for its later rulings regarding health care. The text of the Eighth Amendment, proposed by Congress in 1789 and approved as part of the Bill of Rights, states simply: "Excessive bail shall not be required, nor excessive fines imposed, nor cruel and unusual punishments inflicted." In *Gregg*, the court situated the amendment historically and ultimately progressively. Historically, the Eighth Amendment had, according to the court, "been interpreted in a flexible and dynamic manner to accord with evolving standards of decency" (p. 154). Progressively, the amendment could be evaluated in light of prevailing public sentiments regarding humane treatment (p. 173). In this way, the court argued that the Eighth Amendment was not a "static concept," and that it was applicable beyond the proscription of the "barbarous" methods of punishment prevailing in the eighteenth century (p. 173).

The Supreme Court's ruling in *Estelle* drew on these and other precedents. Although *Estelle* was more consequential than what came before, its factual details were less graphic. And, indeed, in an often-forgotten detail, the court ruled *against* the plaintiff. J. W. Gamble, an inmate in the Texas Department of Corrections, was injured when a bale of cotton fell on him while he was performing his work assignment. He continued to work, but after four hours, the pain had increased, and he was sent to the prison hospital. He was initially evaluated for a hernia and returned to his cell. His pain increased, though, and he returned to the hospital. There he was prescribed pain medication, and the next day, following an evaluation, he was diagnosed with a lower back strain. He was provided with pain relievers and recused from his normal responsibilities, but after about a month, despite his reporting ongoing pain, the physician on staff determined that he could resume light work and rescinded Gamble's work release. When Gamble insisted that he could not work and that his pain was as bad as it was on the first day, he was remanded to administrative segregation. He was also seen by another physician for his back pain, as well as his high blood pressure. A month later Gamble was told that if he did not return to his regular work assignment, he would be sent to the "farm," an undesirable post. Following a period of hospitalization, further examination, and solitary confinement, Gamble eventually sued the state on the grounds of cruel and unusual punishment, both for denying him adequate medical care and for punishing him for refusing to work when he was medically unfit to do so.

In their ruling, the court formulated a standard for assessing medical care in prison considering the obligations of the Eighth Amendment. This standard remains the ruling's most important contribution. The court ruled against Gamble because it did not believe his medical maltreatment rose to the level of "deliberate indifference," the standard they established for judging cruel and unusual punishment. The court noted that the proper forum for litigating a case of medical malpractice was not the Supreme Court and, further, that a case of medical malpractice did not need to be considered under the terms of the Eighth Amendment. In ruling against Gamble, the court emphasized the medical treatment that he did receive, which they regarded as well short of negligent. All told, during a three-month span, Gamble saw medical personnel on seventeen occasions. The court also noted that his injuries were, in fact, treated, as was his high blood pressure and heart problems (though Gamble objected only to the treatment of his back pain). To the court, this suggested that physicians were attuned not only to Gamble's presenting complaint but also to his health more generally, behavior that did not suggest indifference. Delivering health care that was perhaps short of the highest standard for one problem—and a problem that is difficult to treat in any case—did not, to the court's mind, constitute indifferent care. In the decision, though, the court seriously considered Gamble's claim of cruel and unusual punishment and, in the course of doing so, determined the level of care people in prison were entitled to receive. Much rested on the peculiarities of the situation. First, the court argued that inmates relied entirely on prison authorities to meet their medical needs, which is different from how Americans ordinarily receive care in a marketplace that allows for second opinions. The court further argued that denying the medical needs of inmates could result in physical pain or "lingering death," a situation that was not inconsistent with the original intent of the Eighth Amendment (p. 103). Violations of the Eighth Amendment thus rested on "deliberate indifference to serious medical needs" (p. 104), ultimately the most important section of the ruling. Deliberate indifference could be evident when administrators intentionally deny, delay, or interfere with care.

The deliberate indifference formulation remains a crucial safeguard for people in prison, but it introduces two significant sources of ambiguity. The formulation depends on, first, what is considered "deliberate," and second, what medical needs are regarded as "serious." Neither term is clear. Because of its focus on serious medical needs, the formulation would seem to permit neglecting nonserious medical needs, and, absent some clearer standard, the severity of a need rests with the judgment of prison medical personnel. The deference of the court to prison administrators surely extends to prison physicians, especially given the special deference American culture also affords to physicians' medical expertise generally. Indeed, *Estelle* appears to provide especially broad latitude for prison physicians in that even deliberate indifference could be tolerated insofar as the underlying medical need was not deemed significant. Subsequent rulings have clarified somewhat what constitutes a "serious" medical need, with courts generally considering how treatable a condition is, what consequences the condition is likely to have if not treated, and the likelihood of a favorable outcome (Rold 2008, p. 16). This standard, though, will shift according to what medicine is capable of detecting, treating, and curing. Furthermore, not all the elements of this understanding of "serious" are aligned. For example, many conditions are treatable but not terribly consequential, and it still might be worth treating conditions that are unlikely to have an unfavorable outcome.

The reliance on *deliberate* indifference introduces another complication. Because indifferent acts must be deliberate, cases of malpractice do not, in themselves, constitute a violation of the Eighth Amendment. As the court put it, "medical malpractice does not become a constitutional violation merely because the victim is a prisoner" (p. 106). *Estelle* provided little explicit guidance on the concept of deliberate indifference, but subsequent rulings have addressed it more squarely. As developed in case law, deliberate indifference is a high standard, and other rulings have elevated the demands made on a plaintiff in making a successful case. Courts have interpreted *Estelle* to mean a defendant must know of and disregard a substantial risk. This interpretation was especially clear in *Farmer v. Brennan* (Furnham 1994), a Supreme Court case that, in effect, synthesized earlier rulings and established that prisons have a duty to protect prisoners from harm by other prisoners (Schwartz 1995). Like *Estelle, Farmer* is generally seen as foundational for the rights of people in prison, including significant protections against rape. Yet also like *Estelle,* the impact of *Farmer* is diluted by what it requires: the ruling advanced a demanding and, once again, not entirely unambiguous formulation for the concept of deliberate indifference.

The case involved Dee Farmer, a trans woman who, after being transferred from one federal prison to another for disciplinary reasons, was placed in the general male population. There Farmer was threatened, beaten, and raped by another inmate. In her complaint, Farmer alleged that she was transferred despite officials knowing that she was being moved to a prison with a reputation for sexual violence, and that she, as a feminine-appearing trans woman, would be singled out for predation. The case did not involve the delivery of health care, though it was relevant to *Estelle* because the court had already ruled, surrounding *Estelle*, that a standard of deliberate indifference applied to all Eighth Amendment claims regarding prison conditions (see *Wilson v. Seiter* 1991). In addition, *Estelle* was clear in arguing that a successful Eighth Amendment claim required more than negligence. In *Farmer*, the court considered whether the prison was deliberately indifferent to the risk to Dee Farmer, and the long and unproductive gap between *Estelle* and *Farmer* was not lost on the court. The court noted that, prior to *Farmer*, the courts had never sought to clarify the concept of deliberate indifference, despite having used the standard in numerous prior decisions (p. 835). At the time, lower courts were split on the issue of deliberate indifference and the case was petitioned to the Supreme Court.

The Supreme Court ruled unanimously in favor of Farmer but, even so, developed a conservative standard of deliberate indifference. In particular, the court emphasized a distinction between cruel and unusual *conditions*, which they regarded as expected in prison, and cruel and unusual *punishment*, which they regarded as distinct. The court also held that no objective test of deliberate indifference was available and, thus, a determination must rest on a subjective element. It thereby required an investigation of a prison official's state of mind. The court's framework for this subjective test, constituting a standard of subjective recklessness, was multipronged:

> We hold instead that a prison official cannot be found liable under the Eighth Amendment for denying an inmate humane conditions of confinement unless the official knows of and disregards an excessive risk to inmate health or safety; the official must both be aware of facts from which the inference could be drawn that a substantial risk of serious harm exists, and he must also draw the inference. (p. 837)

The court further stipulated that even conspicuous risk was not sufficient for the subjective test, ruling that "prison officials may not be held liable if they prove that they were unaware of even an obvious risk" (p. 826). The decision further specified that juries should be instructed about matters of proof in subjective culpability: it was not enough "to find that a reasonable person would have known, or that the defendant should have known" about a risk (p. 843). Although the court held that the state of mind of an official could be inferred from facts surrounding the case, the emphasis on awareness nonetheless places a burden on plaintiffs and might provide an incentive for ignorance among prison administrators.

The legacy of *Farmer* remains somewhat muddled, as is the case with much prison litigation. Despite the unanimity of the decision and its success in forcing prison officials to address violence in prison, elements of the decision remain controversial and unresolved. In his concurring opinion, Justice Blackmun argued that some prison conditions are unconstitutional regardless of subjective knowledge (and explicitly called for overruling the earlier *Wilson v. Seiter*). Blackmun argued that rape and other violence are tantamount to torture and, therefore, are proscribed directly by the Eighth Amendment. Justice Stevens too wrote a concurring opinion, wherein he noted that prison conditions can be unconstitutional regardless of an official's state of mind. The main text of the ruling itself, written by Justice Souter, is perhaps more notable for spelling out what subjective recklessness is *not* rather than what it *is* (Rifkin 1994–1995).

In general, the *Farmer* decision remains ambiguous because it did not grapple with whether the conditions of confinement—not just the sentence to confinement—are part of the punishment and, therefore, subject to scrutiny under the Eighth Amendment (Cozad 1995–1996). The *Farmer* decision can be interpreted as condoning objectively inhumane conditions of confinement insofar as it rests on a subjective test that is hard to satisfy. In his concurrence, Justice Blackmun argued that much of what makes prisons risky is systematic, institutional, and diffuse and, therefore, will not rest with any one official (see, especially, pp. 855–856). He concludes, "A punishment is simply no less cruel and unusual because its harm is unintentional" (p. 856). Other aspects of the ruling are ambiguous because they do not directly address distinctive aspects of prisons that make subjective awareness even more difficult in the setting. The *Farmer* ruling does not require people in prison to notify prison officials of some risk—indeed, this is among the most significant aspects of *Farmer*. Yet people in prison reside in a culture that demands toughness, and many people in prison are reluctant to report rape or the threat of rape for fear of appearing weak, making it difficult for correctional officers to realize a subjective awareness. In addition, the *Farmer* ruling requires that prison officials respond "reasonably" to risk, though what is sensible under prison conditions is complicated (Rifkin 1994–1995). For instance, in their defense, prison officials might claim they were late in responding to a potential threat because there were no alternative cells available for someone at risk (prisons are often overcrowded) or that in responding to one type of risk, such as the threat of rape, someone could only be moved to a different environment with a different kind of risk, as in moving to solitary confinement (p. 303). In these ways, rulings like *Farmer* introduce significant caveats in the protections afforded by the Eighth Amendment, especially pertaining to the actions, knowledge, and intentions of prison officials. And, as before, the peculiarities of prison loom large.

In the end, *Estelle* provided a narrow and partial prohibition. *Estelle* was fundamentally a ruling against cruel and unusual punishment, but it failed to grapple with the fact that prisons do two things at once: they punish and they protect (Genty 1996). With *Estelle*, the court ruled regarding the former, consistent with the Eighth Amendment, but they did not rule regarding the latter, consistent with an affirmative duty to care. Over time the courts have distilled *Estelle*'s care-related implications to three basic mandates (Rold 2008). First, prisons must provide inmates with access to care, including the ability to respond to medical emergencies. Second, prisons must follow through on the medical care they determine to be necessary for inmates (or continue treatments inmates were receiving prior to admission). And third, prisons must provide a professional judgment regarding medical matters. *Estelle* certainly improved basic access to care in prison, including the material resources necessary for treatment, but the impact of these mandates depends to no small degree on the professionalism and judgment of prison medical staff. *Estelle*, for instance, focused on providing care for serious medical problems, as noted earlier, but the determination of seriousness is made by medical personnel. Similarly, *Estelle* requires the treatment of medical conditions, but decisions regarding what is necessary rest with medical professionals. The prison environment, again, makes this difficult. Although prisons often employ competent and professional medical staff, the prison environment can strain professionalism in a number of ways. It can also strain the capacity of inmates to fulfill their obligations as patients. In considering the actual administration of prison care it is critical to consider the roles and situation of all the people involved.

Dual Loyalty and the Challenges of Prison Health Care

Prisons can foster a sense of dual loyalty among medical staff and prevent physicians from fully engaging with inmates as patients (Pont, Stöver, and Wolff 2012). Prisons and medicine operate with very different prerogatives. On the one hand, prisons require adherence to rules and the close observation of people in custody. People in prison are supervised and controlled continuously, and very few of their actions are private. Additionally, prisons are in the business of meting out punishment, with confinement central to that mission. Medicine, on the other hand, is premised on an ethic of care, consent, and patient-provider confidentiality. Physicians pledge, first and foremost, to do no harm. Physicians encourage patient adherence, to be sure, but they do not require it. In prisons, physicians find themselves at the intersection of all these demands and interests, with little easy way to engage people as both patients and prisoners. In ordinary settings, physicians are, by oath, loyal to patients. In prisons, though, physicians must also be loyal to prison administration, knowing that some of the disciplinary tools of the prison can cause physical or mental harm. And, for their part, prison officials can justify health-harming behaviors as serving their interest in maintaining order, which can reverberate back to health too. For instance, a guard can defend the use of electric shocks by claiming they are necessary to restrain an unruly person. And prison medical staff can be enlisted in service of the other goals of prison administration. For instance, medical personnel can be used to determine whether someone is fit for solitary confinement, even though physicians are aware of the harm even a short stay in isolation can cause. Short of these dilemmas regarding the use of force or affirmatively health-harming punishment, there are other challenges for medical professionals. For example, the prison environment frustrates ordinary continuity of care. Some people in prison are serving long sentences, but most are not. For this reason, medical personnel are usually unable to provide continuous care after someone is released. In ordinary settings, physicians can evaluate a case and develop a treatment plan with a long-term goal in mind, but in prison settings this basic task is much more difficult.

The prison environment is also challenging from the standpoint of patients. Patients in prison differ in important ways from patients on the outside. For one, people in prison cannot choose their providers. Although in ordinary clinical settings patients rarely question the competency of their physicians, patients can seek a second opinion if they find the treatment they receive unsatisfactory or dubious. In addition, outside of prisons, patients can seek over-the-counter treatments on their own if their problems are minor. Competitive pressures of this sort provide a degree of quality control and gatekeeping in medicine, and they also provide patients with some degree of agency over their health. But these options and competitive pressures are entirely absent in prisons. People in prison are dependent on medical staff for even minor medical matters, including such basics as procuring aspirin for a headache. They are also entirely dependent on the medical staff available to them in the facility. Prisons tend to be understaffed and many employ no more than one physician. In addition to limiting options for patients, this situation also means that prison physicians are unable to easily consult with other physicians on staff, something that can promote higher-quality care in other settings, especially given increasingly specialized knowledge.

Prisons are also slow to adapt to a rapidly changing medical landscape, in part because they rarely have the portfolio of medical expertise necessary to address complexity, as might be the case in a hospital. The prevalence of some infectious diseases, especially those that affect prison populations, has increased over time (a topic we return to later). Although prisons have the capacity to respond to these infections effectively, they often move slowly. For instance, prisons greatly improved their treatment of human immunodeficiency virus (HIV)/acquired immunodeficiency syndrome (AIDS) in the early twenty-first century, but they improved much later than the general medical sector, in part because prisons respond primarily to what the law requires of them and *Estelle* encourages a reactive approach. Medicine continues to innovate and the breadth of the medical armamentarium continues to expand. There are many more conditions that can be treated today than could be treated even a decade ago, potentially increasing the obligations of prison medical staff under *Estelle*. The force of case law, however, moves more slowly than the pace of medical innovation, and prisons are slow to adopt the latest treatments when they are not strictly obligated to do so.

Furthermore, the demography of incarceration has shifted in ways that increase case complexity and strain how effectively prisons can adapt to those in their care. The prison population is aging rapidly. Between 1994 and 2011, the number of people in federal prisons age fifty or older increased 330% (Kim and Peterson 2014). For this reason, people in prison are now experiencing all the complex medical problems normally associated with an aging population, and prison staff rarely have the specialized knowledge such a population requires.

The prison population is also increasingly female, shifting the types of medical conditions prisons must address. The situation of pregnant women in prison highlights this issue. Most imprisoned women are mothers and, every year, there are a significant number of births in prison (Clarke and Adashi 2011). By *Estelle*, these women are entitled to care, but when pregnant women in prison are moved to hospitals for birth, they are often placed in restraints for the labor. Recognizing the sharp medical and ethical dilemmas this collision between the hospital and prison presents, a variety of organizations, including the Federal Bureau of Prisons, have created standards for pregnancy-related care in prisons (US Department of Justice 1996). These standards are valuable and consequential. Outcomes for many pregnant women in prison are, in fact, quite good (Martin et al. 1997). But the situation only highlights the more fundamental problem: creating an environment for adequate care required the creation of specific guidelines around the specific health care needs of one segment of the prison population. Absent such guidelines, correctional officers and medical personnel must resolve any dilemmas on their own in an environment of limited consultation.

The Evolving Legal Environment Surrounding Prison Health Care

The protections afforded by case law are weakened further by emerging barriers to prison litigation. There is no doubt that litigation has been an important tool in the cause of advancing the quality of health care in prisons. The use of legal tools, however, presents both opportunities and challenges, and the challenges have begun to outweigh the opportunities, especially given the narrow pathway through which past litigation has been successful.

The Constitution provides a blunt instrument for improving health care in prison. It has certainly yielded improvements in care, but it has not produced an especially nimble or forward-looking prison health care system. In general, prison care is reactive or only narrowly prospective: prison care responds to the problems deemed most important for the prison population or responds to the specific mandates of successful litigation regarding certain aspects of care. In addition, improvements based on violations of the Eighth Amendment tend to center around tertiary care rather than primary care. Successful claims tend to demonstrate specific injury or the threat of "lingering death" through the denial of care. This focus shifts the character of successful claims. People in prison have successfully sued regarding improvements in care for HIV/AIDS, for instance, but they have been much less successful when suing for better preventive care writ large. Medical practice in prisons tends to follow suit. Prison medical personnel are usually concerned more with treating existing maladies than with anticipating all potential health problems.

There are other difficulties with relying on legal tools to improve the quality of care. For one, using legal tools makes people who receive care in prison vulnerable to a changing legal environment. It is difficult to litigate on behalf of people in prison in general. Part of the challenge reflects the long-standing stigma against people in prison, which prevents adequate legal representation. People in prison rarely attract a sympathetic audience, even when they bring a meritorious case. Indeed, a lack of sympathy is, if anything, even more acute in the case of health care litigation than for other kinds of suits. In effect, *Estelle* narrowed the available options. Because the standard of deliberate indifference requires evidence regarding the intentions of prison officials, the impact of mistreatment is likely to be given less weight than the mindset of an official, even regarding the critical question of whether there was "serious" harm involved (Genty 1996). In this legal climate, the focus on harm quickly fades to the background.

In tandem with the long-standing challenges stemming from *Estelle* is the emergence of a more strenuous legal environment for people in prison. Lawsuits brought by people in prison are historically not uncommon. In 1995, people in prisons and jails brought around 40,000 lawsuits to federal court. But after the passage of the Prison Litigation Reform Act (PLRA) in 1996, the number of new filings shrunk by over 40% (Schlenger et al. 2002). The PLRA instituted a number of significant procedural changes. Among other things, it required people in prison to pay regular filing fees and to exhaust all administrative avenues for their grievances. Although even nominal filing fees can be burdensome for those in prison, the so-called exhaustion rule has proven even more significant. The rule requires moving through all administrative options before filing a lawsuit, including appeals. Subsequent case law has expanded the exhaustion rule to render it even more onerous. In 2006, a Supreme Court ruling required people in prison to not only exhaust all administrative avenues but also satisfy all administrative timelines and procedures (*Woodford v. Ngo* 2006). As the court saw it, "exhaustion" should be interpreted not solely in terms of seeking administrative recourse "until administrative remedies are no longer available," but also in terms of what the court regarded as *proper* exhaustion, or exhaustion "in accordance with the applicable procedural rules, including deadlines" (p. 88). The court further noted—with some apparent exasperation—that "exhaustion requirements are designed to deal with parties who do not want to exhaust" and to deal with those who prefer not to "give the agency a fair and full opportunity to adjudicate their claims" (p. 90). The court's decision was split. In his dissent, Justice Stevens noted the difficulties of proper exhaustion in prison, as defined by the court. He noted that most prisons have very short windows on filing, usually no more than fifteen days and occasionally between two and five (p. 118). And he argued that these difficulties could, in effect, override an individual's rights and prohibit filings even for severe constitutional violations, such as sexual assault.

Although the example in Stevens's dissent was hypothetical, there is little doubt the PLRA provides a shield for prison administrators. Taken to an extreme, the PLRA would seem to allow administrators to single-handedly prevent suits. The grievance systems in prisons are usually designed by prison administrators themselves, including relevant details such as deadlines (Human Rights Watch 2009). This prerogative gives administrators significant power, and, indeed, some states have responded to the PLRA by making grievances even more difficult to file properly. Illinois, for instance, revised its procedures after a court found that an inmate had, in fact, complied with its grievance procedures as they were then written. In response to the ruling, Illinois revised their procedures to require much more detailed complaints from people in prison (Human Rights Watch 2009, p. 12). Other states have thwarted exhaustion in different ways. In one case, one person's suit over his alleged assault by a guard was dismissed because he did not file his grievance within two working days, even though, during that window, he was placed in administrative segregation without grievance forms (Human Rights Watch 2009, p. 14). The exhaustion rule is even more difficult to satisfy in a system where people must effectively represent themselves. Although people in prison can be represented by lawyers in a *trial*, the initial grievance process is almost always self-initiated (Human Rights Watch 2009). Technical errors in the process of filing a grievance remain a significant reason for the dismissal of a lawsuit, even though people in prison almost never receive assistance from a legal professional in the process.

Although the PLRA was passed under the assumption that a reduction in the number of filings would increase the merits of the filings that remained, this has not obviously been the case. The PLRA has made it much more difficult for plaintiffs to win cases, but it is not clear that even the successful cases post-PLRA have yielded appropriate improvements in care. Fewer cases are surviving pretrial dismissal. The overall success of prisoner-initiated claims is only around 10% (Schlanger 2003, p. 1594, Table II.A). The nature of health-related suits has changed over time too, but not in ways that adequately address the particular needs of people in prison. For one, the PLRA has circumscribed what the court regards as a legitimate injury. In effect, cruelty has been defined upward, excluding, for instance, some mental health considerations. The PLRA prohibits a federal court from awarding damages to an inmate because of mental or emotional injury, unless they can also show they were injured *physically*. Mental health concerns have historically assumed a second-order position in much of medicine, though in prison litigation the difference is especially sharp. In addition, the PLRA has rendered lawsuits brought by individuals much less likely to succeed than those brought by a class. Although this restriction would seem a limited matter pertaining to how persuasive a case appears based on how many people it affects, it has significant consequences for health care improvement. The two kinds of suits involve different costs and benefits. Successful suits brought by individuals rarely result in systematic changes to the policies and procedures of prisons, whereas successful suits brought by an entire class often do (Wool 2007). Yet class action lawsuits tend to be narrower than individual suits with respect to health outcomes, limited to medical conditions or treatments that affect everyone in a class. Following a successful class action lawsuit, for instance, prisons might be compelled to improve their treatment of HIV/ AIDS, their tuberculosis testing procedures, or their disciplinary procedures for those suffering from psychiatric disorders. But prisons are rarely compelled to make broad improvements that might improve their overall quality of care or prevent indeterminate illnesses in otherwise healthy people. In this light, legal strategies have shifted post-PLRA. Prior to the PLRA, one tactic was to adopt a "kitchen sink" approach, advocating for sweeping remedies regarding the totality of prison conditions, including broad improvements in health care (Schlanger 2006, p. 605). Such a strategy is much less effective today, though there are some notable exceptions, including *Brown v. Plata* (2010). In that case, the US Supreme Court ruled that the California prison system was too comprehensively deficient to benefit from any piecemeal improvement. The state's entire prison health care system was placed in receivership. In most successful suits, however, the rulings are more precise and limited.

Some aspects of the broader policy environment have shifted in ways to improve the situation of people in prison, though usually only in indirect ways. In 1990 Congress passed the Americans with Disabilities Act (ADA), and in 1998 the Supreme Court ruled that the ADA applied to people in prison (*Pennsylvania Department of Corrections v. Yeskey* 1998). Although the ADA provides a supplementary avenue for legal recourse, it has limits as an instrument for wholesale improvements (Paz 2007). The ADA pertains to qualified individuals with disabilities, and it protects those individuals from being denied benefits. In a successful ADA case, the plaintiff must do two things: they must first prove that they have a disability and then prove that their disability was the source of being denied a benefit. This presents only a small opportunity for people in prison. Although someone might successfully claim that the prison *denied* them reasonable accommodation for a disability or treatment of the medical condition behind the disability—and the person would not have to do so under a more strenuous *Estelle* standard— being provided with *inadequate* accommodation or treatment is generally not enough to meet the ADA standard. Similarly, being denied a benefit *that is already in place* is different from requiring a prison to expand the benefits it provides. The ADA does not create a right for any specific rehabilitation service, for instance (*Niece v. Fitzner* 1996). In addition, people in prison still face courts that are inclined to defer to administrators, especially when it comes to judging those in its custody. Some otherwise reasonable ADA accommodations can be interpreted as contrary to a prison's interest in maintaining order and safety, as in the case of allowing for unobstructed entry and exit of a building. Prisons, of course, have no interest in providing easy egress given their mission to confine.

What Do Prisons Provide?

To evaluate the consequences of the legal and professional environment surrounding prison health care, a key question concerns real behavior: what medical personnel in prison in fact do and what they actually provide (rather than the more abstract issue of what *Estelle* encourages or circumscribes). Although policies and procedures vary from institution to institution, there are general patterns. For instance, a medical examination at admission is routine. A brief intake screening occurs upon arrival, with a more thorough exam occurring a week or two later (Faiver 2005). In these exams, people are tested for a number of conditions, but infectious disease is a focus. One survey, for example, found that all state and federal prisons offered testing for HIV and just over 30% made it mandatory (Hammett, Kennedy, and Kuck 2007). Virtually all people in prison are also tested for syphilis and tuberculosis. A much smaller percentage of prisons offer testing for chlamydia and gonorrhea, even though these infections are more prevalent than syphilis. Prisons also provide ongoing treatment, as required. The procedures for receiving care involve several steps, each involving some degree of discretion. Usually a person who is ill submits a slip for a sick call, which is collected at a designated time each day (Faiver 2005). The slip is usually reviewed by a nurse, who, if necessary, can then schedule an appointment with an appropriate provider. Although many medical services are delivered in-house, complicated treatments, including surgery, are usually performed in outside hospitals or in special correctional medical facilities, housed in larger prisons.

In general, prisons do deliver care to those who plainly need it, as would be expected in the legal environment. A nationwide survey of federal and state inmates found that most people in prison with an apparent need for health care received some form of care while institutionalized (Wilper et al. 2009). Although the number of people who are completely neglected is comparatively small, it is not zero; in some institutions it is quite high, and probably underestimated given the disincentives for robust testing and surveillance. There is also substantial variation between federal and state prisons. Of people in prison who report a medical problem, about 14% of people in federal prisons and 20% in state prisons were not examined by a medical professional. Of those who required some type of medication, 21% of people in federal prisons and 24% of those in state prisons were not continued on their medications during their incarceration. Prisons are more proactive when it comes to injuries, as well as medical conditions requiring blood tests. Approximately 96% of people in federal prisons and 94% of those in state prisons who have a problem requiring regular blood tests were continued on those tests while incarcerated, and approximately 92% of those in federal prisons and 88% of those in state prisons were examined by medical personnel following a serious injury. There is also some evidence that prisons provide effective care. Deaths from AIDS have declined precipitously in prisons, in large part because prisons are much better at providing care than they were in the past. Prisons are also generally effective in treating tuberculosis, when it is detected.

Although they are required to provide health care too, jails have somewhat different and more variable procedures than prisons. In addition, jails also have a somewhat different interface with other health care providers, in large part because of high turnover and generally short stays. Although much larger than the average jail, the Los Angeles County jail, operated by the L.A. Sheriff's Department, provides an apt illustration of this interface and the cascade of relevant decisions that condition the outcome (Bechelli et al. 2014). Shortly after making an arrest, a deputy must decide whether the person is physically and mentally safe to detain. The initial decision is based only on what deputies observe and have available to them through records. A deputy knows, for example, whether the person was harmed in the process of arrest and can determine whether the person is behaving erratically. From there, the deputy decides whether treatment—or at least a more professional medical diagnosis—is necessary. If deemed necessary, the person is then taken to an emergency department, where the person sees a medical professional, who, in turn, determines whether the person is safe to detain. These preliminary visits to the emergency room are not insignificant and they are not rare: they occur in about 5.5% of arrests and take, on average, 2.8 hours each (Bechelli et al. 2014). These visits are also motivated by an abundance of caution: only about 3% of visits to the emergency room result in someone being admitted to the emergency room, which is considerably less than the average of 13.3% for all emergency room visits. Under these circumstances, most visits are for the treatment of a chronic condition with no acute symptoms, including hypertension, diabetes, and asthma. In general, jails deliver fewer health care services than prisons, though considering the relatively short amount of time people are held in custody in jail, jails are still substantially involved in the delivery of services (Wilper et al. 2009).

Under most circumstances, prisons pay for the services they provide. In cases where care is provided in inpatient settings outside the prison, Medicaid can sometimes provide coverage (Bainbridge 2012). In addition, a few states have pursued strategies to provide Medicaid benefits for certain people in their custody. The bulk of these health care expenditures concern delivery of services rather than administration: general medical care and hospitalizations account for 57% of the total, while administration accounts for only about 4% (Pew Charitable Trusts 2014, p. 7). Prisons spend on dimensions of care that directly reflect their needs, priorities, and legal mandates. About 19% of the total, for example, comes from mental health care and substance abuse treatment. States that incarcerate many people over the age of fifty-five have higher per-person spending on health care, which also reflects the correspondence between expenditures and the need for care. To the extent that some states have seen a decline in their expenditures, it almost always corresponds with a decline in the size of the prison population rather than a change in per-person spending. Indeed, expressed in terms of spending per person in prison, the upward trends in health care spending are especially pronounced. Between 2001 and 2008, per-person correctional health care spending increased 84% in California, 306% in New Hampshire, and 14% in Alaska, the three states that spend the most per person (Pew Charitable Trusts 2013).

These growing expenditures are not lost on state governments. A large portion of prison expenditures are in the form of fixed personnel costs. Looking for opportunities to cut expenses without reducing the size of prisons, several states have tried to more actively manage prison health care costs (Pew Charitable Trusts 2013). Some of their strategies include the use of telehealth, which allows physicians to access people in prison without incurring the high cost of transporting them off-site. Telehealth is especially popular in states where prisons are far from major hospitals and in situations when someone requires the services of a specialist. Other states have created contracts with outside providers, including public academic medical centers and, in some cases, private for-profit health care companies (see Raimer and

Stobo 2004 regarding Texas's relationship with academic institutions). Other states have adopted some of the same cost control strategies that have been used more generally in the health care sector, including paying a fixed reimbursement rate to providers.

When faced with rising expenditures for prisons, states are often forced to rebalance their budgets. In general, though, spending on prisons does not crowd out spending in other areas. This lack of a relationship is driven, in part, by the comparatively small share that prison spending assumes in state budgets. As a percentage of the total budget, spending on corrections consumes far less than spending on health and education (Ellwood and Guetzkow 2009, Figure 7.1). Although spending on corrections has increased over time, so too has spending in other areas. Spending on health, for instance, has increased enormously over time, from an average of 11% of state budget outlays in 1977 to 17% in 2002 (p. 209). Studies that try to systematically model change in one area of spending as a function of change in expenditures on corrections find a limited relationship: spending on corrections is only associated with declines in welfare spending. In particular, each percentage point increase in spending on corrections is associated with about a percentage point decline in welfare spending (p. 228). Spending on corrections does not generally affect spending on education, health, or transportation.

Although prison health care might be a tempting budget item to slash, it can be very difficult to reduce in practice. For one, those who are involved with the criminal justice system often have urgent needs for care. In addition, the people who are incarcerated are not served especially well by other institutions and state resources. For instance, psychiatric hospitals have slowly disappeared. In 1955, there were approximately 560,000 residents in psychiatric hospitals, compared with fewer than 50,000 in 2005 (Manderscheid, Atay, and Crider 2009). In 2012, there were approximately ten times as many people in prison with serious mental illness as patients in state psychiatric hospitals (Torrey et al. 2014). Some observers see more than a negative correlation in this relationship and draw direct parallels between the decline in psychiatric hospitals and the rise of prisons. In fact, the sum of patients in psychiatric hospitals and people in prisons has remained relatively consistent over time, suggesting some equivalence and the relevance of thinking about the concept of institutionalization in a general fashion (Harcourt 2006). But it is important to be clear about the interface between psychiatric hospitals and prisons. Deinstitutionalization alone cannot explain the rise in incarceration. Although deinstitutionalization was ongoing as the prison population began to swell, studies have estimated that deinstitutionalization contributed no more than 7% of the increase in incarceration between 1980 and 2000 (Raphael and Stoll 2013). In addition, psychiatric disorders are common in correctional settings in other counties as well, regardless of the number of psychiatric hospital beds that are available (Fazel and Danesh 2002). Deinstitutionalization is not an irrelevant consideration. Indeed, a substantial number of people currently in prison would likely be in psychiatric hospitals were it not for deinstitutionalization. In addition, there are other institutional forces that increase the flow of people with psychiatric disorders into prison. These include the growing refusal of some private hospitals to house patients with severe psychiatric illnesses and more restrictive civil commitment laws, both of which have made it more difficult to house severely ill persons in places *other* than prisons (Lamb and Weinberger 1998). Yet it would be incorrect to suggest that the pressure on prisons to provide mental health care would be alleviated simply by returning to an era when we had more psychiatric hospitals.

* * *

There is no denying that prisons are firmly in the business of providing health care. The pressure on prisons to provide adequate care is driven by both the legal mandate they face and the populations they serve. Prisons are legally obligated to provide treatment, consistent with the formulation set in *Estelle*, and many people arrive with pre-existing medical problems, making it difficult for prisons to ignore the demand. Having described the legal and institutional environment surrounding prison health care, we will now turn to what effect incarceration has on the health of incarcerated people. Given everything that has been discussed thus far, it is reasonable to expect some improvements in health or at least no rapid deterioration. But if prisons are also involved in the business of punishment, and the prison environment is often hostile and violent in ways that an obligation to provide care cannot mitigate, what actually happens to the health of people once they arrive?

3

The Effects of Incarceration on the Health of People in Prison

Understanding the effects of incarceration begins with what happens to people while they are incarcerated. On average, people arrive at prison with mental and physical health worse than comparable people who have never been incarcerated. At least with respect to mental health, the reason people in prison suffer from worse health is partly because the symptoms of some psychiatric disorders overlap with behavior that can be the basis of criminal prosecution (e.g., some types of drug addiction). Furthermore, some diseases that disproportionately affect people in prison spread easily in confined spaces. There have been, for instance, numerous outbreaks of tuberculosis (TB) and hepatitis B in state prisons, some in recent years, well after prisons were forced to do more to protect those in their care (Centers for Disease Control and Prevention 2001, 2004). More recently, prisons have been overwhelmed by COVID-19. Half of all Wisconsin inmates have been infected with COVID-19, a rate five times higher than the overall state rate (Swales 2021).

Although there are numerous plausible pathways to poor health among people in prison, it is critical to provide a complete ledger of influences (Sampson 2011). And the ledger has numerous entries, spanning demographic, epidemiological, legal, and cultural influences. There is more to the health effects of incarceration than the architectural design of prisons, the adverse consequences of confinement, or the characteristics of the people who are incarcerated. The legal mandate that has forced correctional institutions to provide higher-quality care has the potential to improve the health of people in prison. Many people experience better access to care while in prison than they did outside. Even in this regard, though, there are reasons to be cautious, as we argued in Chapter 2. The legal mandate to provide care is specific, limited, and open to interpretation, and for this reason it is important to be granular in assessing what dimensions of health are most affected by incarceration. It is also important to think sequentially rather than statically, as understanding the effects of incarceration on health implies changes in health and should therefore be evaluated as a process. And it is important to think about variation in the conditions of confinement as they might relate to variation in incarceration's health effects. In this chapter we focus on average patterns in an attempt to be comprehensive—much of our evidence is drawn from inmates generally rather than select inmates at a specific institution—though in a later chapter we discuss initiatives that have helped some institutions deliver higher-quality care. We also consider influences outside of prison in tandem with those inside. The degree to which prisons detect new conditions, for instance, depends on how comprehensively people in prison were tested prior to their incarceration. In this way— and in ways we elaborate even more in later chapters when we evaluate the spillover effects of the criminal justice system—there are tight connections between the operation of the prison system and the operation of the health care system more generally. There are also tight connections between the multiple missions of prisons and, for instance, how prisons attempt to deal with mental illness among people in prison.

The Detection of Health Problems in Prison

One way to think about how prisons affect the health of people is to consider the previously undiagnosed conditions prisons might detect. Prisons play an important role in diagnosing infections and, therefore, making people aware of their condition before they are released and potentially treating the condition while they are incarcerated. There are several reasons prisons are particularly good in this role. For one, many people in prison are young and medically underserved, and their initial examination in prison might be their first medical checkup in years. In the United States, about 80% of those infected with human immunodeficiency virus (HIV) have been diagnosed, but this percentage drops among both African Americans and younger people, groups that are at much higher risk of incarceration (Iroh, Mayo, and Nijhawan 2015). Furthermore, at least some of the medical conditions people in prison have are asymptomatic and would ordinarily not prompt otherwise healthy people to seek a diagnosis. Some infections can remain symptomless for years, and prisons can be even more effective than regular ambulatory care in detecting diseases of this sort. Prisons are less discerning about their patients and more routine in the application of their procedures. At least on intake, prisons test everyone, not just those with specific symptoms, and they use a standard set of diagnostic tests. In most ambulatory settings, by contrast, those most at risk for HIV are those most likely to get tested. Of course, those at low risk can also be tested for HIV too, and physicians can generally test for anything they deem necessary. In practice, though, routine HIV testing almost always requires a patient to seek a test on their own volition. Patient agency is different in prison settings. In many state prisons, the testing of people for certain infections, like HIV, is mandatory. And even when testing is not mandatory, it often requires effort to avoid. In some states, people are given the choice to opt *out* of testing rather than to opt *in*. By limiting the role of discretion—which remains controversial— prisons enable more comprehensive testing, even as they restrict consent.

For similar reasons, prisons can be highly effective in treating individuals who are ill. This is especially true for infections that demand a long-term and supervised approach. The treatment of TB, for instance, is demanding. It requires an adequate supply of drugs, regular dosing, and the close monitoring of patient adherence. Prisons can deliver treatment and monitor doses very effectively, given that they supervise their patients closely in all aspects of their lives. In fact, prisons have worse treatment outcomes in situations where they exert less control: the success of TB treatment is higher in prisons than jails, in part because in jails most infected people are lost to release before their treatment can be completed (Lobato, Leary, and Simone 2003).

As a setting for routine testing, prisons catch problems that other systems miss. As one example of this phenomenon, studies have explored the detection of undiagnosed cases of HIV among people entering prison. These studies find widely varying levels of previously undetected cases, though they nonetheless point to an important remedial role of prisons in communities where detection is otherwise poor. One study explored undiagnosed HIV among state prison entrants in North Carolina, finding that the vast majority of people who tested positive for HIV were already known to have the disease (Wohl et al. 2013). Only 6% of HIV cases were previously undetected, meaning only one-tenth of 1% of people entering prison were infected with HIV and unaware of it. Other studies in different correctional systems report much higher detection rates, even if they too find that most cases of HIV were already known. A study of New York City jail entrants, for instance, estimated that 28% of those infected with HIV were undiagnosed prior to admission (Begier et al. 2010). A much broader study, using data from sixteen state and city health departments, found a higher rate of detection. In this study, 75% of the cases of HIV detected in correctional facilities were previously undiagnosed (Van Handel et al. 2012). Furthermore—and perhaps even more noteworthy from a public health perspective—about 30% of people in prison who were newly identified as HIV positive were categorized either as being low risk or as having no apparent risk for infection. A recent review of several studies provides an average detection rate somewhere between these estimates but still quite high. The review estimated that, across different settings, about 22% of HIV-infected people were unaware of the infection prior to incarceration (Iroh, Mayo, and Nijhawan 2015).

Prisons are also relatively effective in treating HIV-positive people. Studies have compared the entire HIV care cascade before, during, and after incarceration, involving initial treatment, retention in treatment, and ongoing success in things like viral load. When evaluating HIV treatment in this fashion, prisons can be seen as effective within the confines of their responsibilities. HIV care tends to increase during periods of incarceration and decrease upon release, often to lower levels than prior to incarceration (Iroh, Mayo, and Nijhawan 2015). In one study, about 54% of HIV-infected people received antiretroviral therapy before incarceration, 65% during, and 37% after release. In addition, the majority of HIV-infected people achieved viral suppression while incarcerated but not before or after. About 27% achieved suppression prior to incarceration, 51% during, and 26% after release. Basic adherence to treatment was also much higher in prison, as indicated by treatment retention (defined as at least two medical visits over six months). Approximately 76% of people were retained in treatment while incarcerated, but only 30% after release. Treatment retention is crucial to reducing mortality among those with HIV.

Most people in prison are not HIV positive. Prisons also test people for other infections, and here too they detect and treat many previously undiagnosed cases. Yet prisons tend to be most attuned to the infectious diseases that are prevalent in prison settings or represent a particular threat to the institution. TB is of special concern because it can easily spread among people living in proximity, is often symptomless, and is serious when active. But TB is also an infection where an existing treatment is effective and can prevent contagion. An active infection involves significant symptoms, but a latent infection involves no symptoms and can remain active for long periods. Although only an active TB infection can lead to contagion, a latent infection can become active without treatment, increasing the imperative to treat. Prisons have responded to this epidemiological situation with assertive treatment protocols. The Centers for Disease Control and Prevention have developed guidelines for the prevention and control of TB in correctional settings. These protocols include entry testing, periodic screening after entry, and the treatment of both active TB disease and latent infection (Centers for Disease Control and Prevention 2006). Prisons have adopted many of the Centers for Disease Control and Prevention's recommendations. A study of the Georgia prison system found that of the 142 cases of TB treated during a five-year period, two-thirds of the cases were discovered at prison intake or in a jail prior to transfer to the prison (Bock et al. 1998). In general, a significant number of new cases of latent TB infections in the United States are detected in correctional facilities, in part because people in prison represent a high-risk population (Lobato, Leary, and Simone 2003). Across forty-nine correctional facilities examined in one study, about 17% of TB tests were positive (Lobato, Leary, and Simone 2003). Outside of prison, the treatment of latent TB is not especially common, in large part because patients are not routinely tested. People are ordinarily tested only if their infections become active, they are at high risk, or they suffer from another disease that increases the risk of converting a latent infection to an active one, including, for example, HIV (Getahun et al. 2015). The medical treatment of TB is highly effective, but, as is the case of HIV, it requires intensive therapeutic supervision and, as a result, is treated quite effectively in a prison setting. The primary treatment protocol involves the daily administration of a TB-specific antibiotic for six to twelve months, which is well within the average prison term (if not jail) (Getahun et al. 2015). A similar pattern of detection and treatment in prison pertains to syphilis, which can facilitate the transmission of HIV and can seriously threaten the health of an infected person if left untreated. A study of people admitted to a jail in Baton Rouge Parish found that, among people who tested positive for syphilis, 22% had not been treated before (Kahn et al. 2002). The treatment of syphilis is relatively inexpensive and involves little more than antibiotics, but with infection rates at less than 10 per 100,000 people, testing for syphilis is not usually a primary concern among general physicians unless there are other risks (Centers for Disease Control and Prevention 2015).

The Intraprison Transmission of Infection

Prisons are generally good at treating the infections they detect, those they recognize as serious, or those they are obligated to identify. But the positive role of prisons in treatment does not mean prisons are not also implicated in the intraprison transmission of infection. Any gap between the detection of an active case and its treatment means a person in prison is still capable of infecting others, at least without other precautions. The mandate of *Estelle* is limited and it does not require that prisons test for all possible infectious diseases. Moreover, the prison environment is ripe for the spread of infection. The architectural design common to prisons—housing units stacked together for ease of supervision, as well as shared eating and restroom facilities—makes social distancing almost impossible, especially in the context of significant overcrowding.

A number of studies have examined the intraprison transmission of infections using seroconversion (the development of detectable antibodies in the blood), generally regarded as the best approach for tracing new infections. Similar antibody tests were used widely during the COVID pandemic to test for exposure to the virus in the general population. Epidemiologists refer to new cases as *incident* cases and are interested in the *incidence rate*, or the number of new cases over a defined period. The *prevalence* simply refers to the number of cases in a population, whether those cases are new or old. One study of a Rhode Island prison found no direct evidence for the intraprison transmission of HIV, at least among those who had been incarcerated for twelve months (Macalino et al. 2004). The same study did, though, find an incidence of hepatitis B of 2.7% and of hepatitis C of .4%, which is low relative to the prevalence. In this prison, the prevalence of hepatitis was high, 20.2% for hepatitis B and 23.1% for hepatitis C.

Other studies have found more evidence for the intraprison transmission of HIV. An early study, for instance, found an annual incidence of .41%, which is quite high relative to the prevalence of HIV (Brewer et al. 1988). Another study found that of 271 inmates who tested positive for HIV, 33 had contracted the disease while in prison (Krebs and Simmons 2002). This study also explored the means of transmission and found plausible pathways for intraprison transmission. Of the cases contracted while in prison, most were due to some combination of intravenous drug use and/or men having sex with men.

All these estimates should be interpreted with caution, both because of the difficulties of identifying intraprison transmission precisely and because of the various standpoints from which the magnitude of intraprison transmission can be evaluated. Three findings are clear. First, the prevalence of infectious disease among people in prison is much higher than among people in the general community. Second, most cases of infectious disease among people in prison are contracted outside of prison. But third, intraprison transmission does occur. Ideally rates of intraprison transmission for major infections would be zero. For most infectious diseases, though, there is at least some evidence for transmission in prison, and the impact of even a fractional incidence rate is substantial given the volume of people who move through the system. With the annual churning of state prisons, an incidence of, for instance, 0.4% can lead to the creation of many new cases of hepatitis C, requiring treatment and appropriate long-term planning after release. Furthermore, the approach of prisons to preventing intraprison transmission is not entirely comprehensive. Prisons are probably less effective in preventing the spread of sexually transmitted infections than in preventing the spread of non–sexually transmitted infections. Inmates infected with TB, for example, can be treated well before they pose a risk to others and, if they pose an active risk, can be moved to health-related segregation units. As a matter of course, US prisons prohibit sexual contact among people in prison. For this reason, prisons might regard someone infected with TB as more of a threat to the general prison population than someone infected with hepatitis B or syphilis. Indeed, in a cruel paradox, the segregation of HIV-infected people can increase the risk of a TB outbreak in prison (Spaulding et al. 2002). Segregated HIV-infected people might not contribute to the intraprison transmission of HIV when segregated, but their compromised immune systems make them more vulnerable to acquiring an active TB infection from someone else in segregation.

The COVID-19 pandemic presents a remarkable illustration of the vulnerabilities of prison populations. COVID-19 is airborne and highly contagious. Prisons have been affected virtually from the start. The first known death of a person in prison from COVID-19 occurred on March 25, 2020, at Lee State Prison in Georgia (Marshall Project 2021). As of this writing, there have been at least 377,000 cases and 2,400 deaths from coronavirus among people in prison. Prison staff are affected as well. There have been at least 101,000 cases among prison staff and 181 deaths. There is considerable variation in how comprehensively states have tested for coronavirus in prisons, though accepting reported cases, the infection rates in at least seven states—Michigan, South Dakota, Arkansas, Kansas, Kentucky, Iowa, and Idaho—exceed 5,000 out of every 10,000 people in prison. On the one hand, COVID-19 has revealed the vulnerability of people in prison and the limited administrative and clinical tools prisons have to prevent the spread of the most contagious infections. With overcrowding and confined spaces, for instance, there is little prisons can do to enforce social distancing. On the other hand, COVID-19 has forced prisons to adopt new strategies for preventing harm to those in their care. In particular, the pandemic has shifted the calculus regarding compassionate release (Sandler 2020; Waters 2020). Although the circumstances surrounding COVID-19 are extraordinary, the use of compassionate release for vulnerable people was hastened by the First Step Act, which was passed in 2018, well before the pandemic. The allowances of the First Step Act were expanded further when courts decided to suspend the act's administrative review exhaustion requirements in light of COVID-19. Compassionate release is governed by US Sentencing Commission guidelines, which focus on four main conditions: the age of the person in prison, any serious medical conditions, family circumstances, and other "extraordinary and compelling" reasons, including those that intersect with the other conditions. COVID-19 is related to all of these conditions. Under these guidelines, and in the presence of COVID-19, the number of serious medical conditions expands, as does the relevance of age and the threshold that might be regarded as advanced. Otherwise common and manageable conditions, like hypertension and diabetes, increase the risk of death from COVID-19, and the sharp age patterning in COVID-19 deaths implies a much higher risk of death for aging people in prison than prior to the pandemic. By October of 2020, over 1,600 people in federal prisons had received compassionate release (Blakinger and Neff 2020). Other options for release include home confinement, which has also increased during the pandemic. More than 7,000 people in federal prisons, for instance, were released to home confinement through the fall of 2020, amounting to 4.6% of the prison population (Blakinger and Neff 2020). This too was spurred by a COVID-19 policy change, in this case a federal coronavirus relief bill.

Although compassionate release expanded during the pandemic, release is hardly granted uncritically or generously. An analysis by the Marshall Project found that, between March and May of 2020, 10,940 people in federal prison applied for compassionate release but only 156 were approved by wardens (Blakinger and Neff 2020). Requests were often denied on the basis of skepticism regarding a petitioner's claim of poor health. In general, claims of vulnerability are often ill received by prison administrators. Furthermore, successful cases were generally filed with the assistance of lawyers; few, if any, cases of compassionate release were initiated by the Bureau of Prisons itself. In short, even under the extraordinary circumstance of COVID-19—circumstances that might reveal the criminal justice system's commitment to the health of those in its care—there remains a great deal of resistance to compassionate release. Even successful instances of release betray the failure of prisons to adequately protect people, as well as a lack of confidence in their ability to ensure the health of people going forward.

Mortality in Prison

A review of infectious disease presents a granular picture of the possible effects of incarceration on health. Through this lens, the effects of incarceration can be evaluated in terms of the risks of infection for specific diseases, the likelihood of specific treatments in prison, and the likelihood of continuing those treatments after release. Yet through the lens of infectious disease it is still challenging to think about what happens to the typical person in prison with the usual health profile. A focus on infectious disease can also be misleading. Given the relatively low prevalence of some serious infections, it might be tempting to infer that prison health care is largely inconsequential to the health of people in prison writ large or that prison care results in only small improvements that are limited to an identifiable subset of people (setting aside, for the moment, any benefits that might be realized to the broader community if postrelease infections are also prevented).

A more comprehensive way to evaluate the sum of risk and protective factors is to think about overall mortality. Given the average age of US prisoners, mortality in prison is generally quite low. Regardless of where they reside, people in their twenties and thirties have lower mortality than people over the age of sixty-five. As a percentage of all inmates, very few inmates are serving life sentences or even sentences longer than twenty years. Mindful of this, several studies have estimated mortality in prison relative to mortality among demographically comparable people residing in the general community (Patterson 2010). Here too the findings speak as much to the nature of risk and mortality outside of prisons as inside. In exercises of this sort, it is crucial to consider sex and race. In general, incarceration is worse for mortality among women than among men. Compared with women of the same age living in the community, mortality among women in prison is between 16% and 76% higher, depending on the time period. Although the difference has declined somewhat over time, it remains significant. For men, these patterns are different, and the effects of incarceration on mortality vary substantially by race. Among Black men, mortality in prison is *lower* than mortality outside of prison. In contrast, among white men, mortality in prison is somewhat higher than mortality outside, though the inside/outside difference among men is nowhere near as large as the difference among women. In her study of race differences in the effect of prisons on mortality, Evelyn Patterson focused on a specific quantity: the expected number of years of life lost to death between the ages of eighteen and sixty-five. This number provides a plain metric for interpretation and reveals that the positive effects of prison are hardly small. Among Black men, the number of years lost in prison is 3.068, whereas outside prison it is 6.024. Among white men, meanwhile, the comparable figures are 2.850 and 2.597. Another way to interpret these comparisons is in terms of the overall Black-white difference in mortality: though Black men have a significantly higher risk of mortality outside of prison, something closer to racial equality prevails inside prison.

The relative difference in overall mortality among Black men in prison can be partitioned into specific causes of death. The most relevant causes for understanding the difference are those that are uncommon in prisons but common outside. Deaths caused by firearms and motor vehicles, for instance, are frequent outside of the prison but virtually nonexistent in an institutional setting. While deaths from these causes account for some of the total difference in mortality, age patterns are also important. The mortality-reducing effects of incarceration for Black men are strongest at younger ages, a time when homicide and accidents are otherwise leading causes of death. But these causes do not account for the entire difference. Prison health care also plays a role, and other studies have demonstrated that causes of death that are amenable to care are important (Mumola 2007). Overall mortality in prisons is about 19% lower than in the general adult US population, but the most common causes of death are very similar in the two settings. As with the general population, the leading causes of death in prison are heart disease and cancer, followed by liver disease, acquired immunodeficiency syndrome (AIDS), and suicide. Together cancer and heart disease make up just over half of all deaths in prison (50.6%), while liver disease, AIDS, and suicide follow distantly behind, at 10.1%, 7.2%, and 6.1%. Other "external" causes of death—causes of death related to a process outside the body, which an especially secure and supervised environment might be expected to prevent—account for only a small percentage of deaths in prison. Homicide, for instance, accounts for 2% of deaths in prison and overdoses account for 1%. Another way to consider the role of prison health care is in terms of deaths from ailments that predate incarceration. About two-thirds of deaths in prison are from conditions that were present at the time of admission but advanced beyond treatment over the course of a sentence. Among those who died, 93% received medication for the illness that would lead to their death.

The significance of prison care can be evaluated in other ways as well. Some studies have tracked improvements in prison mortality that correspond to improvements in care. For instance, a study of mortality in the Texas prison system spanning more than a decade found declines in mortality from infection, cardiovascular disease, liver disease, and respiratory disease (Harzke et al. 2011). Although mortality from cancer increased, this was largely because the proportion of older people in prison grew. Those causes of death that declined the most were those most amenable to medical treatment or those that were explicitly targeted for better case management. In Texas prisons, health care is contracted with academic medical centers, which generally provide high-quality treatment.

Although these studies suggest seemingly low mortality in prison, perhaps rooted in the effective delivery of health care or, short of that, protection from external mortality, these studies are difficult to reconcile with the facts surrounding recent prison litigation. Discovery in successful lawsuits has revealed a good deal of inadequacies regarding prison health care. In light of these apparent inadequacies, critics have sought other explanations for the apparent positive effects of incarceration, starting with a consideration of whom prisons admit and release rather than what treatments people in prison might receive. In this vein, at least one lingering concern for causal inference is compassionate release, which could introduce bias in favor of demonstrating an apparent mortality-reducing effect of incarceration. In the presence of substantial compassionate release, mortality might appear lower among people in prison than among comparable men on the outside, but this difference would reflect the release of people who are in poor health rather than the delivery of effective treatment while they are incarcerated. This possibility is especially likely if prisons are keen on releasing people who are costly to treat or nearing death. Although compassionate release remains uncommon and is generally underutilized, even small amounts of health-related release can be sufficient to produce a seemingly beneficial effect of incarceration, especially in some limited settings. One study of Georgia prisons, for example, explored the role of release and concluded that compassionate release accounted for *all* of the apparent protective effect of incarceration on mortality, even though there were relatively few such releases (Spaulding et al. 2011). In Georgia, there are approximately ten to twenty-two compassionate releases per year, a number that can account for the apparent mortality-reducing effects of incarceration in a single prison system given the relatively small number of deaths.

Although this study casts doubt on claims that health care in prison reduces mortality, it should be interpreted in context. As we have emphasized elsewhere, accurately understanding the effects of prison on health requires a comprehensive approach to characterizing the environment inside and outside prison, including the policy environment. Compassionate release can be a source of bias in studies of this sort, but it is also, in itself, a process that reveals the uneasy collision of prisons and health, as well as the unresolved tension between punishment and care. For one, the nature of compassionate release varies between states, so what applies to Georgia need not apply to other states. All states set a high bar for release. A petitioning inmate must pose no risk to society and have a terminal condition that cannot be treated appropriately in the prison (Beck 1999; Williams et al. 2011). Some states impose supplementary criteria, raising the bar further by demanding reassurance regarding both the inevitability of near death and the risk of recidivism. New York, for instance, explicitly blends medical considerations with expectations about the risk of future criminality. In New York, inmates must be terminally ill, severely restricted in their ability to walk, *and* severely restricted in their ability to care for themselves (Beck 1999). Florida imposes a similar set of criteria, demanding permanent incapacitation. In general, across all prison systems, only a small percentage of people nearing death are released. Among those who seek compassionate release, many die awaiting review. In New York, for example, fewer than one in ten petitioners is released before death (Beck 1999). Data from the Federal Bureau of Prisons in

2008 indicates that there were 399 deaths in federal prisons but only twenty-seven approved requests for compassionate release (Williams et al. 2011).

Beyond strict criteria for release, there are administrative reasons that compassionate release likely plays a small role in mortality statistics. Compassionate release is never an easy matter, in part because it involves a complex medical prognosis set in an ill-suited bureaucratic process. In the federal prison system, for example, there are four levels of review, after an initial medical evaluation. Medical personnel must determine whether a person's condition is terminal. Predicting how long a patient will live is never a simple matter and physicians routinely overestimate prognoses in oncology, for instance (Christakis 1999). But in a prison setting there are reasons to suspect that physicians might be even more conservative. To meet most guidelines for compassionate release, people in prison must have a *predictable* terminal prognosis, meaning the person is expected, with unusual certainty, to die shortly following release. There is considerable unpredictability surrounding prognosis, and this uncertainty is, if anything, greater for the kinds of medical conditions that are common among people in prison, including liver disease. One reason there are few cases of compassionate release, then, is the tension between the humanistic goals of compassionate release and the difficulties of its proper and generous administration. The difficulty falls on petitioners too. If a person in poor health applies too soon, a medical officer might conclude they have too long to live, but if they apply too late, they will very likely die during the process. Some states, like California, are firm in matters of timing, stipulating a life expectancy of precisely six months or less, well within the window it might take for a petition to be adjudicated.

Overall, the evidence indicates that prisons reduce mortality, especially for populations that have high mortality outside of prison or are otherwise medically underserved. But this broad conclusion requires some caveats and further elaboration. To this point, the evidence we have presented on the health-promoting effects of incarceration has been limited to low-incidence infectious diseases and mortality among people mostly under the age of sixty-five. Even if we accept that violent deaths are less common for some groups in prison than the same groups outside, this should not be taken to mean prisons are free of assault. Clearly prisons are not entirely safe environments, and most assaults do not result in death. Furthermore, even if we accept that prisons can, under some circumstances, improve physical health, this does not mean that prisons are conducive to better mental health. Indeed, some of the things that might reduce violence in prison, like administrative segregation (or even the threat of using such segregation), are damaging to mental health. Before turning to the effects of incarceration on mental health, the issue of prison violence deserves special attention, as it sets the stage for thinking about the psychological climate of prisons.

Prison Violence

Prison violence is implied in some of what we have discussed already. For instance, the single most common mode of transmitting HIV in prison is men having sex with other men. Although some of this is consensual, much of it is not. A comprehensive study conducted in 2011 and 2012 explored sexual victimization in prisons using a national survey. The data were gathered independent of prison administrators, ensuring some degree of candor in what people reported to researchers. The study effectively put to rest the notion that sexual victimization in prison is rare, finding that about 4% of people in state and federal prisons experienced one or more incidents of sexual victimization in the preceding year, with most victims reporting that they were repeatedly abused (Beck et al. 2013). In instances where victimization occurred, the perpetrator was not always another inmate. Whereas 2% of people reported an incident with another inmate, 2.4% reported an incident with staff. Projected over the entire prison population in the United States, these percentages imply nearly 60,000 victims of sexual victimization per year. The same study, however, found that prison facilities varied enormously in the amount of sexual victimization that occurred within their walls. In some facilities, *no* person who participated in the survey reported victimization. In other prisons, the frequency of sexual victimization was at least 55% higher than the overall average. Although a skeptic might worry that people in prison fail to report violence for fear of retaliation, and that this fear might be greater in some facilities than others, all participants were assured that prison officials could not see their responses to the survey. There is no obvious reason to doubt the veracity of differences between facilities, even if we accept that reports of violence are generally biased downward.

Sexual victimization is a form of violence. While it rarely results in death, it causes great physical and mental harm. But there is more to this relationship—the connections between sexual violence and health reflect more than a one-way path. Sexual victimization is usually the result of predation, and health is strongly implicated in who in the prison population is targeted. People suffering from psychiatric disorders report much higher rates of sexual abuse. Among those with an anxiety or mood disorder—among the most common psychiatric disorders—2.8% experienced inmate-on-inmate abuse and 3% experienced staff abuse, compared to 0.7% and 1.1% among those with no disorder (Beck et al. 2013). Among those experiencing serious nonspecific psychological distress—defined as significant symptoms that may or may not be attached to a psychiatric disorder—the percentages are even higher: 6% experienced inmate-on-inmate abuse and 5.6% experienced staff abuse. Because a large percentage of people in prison suffer from psychological disorders, and because prison conditions themselves might cause significant psychological distress, the number of at-risk people is considerable. About 37% of people in prison report having been diagnosed with a psychiatric disorder by a mental health professional, a threshold higher than the percentage likely experiencing psychological symptoms.

Although violence from staff and other inmates receives the bulk of attention, psychiatric disorders are also related to self-harm. People in prison are generally more likely to hurt others than themselves, but the frequency of self-harm varies by the conditions of confinement. For instance, one study of the New York City jail system, conducted over a three-year period, found that only 0.05% of individuals harm themselves, but that the risk of self-harm increased considerably when people were held in solitary confinement (Kaba et al. 2014). Most incidences of self-harm (53.3%) occurred in the context of solitary confinement. Self-harm also includes suicide. Suicide remains a common cause of death in prison, though its frequency varies by the conditions of confinement, and in particular, jails differ from prisons. Between 2000 and 2009, suicide was the single leading cause of death in jails, accounting for 29% of deaths, followed by heart disease, at 22% (Noonan and Carson 2011). In prisons, however, suicide accounted for only around 6% of deaths, whereas heart disease and cancer accounted for around half. One reason for this difference, of course, is that prisons hold people longer than jails—with aging, the causes of death among people in prison begin to resemble the causes of death found in nonincarcerated populations. The difference also, however, reflects administrative and institutional differences between prisons and jails (Chammah and Meagher 2015). The initial shock associated with confinement increases the risk of suicide in the first few days and even hours of incarceration. Relative to people in prison, a much larger number of people in jail are in this "initial" period at any given time. About 47% of all jail suicides occur in the first seven days or less, and about 62% of all jail discharges occur in the same amount of time (Noonan 2010). Consistent with the idea of a shock, far more suicides occur among people in jail who have never been convicted of a crime, suggesting they have limited (or no) prior exposure to the criminal justice system and fewer tools for coping with the trauma. In addition, many jails are poorly equipped to identify people at risk for suicide, especially if their intake procedures do not involve especially thorough mental health diagnostics or rely entirely on pre-existing diagnoses. The suicide rate in jails holding fewer than 50 people is more than five times higher than the suicide rate in jails with 1,000 or more (167 suicides per 100,000 people, relative to 33). The vast majority of large jails provide training in suicide risk assessment for their staff, but in small jails only 54% provide such training (Noonan 2010).

In prisons, the risks associated with a psychiatric disorder assume a somewhat different character. In the general community, those who suffer from a disorder are at a higher risk of both suicide and being the victim of a crime. These associations are also apparent in prisons too, but the prison environment shapes which psychiatric disorders are more consequential. Understanding what incarceration does to people requires a nuanced understanding of what makes the prison environment unique. Table 3.1 presents estimated change in the odds of victimization after accounting for a variety of factors known to be related to the risk of victimization, including the type of prison, the age of the person, race, marital status, height, the presence of any disability, and a variety of background characteristics, including prior incarceration or earlier sexual abuse. The table highlights the effects of specific psychiatric disorders and symptoms on victimization. Additionally, it looks at the risks associated with specific disorders by gender. In general, the risks associated with psychiatric disorders are stronger for men than for women. For instance, a depressive disorder increases the odds of victimization among men in prison by 53%. Except for a psychotic disorder, all disorders are associated with an increased risk. Among women in prison, however, most disorders are unassociated with victimization.

In general, incarcerated women with psychiatric disorders seem to face a slightly lower risk of victimization, but the relationships are small. Once we

Table 3.1 Relationship between Psychiatric Disorders
and Victimization in Male and Female Inmates

	Men	Women
Disorders		
Depressive disorder	53%*	−10%*
Bipolar disorder	51%*	−8%*
Psychotic disorder	7%	−8%
Posttraumatic stress disorder	37%*	−28%*
Anxiety disorder	39%*	−19%*
Personality disorder	72%*	−38%*
Symptoms		
Sadness	40%*	−24%*
Anger	53%*	134%*
Agitation	20%	22%
Delusions/hallucinations	27%	53%

*Denotes statistically significant sex difference, at $p < .05$

Note: Estimates derived from Tables 4 and 5 in Schnittker and
Bacak (2015).

separate symptoms from disorders, however, we can better understand the
nature of this sex difference. Anger is a symptom of a variety of psychiatric
disorders. It also plays a role in provoking violence in prisons. Yet the relationship between anger and victimization is much stronger among women
in prison than among men in prison, increasing the odds of victimization by
134% among women but only by 53% among men. Sadness, however, is very
different. Women who experience sadness are about 24% *less* likely to be victimized, while men with sadness are 40% *more* likely to be victimized. Other
symptoms, such as agitation and delusions, show no significant differences
by sex.

These patterns likely reflect how psychiatric symptoms are interpreted by
others in a prison setting. On the one hand, the presence of a psychiatric
disorder signals weakness and, therefore, increases the risk of victimization. As is true on the outside, those in prison with a psychiatric disorder
are more vulnerable to violence. On the other hand, psychiatric symptoms

can often be interpreted relative to how far they diverge from traditional gender norms, that is, in terms of larger notions of deviance. Depression in men, for instance, signals weakness much more than depression in women. And indeed, in some circumstances, women in prison with mental illness might be at a lower risk of victimization than those without. Anger, however, is far more bound up with traditional heteronormative masculinity (Stanko and Hobdell 1993). Consistent with this, the relationship between anger and victimization may be much stronger in women than men in a prison context. When thinking about the risks of victimization posed by a psychiatric disorder, it is important to consider what the disorder might signal to other people in prison as much as the behavioral consequences of a given disorder. The relationship between anger and victimization is not surprising if we assume that psychiatric disorders can provoke a violent response from others, but the fact that anger is more consequential for women in prison suggests that symptoms are interpreted through the lens of gender. Prisons are gendered organizations that both reflect and reproduce existing inequalities (Britton 1997). And research has shown that prisons tend to reinforce gender norms in surprisingly powerful ways, by, for instance, encouraging hypermasculinity among men and a heteronormative vision of femininity among women. In the past decade, research has begun to document the experiences of transgender prisoners in such settings, particularly trans women, like Dee Farmer, who are housed in men's prisons (Sexton and Jenness 2016). The gender culture of prisons is a significant factor when thinking about how prisons undermine health and well-being.

The Treatment of Psychiatric Disorders in Prison

An important consideration for understanding the effects of incarceration on mental health is the adequacy of the psychiatric services incarcerated people receive. Obviously, this parallels our consideration of the treatment of physical problems, though psychiatric disorders present their own complications. Most prisons provide screening for psychiatric disorders, but the challenges of providing mental health care are daunting. For one, the problem of dual loyalty is especially pressing in the case of mental health. The concept of dual loyalty focuses on the challenges of providing care in a setting that is focused overwhelmingly on security. Prison medical personnel sit between these missions, and because psychiatric disorders can be interpreted in multiple ways, disorders cross these missions in a way that is difficult to reconcile. Psychiatric disorders can be interpreted as revealing a medical problem, a character problem, or a threat. The interpretation that prevails depends greatly on the circumstances, perhaps more so than the symptoms themselves. An episode of acute psychosis, for instance, is ordinarily a medical emergency and treated in a clinical fashion, but in the context of a prison, it is also a disciplinary problem and treated with force. Psychiatric disorders are implicated in disciplinary infractions. One nationwide study found that 58% of incarcerated people who suffered from a psychiatric disorder had been charged with a rule violation, relative to 43% of those who did not suffer from a disorder (James and Glaze 2006). Reports of verbal assault were especially common among those with a disorder.

Dual loyalty is not an abstract matter with few practical implications. A study of the New York jail system found that mental health staff routinely reported dual-loyalty concerns (Glowa-Kollisch et al. 2015). More than a third of staff, for instance, reported that their ethics were compromised on a regular basis. For their part, incarcerated people were more likely to say that mental health staff were part of the security apparatus than the medical staff. In this study, prison mental health staff were asked to evaluate six hypothetical situations, presented as vignettes, after which they were asked about the frequency of their experiences with these situations in actual day-to-day encounters. One vignette, for instance, depicted an injury report that falsely claimed an incarcerated person was attacked by another incarcerated person when, in fact, they were injured by a guard. More than 90% of prison medical staff reported encountering or at least hearing about something similar. Short of possibly condoning abuse by other staff, mental health personnel participate in routine activities that involve significant ethical dilemmas. Mental health staff, for example, are frequently used to approve people for transfer to solitary confinement. In these circumstances, staff are asked to rule whether the person is mentally fit for solitary confinement, knowing full well that its conditions are detrimental to well-being and fitness is likely to be fleeting. There is little evidence they are screened with medical interests in mind: incarcerated people with psychiatric disorders are disproportionately represented in solitary confinement, a practice that surely exacerbates their symptoms (Human Rights Watch 2015).

Dual-loyalty issues are also evident in routine diagnostic practices. A crucial aspect of delivering effective mental health services is, of course, making an accurate diagnosis. In a prison, the blending of concerns regarding health and discipline contaminate diagnostic practices. Using an ethnographic approach, Lorna Rhodes (2000) studied how psychiatric nomenclature is used in prison settings and, in particular, its function. Rhodes finds that diagnoses are deployed to signal the threat someone poses as much as to provide an accurate appraisal of an underlying disorder. In particular, she finds regular use of the term "psychopath," despite the concept's opaque definition and lack of formal recognition. Although the term has psychiatric origins and can be used to describe a certain category of symptoms, it is used in prisons to refer to people who are threatening and, at that, is used to describe the *character* of people more than the nature of their dysfunction. The label implies that the person has little control over dangerous impulses and lacks a recognizable morality (even though formal psychiatric nomenclature explicitly eschews forensic considerations). Rhodes also demonstrates how the label has consequences that stretch far beyond the appropriate tailoring of services to a case. In particular, and consistent with the tenets of labeling theory, she shows how the label loops back to the inmate, providing a convenient and all-encompassing explanation for behavior. Indeed, the label is often used to explain a range of actions, both deviant and seemingly ordinary. Moreover, the label carries extraordinary power. People who have been labeled as psychopaths are greeted with suspicion, even when their behavior is not obviously threatening. A calm demeanor, for instance, is interpreted as concealing something more nefarious, while mere frustration is interpreted as insidious rage.

Although mental health staff lean on the specific concept of psychopathology more than is warranted, misdiagnosis in prison stretches beyond this single disorder. Across a variety of diagnostic categories, errors are more common in prison settings than elsewhere (Martin et al. 2016). Approximately 10% to 15% of people in prison, for instance, are incorrectly diagnosed in an elementary way: accurately determining whether they have a disorder or not. In addition, many people in prison who are diagnosed with a disorder receive the wrong diagnosis. Although the problem of misdiagnosis is not entirely the fault of mental health staff, it does reflect the peculiarities of the prison environment. Many incarcerated people who would normally meet the diagnostic criteria for a disorder are not properly diagnosed because they fail to report their symptoms accurately, either because they fear being seen as weak or because they had poor experiences with psychiatric services prior to incarceration (Morgan et al. 2007). On the provider side, mental health assessments in prison are often done quickly with little follow-up. Evaluating people at intake—ordinarily a proactive approach—presents another problem in the sense that people sometimes display symptoms at admission that will fade over time, especially given the shock of arrest or initial confinement. In fact, the adequacy of detection *within* prison depends a great deal on the adequacy of detection *outside* of prison. A study of jail detainees found that the strongest predictor of detecting mental illness is a diagnostic history available in medical records at the time of intake (Teplin 1990). Indeed, in this study a record of psychiatric treatment mattered more than the nature of the arrest or even the overt presence of symptoms. In addition, staff are also much more likely to detect disorders that present a challenge to administrators. For instance, staff are much more likely to detect schizophrenia than depression, a disorder often characterized by psychomotor retardation. Among inmates who suffer from depression, fewer than one in ten cases is accurately detected.

The concept of dual loyalty was developed with prison medical staff in mind, but in correctional settings the dilemmas of properly addressing mental health apply to other staff members as well, pointing to larger institutional considerations. Correctional officers are trained to assess threats and secure inmates (Human Rights Watch 2015). In securing the social environment, they demand obedience and assume those in their custody behave in accountable ways. Correctional officers certainly recognize that people in prison can suffer from mental health problems, but they are rarely trained to address psychiatric disorders with clinical acuity. For instance, correctional officers are not trained to discriminate between behaviors that result from a psychiatric disorder and behaviors that do not. When restraining incarcerated people, officers generally employ the same tactics, irrespective of a person's mental health. Disciplinary hearings involve the same indiscriminate approach. Hearings rarely consider mental illness explicitly, and people who are suffering with mental illness generally receive the same sanctions as those who are not (Fellner 2006). For prison officials, this approach is surely blunt but it may also be strategic, rooted in intuitions regarding the credibility of mental illness among people in prison. If mental illness is regarded as an extenuating factor in disciplinary matters, officials fear that others will fabricate symptoms to circumvent punishment. Indeed, a survey found that some prison officials believe that allowing for consideration of mental illness in disciplinary matters will *accentuate* problems of dual loyalty. If mental health staff, for instance, were called upon to make forensic evaluations, incarcerated people might retaliate if those staff failed to support their claim to being ill (Krelstein 2002). In some states it is official policy that mental health staff should not communicate with officials presiding over disciplinary hearings.

Beyond the peculiar situation of prison staff, there are larger institutional issues preventing adequate mental health treatment in prisons. The American Medical Association (AMA) has developed standards of prison health care through the long-standing National Commission on Correctional Health Care. In 2015, the commission created a Mental Health Standards document that paralleled their more general Standards for Health Services in Jails. Although the creation of these standards reveals a serious concern with adequate care for incarcerated people and a growing alignment of physical and mental health, the emphasis on prison care has been a relatively small part of the AMA's portfolio. The American Psychiatric Association has also devoted attention to mental health care in prisons but has generally focused more on services for re-entry than services for those in custody. Staffing issues can also pose challenges. For instance, most prison medical staff are generalists rather than specialists, and many staff who focus on mental health tend not to be medically trained. It is generally difficult to attract psychiatrists and psychologists to correctional settings, in part because the salary differential between prisons and community settings is considerable (Human Rights Watch 2003). Prisons certainly pay less than private practice, but prisons also pay less than many schools.

Oversight is difficult as well, in large part because it can rest on political entities rather than professional ones. In response to a class action lawsuit, for instance, Florida created the Florida Correctional Medical Authority in 1986. The authority was designed to oversee health care in its prisons, but it was effectively disbanded in 2011, when the Florida legislature eliminated funding for it. Political willpower matters as well. In general, states are reluctant to create oversight agencies of their own accord, instead acting only in response to litigation (Deitch 2012). Comprehensive independent agencies are rare, and even when they exist, they face problems related to jurisdiction. Perhaps the best example is the California Inspector General, which oversees all California state prisons. This is a substantial remit for the agency, but there is no equivalent statewide unit that oversees California's *jails*, even though the volume and churn of people in jail implies a potentially large impact of improved care (Deitch 2010).

Psychiatric Disorders as a Cause of Offending

One argument for providing mental health services for people in prison is that better care can reduce recidivism. There is a relationship between psychiatric disorders and offending—a relationship that partly explains the prevalence of psychiatric disorders in prisons—but the relationship is multifaceted. The strength of the relationship depends on the specific type of disorder and its symptoms, as well as how the disorder interacts with other characteristics. Even for psychiatric disorders strongly related to offending, the disorder itself is seldom the determining behavior. Some psychiatric disorders involve impulsive or even directly criminal behavior. Substance abuse disorders, for instance, can entail criminal behavior in the sense that driving under the influence of alcohol and possession of a controlled substance are crimes. In addition, some disorders involve feelings of threat or insecurity that might trigger offending, including violence. Yet mental illness per se is only the tip of the iceberg and we risk misplaced specificity when attempting to attribute offending to mental illness.

For one, mental illness and criminal behavior are often determined by the same factors, rendering the relationship between the two spurious. Criminologists have long appreciated that stress and weak social support can lead to violent behavior, while epidemiologists have recognized that the same factors can increase the risk of developing a psychiatric disorder. Because of this codetermination, much of the apparent effect of psychiatric disorders on violence is likely attributable to stress and social isolation. Indeed, about a third of the relationship between a major psychiatric disorder and violence is due to stress and diminished social support rather than the disorder per se (Silver and Teasdale 2005). Social support is especially significant in this regard. Strong social bonds have long been known to reduce crime, explaining why, for example, married people offend less than single people, and why adults, embedded in networks of obligation, offend less than younger people (Sampson and Laub 1993). The significance of social bonds is no less among those suffering from a psychiatric disorder. For example, one study explored recidivism among those acquitted by reason of insanity (Callahan and Silver 1998). If mental illness was *the* most important factor in offending, then reoffending should be determined by no factor other than mental illness. Yet among people acquitted by reason of insanity, those who were married were much less likely to reoffend than those who were not.

The relationship between psychiatric disorders and offending is complicated in other ways. Although it is easy to imagine a relationship between a specific disorder and offending—as in, for example, an impulse control disorder that motivates theft—evidence indicates that specific symptoms often matter more than the set of symptoms that compose a disorder. In this vein, one study explored the relationship between psychiatric disorders and violence and found that the presence of a psychiatric disorder per se mattered much less than the presence of a specific cluster of symptoms (Link et al. 1999). In particular, threat-control override symptoms, characterized by feeling threatened and not in control, had an especially strong relationship with violent behavior. Such symptoms explain much of the relationship between the presence of a disorder, especially bipolar disorder, and violence. Those suffering from bipolar disorder but not experiencing threat-control override symptoms were essentially no more prone to violence than someone not suffering from a psychiatric disorder at all. The beliefs associated with threat-control override may have no rational basis—a person who feels they are being pursued by secret agents, for instance, probably has no rational basis for that belief—but these beliefs do help to explain why the person might be motivated to act aggressively. Yet such beliefs represent only a subset of the symptoms that make up bipolar disorder. Moreover, these particular symptoms are not essential for meeting the diagnostic criteria for the disorder and they are not present in all people suffering from the disorder.

In a similar vein, other studies have demonstrated that any single disorder might matter less than certain *combinations* of disorders (Copeland et al. 2007). A study linking childhood psychiatric disorders to offending among young adults found that comorbidity among disorders was especially important. Young adults with *both* emotional and behavioral disorders were more likely to offend than young adults with either disorder on its own. Having depression, for example, doubles the odds of committing a violent offense, and having a substance use disorder increases the odds by a factor of

3.5, but the multiplicative effect of having *both* disorders increased the odds of a violent offense by more than a factor of 12. The most consequential pairings of disorders involve conduct and substance use disorders in combination with anxiety and depression. One interpretation of this pattern is that a proclivity toward criminal behavior, as in a conduct disorder, is conducive to criminal behavior only when experienced in combination with a sense of unease, as in an anxiety disorder. Confluences of this sort are unusual in someone who only suffers from anxiety.

Perhaps the most thorough study of its kind explored, in an especially granular fashion, the symptoms and crimes of more than 100 people in prison with mental illness (Peterson et al. 2014). The researchers paid close attention to the question of whether the symptoms could plausibly have motivated the crime, using indicators such as how closely in time the symptoms and the crime were experienced, as well as how reasonably the specific symptoms might explain the criminal behavior. The results were revealing. Almost two-thirds of the crimes were judged to have occurred entirely independent of the disorder, and only about 8% could be considered a direct result of the disorder. Even for people suffering from the most severe psychiatric disorders, the relationship between the disorder and the crime was comparatively weak. Among people suffering from bipolar disorder, for example, 62% of their crimes were unrelated to the disorder. Similarly, among those suffering from schizophrenia, less than a quarter of their crimes could be considered completely or mostly related to their symptoms. Of those people who were determined to have committed at least one crime because of their disorder, two-thirds *also* committed a crime that was unrelated to their disorder. A mere 5% committed *only* crimes that could be related to their disorder. Even if we grant that there is some relationship between psychiatric disorders and offending, it does not appear to explain much of the total criminal behavior. One study examined the impact of psychiatric disorders on violent crime, based on administrative data collected in Sweden (Fazel and Grann 2006). It found that only about 5% of violent crimes could be attributed to severe mental illness. Even among men ages fifteen to twenty-four—the most violence-prone age group in general—mental illness explained only 3% of the group's violent behavior. The authors argue that mental illness might explain more of the violence committed by women, but because women are far less likely to be violent than men, the total number of incidents explained by mental illness is very small.

Another way to think about the relationship between psychiatric disorders and offending is less in terms of the likelihood of criminal behavior than in terms of the likelihood of arrest. Relative to those who do not have a disorder, those with psychiatric disorders might be only somewhat more likely to engage in criminal behavior but much more likely to have contact with the criminal justice system when they do. Those with psychiatric disorders might, for example, commit more visible crimes, including, for instance, crimes in public places. In addition, they might face more stigma because of their disorder, behavior, or both, making them more likely to be remanded to jail when arrested. The evidence on this possibility is not terribly strong, though it is certainly the case that many acutely mentally ill persons come into contact with the police (Lamb and Weinberger 1998). When presented with an obviously disordered person, police have relatively few options: they can refer the person to a psychiatric hospital if space is available, they can take the person to jail, or they can do neither and release the person. But mental illness complicates the availability of these options and contravenes discretion. Many arrestees end up in jail, especially if they are unhoused and lack other forms of material support.

Understanding the Effects of Incarceration on Psychiatric Disorders

Returning to the central question of this chapter: what can be said about the effects of incarceration on mental health? It is clear that the prevalence of psychiatric disorders among people in prison is considerably higher than among the US population generally. Yet the effects of incarceration on mental health are less certain. If the conditions of confinement are sufficiently adverse, incarceration might lead to the creation of new disorders. Incarceration might also worsen existing disorders, including through a process whereby an active mental illness contributes to victimization in prison. Yet evaluating the effects of incarceration on mental illness deserves special consideration, perhaps even more so than when evaluating the effects on physical health. As before, it is important to consider the complete ledger of influences, including the psychiatric disorders that predate incarceration, the disorders that prisons detect and treat, and the ways a prison environment compromises mental health. With this set of influences in mind, one major review concluded that evidence regarding the so-called pains of imprisonment—a phrase used to describe the many aspects of imprisonment that can undermine mental health—was inconclusive (Bonta and Gendreau 1990). But variation in the effects of incarceration is critical. Not all prisons will be equally stressful, some conditions of confinement are especially bad, some inmates will cope much better than others, and mental health has multiple potential dimensions (Haney 2006).

Evaluating the effects of incarceration begins with a discussion of the prevalence of psychiatric disorders in prison. It is clear that psychiatric disorders are more common among people in prison than in the community, although estimates can vary significantly between facilities. The percentage of people in prison who suffer from major depression, for instance, ranges from 9% to 29% (Prins 2014), whereas in the general community the prevalence of major depression is just under 7% (Kessler et al. 2005). Similarly, anywhere from about 6% to 16% of people in prison suffer from bipolar disorder, an especially debilitating mood disorder, whereas fewer than 3% of those in the general community suffer from the same. Schizophrenia is ordinarily found in about 1% or less of the general population, but among people in prison the prevalence is between 2% and 6.5%. For the most common psychiatric disorders, the lowest reported prevalence in prison is still higher than what is found in the community.

All these estimates pertain to diagnosed or diagnosable disorders; that is, they indicate the percentage of people in prison whose symptoms are sufficiently severe to be detected or meet the diagnostic threshold for a formal psychiatric diagnosis. Another way to think about mental illness, though, is to think in terms of symptoms, irrespective of whether they are sufficient for a specific disorder. It is possible, for example, that even if most people in prison do not suffer from major depression, many are still sad, anxious, or irritable, well beyond what is found on the outside. Some studies have explored the prevalence of specific symptoms in prisons, and they point to especially high levels of nonspecific psychological distress (James and Glaze 2006). About 49% of people in state prisons and 60% of people in jails suffer from at least one symptom of a psychiatric disorder. The most common symptoms, experienced by just under half of all people, are consistent with either major depression or mania. In addition, just under half of all people in jail report feeling persistently angry or irritable, and nearly 20% report a delusion. People in state prisons fare somewhat better but still report considerable suffering. Around a third report feeling, for example, persistently sad, numb, or empty. Only about 30% of people in state prisons and 23% of people in jail report no symptoms of depression at all. Evidence links the prison environment itself to these symptoms. Prisons are stressful, though in discontinuous ways over time. Evidence indicates that the first month is the most stressful period, after which many people appear to adjust (Zamble 1992). Suicides are much more common in the first month than later. This does not imply that people grow well after an initial period of adjustment, but debilitating depression or anxiety appears to fade as people in prison adapt to their circumstances. Criminologists refer to the process of *prisonization,* which refers to the successful adaptation to the norms and routines of prison life, or, alternatively, *institutionalization,* which describes the ways in which institutionalized persons—whether people in prisons, psychiatric hospitals, or the military—adapt to an all-encompassing environment (Paterline and Petersen 1999; Thomas 1977).

Other aspects of the prison environment are not conducive to well-being and do not fade with time or adjustment. One dimension of prisonization is how people successfully learn to prevent predation, as when they learn an informal code. Yet it is difficult to eliminate the risk for violence entirely. As discussed earlier, assault is not uncommon in prisons, and assaults can have lasting effects on mental health. Victims of violence continue to suffer long after the physical pain of an assault has subsided, largely because they fear an assault happening again (Resnick, Acierno, and Kilpatrick 1997). Even if someone can successfully avoid another assault, the behaviors that prevent assault can themselves erode well-being. People in prison often maintain a heightened sense of anticipatory fear, which may well preserve their physical safety but leads to a persistent state of physiological arousal.

Other aspects of confinement are detrimental to mental health as well. Prison overcrowding undermines mental health (Cox, Paulus, and McGain 1984). Studies following people in prison over time find that an increase in overcrowding is associated with a variety of indicators of worsening mental health, including higher suicide rates, more disciplinary infractions, and more self-mutilation. In addition, large open housing—common in over-crowded prisons—is associated with negative psychological reactions. Although it is unclear what produces these reactions, research points to how overcrowding increases uncertainty and frustration. Indeed, the psychosocial effects of overcrowding can be quite broad: they can be manifest in aggressive behavior, as might be expected if inmates become vigilant, but also depression and anxiety, as if acknowledging defeat. Prison overcrowding is also detrimental in making it more difficult for people to assess threats. For instance, one study found that people in prison who experienced overcrowding were more likely to interpret behavior as aggressive and violent relative to those in less crowded prisons (Lawrence and Andrews 2004).

Perhaps not surprisingly, another aspect of incarceration that has been associated with worse mental health is solitary confinement (Arrigo and Bullock 2008). In 2011 and 2012, about 4.4% of people in prison were held in either solitary confinement or some other form of administrative segregation (Beck 2015). People in prison, however, cycle in and out of segregation. Considering the totality of their time in prison, nearly 20% of people in prison have spent at least some time in solitary confinement and 10% have spent thirty days or more. People who have spent time in administrative segregation are much more likely to experience serious psychological distress. Among all people in prison, about 15% experience serious psychological distress, but among those who had spent time in solitary confinement, about 29% had (Beck 2015). In principle, those who suffer from an active psychiatric disorder should not be placed in solitary confinement. Yet having a psychiatric disorder is positively related to the likelihood of solitary confinement, in large part because psychiatric disorders are associated with disciplinary infractions. Among those who were ever told by a mental health professional that they had a psychiatric disorder, about a quarter had spent time in solitary confinement, relative to 14% with no disorder. Among those who had *any* indication of a past mental health problem— not necessarily a formal psychiatric diagnosis—the difference was much the same. About 24% had spent time in solitary confinement, relative to about 14% among those with no indication of a problem. Solitary confinement involves several deprivations at once, but among its most potent is isolation. As many learned during the COVID-19 pandemic of 2020, the effects of isolation are strong regardless of the reason for that isolation (VanderWeele 2020). Living alone, for example, is a strong risk factor for depression, but it is often a matter of choice. The isolation of people in solitary confinement is different and especially severe and consequential (Haney 2003). One clear indicator of poor mental health in solitary confinement is the large number of suicides that occur there relative to elsewhere in the prison (Patterson and Hughes 2008).

Although solitary confinement is nominally blunt in its operation, the psychological effects of solitary confinement can be nuanced and subtle. Some studies highlight the unique cluster of symptoms associated with solitary confinement. One study explored the psychological experiences of fourteen people exposed to solitary confinement, with a median confinement of two months (Grassian 1983). The study conducted in-depth interviews, revealing considerable nuance, the kind that might not be apparent in standard psychiatric workups or nomenclature. Many people held in solitary began their interview by noting that solitary confinement did not bother them, and many also outright denied the significance of solitary confinement. Only with subsequent questioning—perhaps reflecting the instinctive psychological reticence of institutionalized people—was the researcher able to uncover symptoms of panic, fear, and paranoia. Eventually the interviews revealed a consistent set of patterns, including hypersensitivity to stimuli, such as noise; perceptual distortions, including hearing voices; free-floating anxiety; difficulties with concentration; and aggressive and paranoid fantasies, including of revenge.

Some empirical evidence on solitary confinement is not as damning, at least on the effects of solitary confinement relative to general prison confinement. In one of the more comprehensive studies of its kind, researchers explored the effects of administrative segregation over time, testing whether those held in solitary confinement showed greater deterioration relative to comparable people held in the general prison population (O'Keefe et al. 2013). The study also compared those with and without mental illness at baseline, allowing the researchers to discern whether the effects of solitary confinement were worse for those already suffering from a disorder. The study tracked a variety of symptoms at various points in time. In contrast to most previous studies, the authors found no differences between the groups they identified. Those held in solitary confinement did not show more deterioration over time, regardless of whether they had a pre-existing disorder. The study had significant limitations, however. Because the study focused entirely on people who faced the possibility of administrative segregation, selection problems limited the generalizability of the findings. All those who participated in the study were involved in an administrative segregation hearing: some were later sent to solitary confinement and others were not, but all were initially sent to disciplinary segregation pending the outcome of their hearing. This muddles the distinction between those who are treated in the study as experiencing solitary confinement and those who are not (Kapoor 2014). Given the possibility of shock effects, all the participants might have already experienced the negative effects of solitary confinement, even though the study found that more such confinement might not make things worse.

There are other difficulties to studying solitary confinement. In particular, the effect of solitary confinement is difficult to evaluate given how solitary confinement is situated in the overall prison environment. The active ingredients of solitary confinement are difficult to identify uniquely, because some elements of solitary confinement are also characteristic of the general prison environment. For instance, people in solitary confinement receive very little in the way of intellectual or sensory stimulation (Grassian 1986), but this applies to many general population incarcerated people too, especially as prisons have shifted their focus from educational and vocational activities to supervision and control (Feeley and Simon 1992; Jacobs 1977; Kruttschnitt and Gartner 2005). The Bureau of Justice Statistics reports that nearly 40% of people in prison have no work assignment (McGuire and Pastore 1993). Further complicating matters is the relationship between the use of solitary confinement and other severe forms of discipline. Prisons that use solitary confinement extensively also tend to have higher levels of social disorder and lower levels of trust in correctional officers (Beck 2015). Although solitary confinement is unique in that it involves severe and often prolonged isolation, even people in the general population are socially isolated from others in ways that can undermine mental health. The entirety of a prison sentence involves separation from friends and loved ones.

One way to interpret the seemingly mixed evidence surrounding solitary confinement is that it reveals less about the average harms of severe isolation and more about how some people successfully cope with circumstances that be construed in a few ways. Even studies that demonstrate negative effects of solitary confinement on mental health find a range of consequences—*some* people in solitary confinement show no apparent symptoms (Grassian 1986). This range is partly due to how individuals interpret their experience. If solitary confinement is interpreted as punishment, it has more negative psychological consequences. But if it is interpreted as protective—as, for instance, time away from other people in prison who may do you harm—it has fewer such consequences. Even if solitary confinement is intended as protective by correctional officers, it may not be by the person sent there. The range also reflects the risks people carry with them into administrative segregation, not all of which will be legible to administrators or medical staff (or researchers). Virtually all the evidence indicates that a pre-existing psychiatric disorder increases the pains of imprisonment. People who are able to adjust to life in prison are usually those who suffered no depression or anxiety prior to admission. In addition, those who are able to avoid violence in prison are usually those who do not harbor any psychiatric symptoms. Unusually and outwardly robust people can adjust to life in prison as well as they adjust to life on the outside.

As reassuring as this might seem, these patterns point to deeper institutional problems, ones that lie at the heart of this book. To mitigate the psychological harm of incarceration and solitary confinement, prisons must adequately treat those in their care, a goal at odds with their mission to punish those in their custody. Still, some prisons do treat well, as is evident, for instance, in the percentage of inmates with a psychiatric diagnosis who continue to receive their medications while incarcerated. But many prisons do not screen well, especially when it comes to psychiatric disorders. Without a prior diagnosis, a new disorder is unlikely to be detected. Adequate screening in prison requires an enhanced screening process that few prisons are able or willing to provide. And the enhancements that are required are particular to prison environments, not just enhanced beyond the standard for ordinary medical care. For instance, studies of the effects of solitary confinement reveal that people in prison have a difficult time admitting fear, anxiety, or depression, especially in the initial part of an interview. Only with time, patience, and familiarity do reports of symptoms begin to emerge. In addition, some of the symptoms associated with solitary confinement do not cohere well with traditional psychiatric nomenclature. For these reasons, identifying vulnerable inmates requires unusual sensitivity, with respect to both the symptoms to ascertain and how people in prison report them. In this sense, reducing the pains of imprisonment likely requires a thoroughly enriched approach to evaluating mental illness and risk. In a cruel irony, some common symptoms of mental illness involve precisely those behaviors that will remand a person to solitary confinement.

Given the role of subtle personal characteristics and prior disorders in how people in prison experience their environment, evaluating the effects of incarceration on mental health is difficult. Put in the language of causal modeling, the treatment and effect are closely aligned. The best empirical design would be one where individuals are assigned to prison irrespective of personal characteristics—as in a randomized experiment—and one where the evaluation of mental health is not conditioned on variation on perceptions of the need for services. Of course, such a study is neither ethically acceptable nor feasible. There is, however, evidence from so-called natural experiments, providing *as if* random conditions, based on significant policy changes. In one study, the effects of a change in criminal justice processing times—if not incarceration itself—was used to evaluate the effects of incarceration on mental health (Baćak, Andersen, and Schnittker 2019). The study used Danish administrative data, amounting to information on every person in prison in Denmark over a window of time, including information on health care utilization. Timing was critical to the design. Because of a 1994 policy change, people in the criminal justice system in Denmark were processed and sentenced faster than before, resulting in earlier incarcerations for first-time offenses post-reform relative to pre-reform. As a "dose" the effect of this change was seemingly small, implying an acceleration of only a few months, from an average age of twenty down to nineteen and a half. But the change was broad enough to affect people of all ages and, on average, occurred around a developmentally meaningful margin. The late teen years provide a significant turning point in the lives of young people, representing the transition to adulthood and also the age at which many psychiatric disorders begin to emerge. If incarceration is detrimental to mental health, especially as a shock, as much of the evidence suggests, even a small shift in the age of first incarceration should result in worse mental health than would be apparent if it came later. In this case, the shift to younger incarceration is entirely unrelated to the personal characteristics of the person who is sentenced, as it reflects a sweeping policy change. Under normal circumstances this is not, of course, the case.

The policy change did result in worse outcomes. The researchers explored the use of psychiatric services and found that the percentage of those who used mental health services after the policy change was 5.3%, but among those charged before the change the percentage was 1.5% (service use was indicated by receiving any services within five years after being charged). In short, being incarcerated even six months earlier during a vulnerable window resulted in a near tripling of the risk of a mental health problem. Ten years later 10.3% of the earlier-incarceration group had used mental health services relative to 4.7% of the later-incarceration group. This difference cannot be attributed to anything other than incarceration at a younger age. Because of the sharp nature of the policy shift—down to a day—there are no other differences between the two groups that might explain the greater disadvantage of being incarcerated at a younger age. The criminal histories of the two groups were similar, as were their socioeconomic backgrounds. Those who were incarcerated at an earlier age were not incarcerated earlier because of any pre-existing conditions. In Denmark, mental health services are provided as part of national health care. Denmark and the United States differ in many ways, of course. But studies of this sort provide strong evidence that incarceration damages mental health in ways above and beyond any pre-existing risks people in prison might have. If anything, the results from this study are conservative relative to what might be apparent if a similar natural experiment could be conducted in the United States, as the prevalence of psychiatric disorders is considerably lower in Denmark than the United States, the prison system is less regulated in the United States, and the mental health treatment system of Denmark is more robust. The environments outside of prison are also very different, likely diminishing the long-term impact of incarceration in Denmark. As we will discuss in the next chapter, early incarceration can set off a chain of events that results in progressively worse socioeconomic conditions over the life course. This chain of events transpires in Denmark too, though with a stronger social safety net and more robust health care, the impact on incarceration is likely more tempered. All these between-country differences center the interpretation of the effects of incarceration on a set of common within-prison influences. People in prison, in Denmark and the United States alike, experience isolation, confinement, and the loss of autonomy. And these factors play an important role in understanding how incarceration undermines mental health.

* * *

This chapter has focused on the relationship between incarceration and health, focusing on the situation of people in prison. The relationship between incarceration and health is, however, dynamic and long term. A full appreciation of the connection requires understanding the enduring effects of incarceration, including especially what happens after release. The most damaging consequences of incarceration might only transpire after release, when the availability of health care changes abruptly and people struggle with a new set of challenges, including the stigma of a criminal record, the difficulty of finding employment, and the struggle to re-establish social connections. The postrelease environment is, in some ways, as emotionally challenging as the prison environment.

4

The Effects of Incarceration on Health after Release

The health effects of incarceration on those currently in prison are very different from the effects of incarceration that emerge after release. Although prisons provide health care, that level of access to care usually ends at release and there is no guarantee that released people will continue to receive treatment once they are in the community. Many of the immediate pains of imprisonment are alleviated a few weeks after returning to the community, but a criminal record is difficult to hide, and there remain sources of stress that can be traced back to incarceration. In addition, the sort of mindset that might allow some people to cope with incarceration can often become counterproductive after release. People who have been released from prison must also deal with the negative reactions of those in their community. This arises in both immediate face-to-face interaction and in what sociologist Sarah Lageson calls long-term "digital punishment," enhancing stigma and expanding the reach of a diminished reputation (Lageson 2016).

Understanding the effects of incarceration on health after release requires thinking about how incarceration impacts health in a somewhat different way from thinking about how it impacts health immediately. It involves, first, thinking about the process of release. It then involves thinking about the range of potential mechanisms that might provide a link between incarceration and health, even years after release, through processes operant outside the prison walls.

The Process of Release

Even the meaning of *release* from prison is ambiguous—and potentially a misnomer—as people returning from prison to the community often remain ensnared in the criminal legal system. Historically, the parole system served as a bridge between the prison and the broader community, easing the transition for people released from prison while protecting the interests of other citizens in the form of ongoing supervision. In earlier decades, these two interests were often in balance, as the public saw the potential for reforming people and the criminal justice system devoted resources to promote reintegration into a relatively more accepting society. Starting in the late 1970s, however, the parole system became more closely aligned with law enforcement. This realignment has happened in a variety of ways.

Among other things, the parole system has cut back on social and vocational support, while simultaneously increasing monitoring, surveillance, and reporting requirements. Today more people are released "conditionally" under probation or parole. In 2019, for instance, over 71% of those released from prison were under some kind of supervision, compared to 56% in 1960 (Carson 2020a; Travis and Lawrence 2002). At the same time, many states have reduced or eliminated discretionary parole, so more people must now "max out" by serving the entire duration of their sentence. The nature of supervision has changed as well, with many more people being returned to prison for "technical" violations. The conditions surrounding probation or parole supervision are often demanding. The number of releasees remanded back to prison for having violated the conditions of their parole has increased more than sixfold since the late 1970s (Travis and Lawrence 2002). The total impact of these violations is not small: the majority of people who return to prison for any reason are reincarcerated for technical violations rather than for new crimes (Kaeble and Alper 2020). The difference between technical violations and ordinary violations of the law is sharp. Technical violations can be triggered by a broad range of behaviors—failing a urinalysis, consuming alcohol, being in the presence of others convicted of a crime—that do not normally result in criminal proceedings for those not under correctional supervision. Furthermore, the application and enforcement of technical violations is often particular to local parole offices and individual officers. Some officers require, for example, that the person on parole maintain gainful employment and meet family obligations, whereas others require only that they meet regularly with the officer (Rhine, Smith, and Jackson 1991). Although remanding a higher-risk parolee back to prison for a technical reason can sometimes be justified as crime prevention (e.g., a failure to participate in treatment for those with histories of criminal sexual behavior or heavy drinking for those with repeat drunk driving convictions), there is little evidence that technical violations are related to actual criminal activity (Travis 2005). Furthermore, the responsibility of meeting the conditions of supervision often represents an additional stressor for people at re-entry, adding to their many other challenges.

The Challenges of Reintegration

Upon leaving prison, many people struggle to find a place to live, in part because incarceration undermines long-standing relationships. The social connections that form the cornerstone of a residential life frequently dissolve in prison, as many partners, parents, and friends simply "move on" and away from incarcerated people. Those who are or were once incarcerated have an increased risk of divorce, as well as the dissolution of other long-term relationships (Apel et al. 2010; Massoglia, Remster, and King 2011). Although the loss of certain relationships sometimes presents an opportunity or turning point—allowing former inmates a fresh start and a new path, away from the influences that might have led them to prison in the first place—it more often leads to isolation and disadvantage.

There are numerous structural challenges related to residential mobility. The consequences of incarceration for mobility vary by race (Massoglia, Firebaugh, and Warner 2013). Only one in five people returning from prison is able to return to their old neighborhood, and the pathways to new neighborhoods are variable. Although Black people returning from prison tend to return to neighborhoods that are roughly as disadvantaged as those they came from, white people returning from prison tend to move to more disadvantaged neighborhoods. Perhaps not surprisingly, homelessness is common among people released from prison. One study found that 11% of people released from New York state prisons had entered a homeless shelter within two years of release (Metraux and Culhane 2004), and a 2016 study estimated that formerly incarcerated people are ten times more likely to be homeless than the general public (Couloute 2018). Formerly incarcerated people living in homeless shelters are much more likely to return to prison than to find stable housing. Homelessness is not necessarily the end of a long road after release: in some cases, the use of a homeless shelter happens almost immediately after release, as people find they have nowhere else to go.

In addition to social and geographic barriers to housing, there are legal barriers. Federal housing policy prohibits most people with felony records from receiving subsidized housing (Uggen and Stewart 2015). In addition, many regional housing authorities exclude people with a prison record from renting, a legalized form of residential discrimination. Apart from these exclusions, other legal barriers restrict where people released from prison can live. Some regions prohibit people with a prison record from entering school zones or drug- or prostitution-free zones. As defined by a municipality, the boundaries of these zones can be broad. Other geographic restrictions are narrower in intent but still expansive in their impact. People convicted of violent, predatory, or sex offenses are frequently banned from living near schools, though the definition of "near" varies and is often capacious (Barnes et al. 2009). For instance, one study in Orange County, Florida, found that especially broad geographic restrictions effectively limited the potential residences of convicted sex offenders to only about 5% of parcels in the area (Zandbergen and Hart 2006).

Just as formerly incarcerated people transition from one residence to another, they must also transition between health care providers. This is obviously a very different kind of challenge, but it can be no less daunting and consequential. The health benefits that prisons are obligated to provide end with release, and, on the outside, being uninsured is a critical barrier to care. Most Americans who have health insurance receive benefits through either their own employer or their spouse's employer. People released from prison are much more likely to be unemployed and unmarried. Although public insurance programs like Medicaid are available to those who qualify, enrollment is not easy. Even under the best circumstances enrollment takes time—often months—and the speed with which former inmates can re-enroll varies between states, depending on their formal procedures (Wakeman, McKinney, and Rich 2009). These procedures for re-enrollment reflect not so much the law as a state's stance regarding compliance. Since its inception in the 1960s, federal law has prohibited the use of Medicaid to treat people in prison. States have used one of two strategies to ensure compliance: they either terminate a qualifying person's benefits once they enter prison or have those benefits suspended, with suspension imposing a less onerous burden for re-enrolling after release. Uninsurance is common among people formerly in prison and varies by state, often in ways that do not reflect a state's general approach to the social safety net. California, for instance, provides a strong health care safety net, but one study found as many as 60% of jail releasees in San Francisco were uninsured after release (Wang et al. 2008). Other studies suggest even higher levels of uninsurance. A study of prison releasees in Illinois, for example, found that 85% had no insurance even sixteen months after release (Mallik-Kane 2005).

Being uninsured can pose a major barrier to care for anyone, especially in the context of rapidly rising costs of care, but access problems for people released from prison stretch beyond their ability to pay. For one, people nearing release are unlikely to receive any kind of health-related discharge planning, which can ordinarily encourage better health behavior and appropriate re-engagement with the health care system. Even under the best conditions, people released from prison seldom continue with whatever treatments they were provided before. As discussed earlier, many people in prison have a chronic medical problem or psychiatric disorder, but as few as 15% visit a physician in the year after release. In addition, if people released from prison report a regular source of care at all, they usually report visiting an emergency room rather than a clinical setting (Mallik-Kane and Visher 2008). People can be encouraged to seek primary care in a regular ambulatory setting, but that encouragement works best when people in prison are provided with access immediately upon release (Wang et al. 2012). Even a short gap in care can have detrimental effects. Studies that follow people over time find that the benefits of medical therapy that were realized in prison often disappear after release. One study found that among people in prison with human immunodeficiency virus (HIV), treatment within prison was highly effective (Springer et al. 2004). Indeed, as many as 59% of HIV-infected people had undetectable viral loads by the end of their incarceration. Yet the same study found that most of these improvements were lost upon release, either because of a failure to continue with treatment or because of inconsistent treatment.

These failures are not always for lack of access. A related study explored what happens to HIV-infected people in Texas prisons who were receiving antiretroviral therapy (Baillargeon et al. 2009). From the standpoint of discharge planning, these people were in a relatively good position: on the day of their release, they were instructed to obtain an initial thirty-day prescription; they were also provided instructions and contact information for doing so; and a few were also assigned a discharge coordinator, who completed and submitted required application forms. Yet even with this support, planning, and intervention, only 5% filled their prescriptions in time to avoid an interruption in treatment. The typical interruption was not brief. Only 30% filled a prescription within sixty days. With antiretroviral treatment, even short interruptions can lead to much poorer outcomes. Interruptions can also create more drug-resistant strains of HIV, increasing the likelihood of transmitting the virus to others.

For other diseases, release from prison presents a different set of challenges. Opioid dependence, for instance, is relatively common among people involved with the criminal justice system (Winkelman, Chang, and Binswanger 2018). If dependence is regarded as a medical problem, it logically follows that it should be approached as a chronic disorder and treated consistently, especially because release from prison increases the risk of relapse (Howell et al. 2021). Yet there is considerable controversy regarding the best way to treat dependence in correctional settings, given how dependence straddles the line between legal and clinical frameworks. Methadone is a treatment for opioid dependence, but most prisons discontinue methadone, often abruptly, when a person is incarcerated (Rich et al. 2015). Discontinuing methadone is not unreasonable from the standpoint of law enforcement: although it works for maintenance therapy, methadone is an opioid with many of the same risks of other narcotics, including death from poisoning. In addition, methadone is regulated like other controlled substances and has a street value. Yet methadone is a clinically effective treatment for dependence, both inside prisons and out. Evidence indicates that people who are continued on methadone in prison are less likely to experience the symptoms of withdrawal, which can ordinarily last for months. Furthermore, people treated with methadone have better outcomes after release. They are much more likely to continue treatment once released, less likely to return to using opioids, and less likely to return to prison (Rich et al. 2015). Yet some correctional officials worry about treating one addiction with a different drug. For this reason, forced withdrawal—without the aid of other medications—remains the default treatment in prison. People actively involved with the criminal justice system—or even potentially involved with the system—are aware of how addiction is treated in prisons, setting the stage for spillovers from prison to the community: a significant number of opioid users in the community are reluctant to enter methadone treatment precisely for fear that their treatment will end if and when they are incarcerated (Fu et al. 2013).

Psychosocial Mechanisms Linking Prior Incarceration to Health

Although for people released from prison finding a place to live and securing appropriate health care represent significant challenges, stress comes from many sources. People returning from prison are tasked with no less than reintegrating into society. The challenges of reintegration are stressful and there is already evidence that some experiences common to those released from prison are detrimental to health. Poverty, for instance, is associated with worse mental and physical health. The experience of discrimination is, likewise, detrimental to health and well-being. And poor social support increases mortality. An especially keen problem with the combination of incarceration and release is that it simultaneously exposes people to multiple forms of stress while also undermining their ability to cope. Sociologists refer to this process as stress proliferation, and while it is not unique to people released from prison, it is certainly characteristic of their situation (Pearlin, Aneshensel, and Leblanc 1997; Turney 2014).

Finding and keeping a job is one significant source of stress, ranking among the most important challenges at release. As many as 30% of people released from prison are unemployed, and among those who find a job, few find one that provides more than the minimum wage (Kling 2006). Although the static picture is grim, it is even worse when considering employment stability. Any economic security people released from prison can find is often fleeting (Harding, Morenoff, and Wyse 2019; Harding et al. 2014). Upon release, people often manage through a combination of resources, including income from a job, the support of family, and assorted public benefits. Indeed, very few people find economic security only through a single job, and reliance on social support and public benefits has, if anything, grown over time.

Scholars who study reintegration frequently leverage the concept of a *turning point*. A turning point refers to a moment when someone gains a new foothold in society, often through a life course transition, such as a new job, a new relationship, the birth of a child, or military service. Turning points provide new opportunities and can help people transition to new roles and adopt new identities. For people released from institutions, turning points of this sort are disappearing. Job opportunities are scarce and military service is often unavailable (Lundquist, Pager, and Strader 2018; Western 2006).

Some states have made these transitions even more difficult. Many states, for instance, ban those with felony convictions from receiving benefits such as Supplemental Security Income (SSI), food stamps, and public housing (Ewald and Uggen 2012; Travis 2005). In some states these bans are temporary and are lifted in time, but when the riskiest period is immediately after release, even a short spell of ineligibility can do lasting harm. The structure of these bans is also relevant. Some eligibility criteria, for instance, are especially severe for drug offenses. Other criteria are not targeted directly at people involved with the criminal justice system but nonetheless impact them. Some federal supplementary benefits, for instance, are provided only to families with dependent children, effectively eliminating the young single men who move through the prison system.

Although it is difficult to attribute all these difficulties to incarceration alone, evidence indicates that incarceration certainly plays a role. In some cases, people released from prison would be undesirable employees irrespective of their incarceration history, but high-quality studies reveal that discrimination based on a criminal record is real and consequential. Perhaps the best evidence of the effects of incarceration on employment opportunities comes from audit studies. In an audit study, researchers randomly assign an indicator of prior incarceration or criminal justice contact to the résumé of alternating auditors, who otherwise present themselves in identical ways. Studies of this sort find that a criminal record strongly reduces the likelihood of receiving a callback from employers, ordinarily the first step in securing a job. One study, for instance, found that the likelihood of a callback was reduced by about half among white applicants with a felony conviction and by about two-thirds among Black applicants with the same (Pager 2003). While a felony conviction might be an especially strong deterrent, other evidence indicates that even superficial contact with the criminal justice system is damaging. One study, for instance, explored the effects of a three-year-old misdemeanor arrest and found similar results. In this case, the arrest was for disorderly conduct, a minor charge that makes up about 5% of all arrests. Even an arrest on a minor charge reduced the likelihood of a callback by about 10% among white applicants and 15% among Black applicants (Uggen et al. 2014).

Such examples reflect the real-world practices of employers. When employers decide whether they are interested in an applicant, they are increasingly using contact with the criminal justice system as a criterion, engaging in discrimination. Yet in some occupations those with a criminal conviction face lawful discrimination as well, especially in occupations that are highly regulated or those that require licensing, such as health care. Policies at the state and federal levels, for instance, ban people with felonies from working in some public sector jobs, such air transportation and real estate. People with criminal records may also be excluded from some of the trades they have learned while incarcerated, such as cosmetology (with most states stipulating that they "may" rather than "shall" ban). Other occupations require good character testimony that, while not explicitly excluding felons, allows for the consideration of a criminal record and, thereby, disqualifies applicants.

Criminal records also affect educational attainment, which has a strong relationship with health and life expectancy. Indeed, the evidence linking education to health is even stronger than the evidence linking income to health. And education ranks also among the strongest predictors of longevity. Compared to those with less than a high school diploma, those with a college degree have more than a decade of additional life expectancy (Hummer and Hernandez 2013). Though it might seem implausible to think about incarceration undermining education—after all, the incarceration of adults usually happens after the age that someone would graduate from high school—researchers have shown clear evidence of discrimination. A recent audit study found that the college rejection rate for applicants with criminal records was 2.5 times higher than for matched applicants who did not have criminal records (Stewart and Uggen 2020). The same study found that over 70% of colleges required criminal history information, which helps explain why former inmates have difficulty returning to school. The criminal history information is often extensive. After college applicants report their convictions on an application they are often required to submit additional documentation, including letters from criminal justice officials. Similar procedures pertain to receiving federal student aid, meaning that even if a former inmate is admitted to college, there is no guarantee they can secure financial aid or on-campus housing.

Incarceration also disrupts social support, which is a very strong predictor of health (House, Landis, and Umberson 1988). The health effects of social isolation, for instance, rival those of smoking. Furthermore, men who are married live considerably longer than men who are not. Although it is not entirely clear why social support is such a powerful predictor of longevity, there is evidence that close friends encourage healthy behavior (something that particularly benefits men) and that socially integrated people report lower levels of stress, as indicated by assorted biomarkers. In short, the need for social connection appears to be so strong that its frustration undermines the integrity of human physiology. Social integration with family, friends, and neighbors is an enormous challenge for people returning from prison. In the first instance, incarceration separates people from those close to them. People often serve their sentences far removed from their communities, including in rural areas distant from the cities in which they live. This presents challenges for those who might wish friends and family to visit them, but after release there are additional challenges beyond simple geography. In some respects, people released from prison would appear to be in a good position to recover their social lives. On average recently released people are relatively young and otherwise socially active. Prior to incarceration, they report high levels of social involvement, and on the day of their release the first thing many people do is spend time with family and friends (Western et al. 2015). Yet these contacts can quickly fade as the challenges mount. A large percentage of people released from prison report living with family members at some point, but this percentage declines over time, while the percentage residing in temporary housing increases. People who find themselves isolated in their initial period of release tend to remain isolated, rarely receiving ongoing support from family and usually finding only temporary housing. Many face protracted struggles in this regard, in part because of the enduring stigma of a criminal record. One long-term study of incarceration and marriage, for instance, linked disadvantage in the marriage market to incarceration that occurred over two decades prior (Huebner 2005).

Sexually transmitted infections among formerly incarcerated people are more common than among the general population. Although it is tempting to infer that the elevated prevalence is due either to conditions acquired before incarceration or to transmission within prison, as we discussed earlier, there are some risks that pertain only to the period after release. When longstanding relationships are disrupted, for example, people are more likely to have sex with new partners or to engage with multiple partners simultaneously. Studies of recently released people find an elevated risk of new sexually transmitted infections (Wiehe et al. 2015). The effects of incarceration are especially strong among the most common infections, including chlamydia and gonorrhea. Among recently released people the annual infection rate for chlamydia is 2,968 per 100,000 people, relative to 759 among those who have not been incarcerated, and, for gonorrhea, the same rate is 2,305, relative to 350. Understanding the processes that link incarceration to health, including the way it disrupts social networks, necessitates a consideration of the social and psychological dimensions of stigma.

The Social and Psychological Context of Incarceration Stigma

Many of the challenges faced by people released from prison can be interpreted in terms of stigma. Employers might not hire former inmates because of expectations of poor work performance, and friends might avoid them because of fear, discomfort, or "guilt" by association. And if people released from prison are still on parole, they might be prohibited from associating with others who have criminal records, introducing uncertainty into their interactions with other people. Focusing on the stigma of incarceration alerts us to several things.

First, it suggests that the meaning of incarceration is shared, both by released individuals and by members of the communities to which they return. It also implies that incarceration is understood to be significant. One reason incarceration is such a strong impediment to employment, for instance, is because employers greatly exaggerate the severity, significance, or danger represented by a criminal record. Individuals released from prison too understand this and so apply to jobs less frequently than they should, fearing the added scrutiny. The fact that these beliefs are inaccurate does not diminish the threat that lingers in the air. But the fact that these are expectations also implies that they can change, elevating the importance of one-on-one contact. To this point, once people with criminal records meet employers, such fears tend to recede, which is one reason audit studies consistently show that job applicants who get a chance to interview with hiring authorities greatly improve their chances of another callback (Pager 2008; Uggen et al. 2014).

Second, a focus on stigma reminds us that some of the effects of incarceration stem from having been *in prison*, rather than from other characteristics that people released from prison might have. In this sense, having been in prison is worse than having merely committed a crime or only having been arrested, or even the underlying behavioral issues that might have led to arrest. Related to the mark of incarceration is the idea that the mark is difficult to cover or remove, particularly in the era of digital punishment (Lageson 2020; Uggen and Blahnik 2016). Although mortality research suggests a relatively brief postrelease period of exceptionally high risk, stigmatization lasts much longer. Avoiding the negative associations of incarceration is a protracted process, paving the way for long-term consequences related to chronic disease and recurrent psychiatric disorders. There are no easy ways for those released from prison to conceal a criminal record or diminish its consequences.

The challenges of stigma may be getting worse over time. The public has increasingly negative views of people in prison, even as incarceration has grown more common. In addition, how people in prison are portrayed in news media has also changed over time, in ways that accentuate a criminal record's impact (Sloop 1996). In the 1950s, the typical inmate was seen as a white male who might be down on his luck but who shared many of the values of conventional society and so was redeemable given proper guidance. In this context, many Americans could easily imagine the prison system as a site of rehabilitation rather than retribution. As the prison system grew, however, this image changed. By the 1980s, the typical inmate was stereotyped as a Black male, prone to violence, and essentially only "serving time" with little real hope of rehabilitation. In 1968, for example, nearly 75% of Americans felt that rehabilitation was the goal of the prison system, but by 1982 this number had declined to just over 40% (Cullen, Fisher, and Applegate 2000). Furthermore, despite the unprecedented growth of the prison system, most Americans continue to think the criminal justice system is too soft on crime. From the 1970s to the 1990s, around 80% of Americans believed that courts did not deal harshly enough with criminals (Cullen, Fisher, and Applegate 2000). Over the past two decades, the share that would prefer more lenient courts has risen, from about 3.5% to over 20% in 2016 (Uggen and Larson 2017). Still, beliefs about courts differ from beliefs about the people they judge: the overwhelming majority of Americans regard imprisonment as an appropriate punishment for most crimes (Innes 1993; Warr 1995). When survey questions on punishment are framed in terms of what is best for "the good of society" or in terms of guilt versus innocence, the public's tough-on-crime stance remains pronounced. Over 90% of Americans, for example, believe that criminals should be incarcerated to protect "innocent citizens" (Cullen, Fisher, and Applegate 2000).

Although some of the evidence for the stigma of incarceration pertains to public beliefs about crime and prisons, other evidence focuses on those it affects. One way to approach the study of stigma is to consider how those who were once in prison see themselves and think about their status (Schnittker and Bacak 2013). The public might very well hold negative beliefs about people with criminal convictions, but the concept of stigma goes a step further and presupposes that the stigmatized and the stigmatizer share the same mindset, such that the stigma of incarceration is internalized. If the stigma of incarceration is sufficiently strong, former inmates should think of themselves as somehow less than the average citizen, much like the public at large. A popular way to measure relative subjective status is through the so-called ladder measure of relative rank (Adler et al. 2000). The ladder is a survey measurement tool that presents respondents with an image of a ladder with ten rungs. In one version, respondents are told the ladder represents where people stand in the United States. In another version, they are told it represents where people stand in their community. Respondents are told to think of people at the top as those "who are the best off—those who have the most money, the most education, and the most respected jobs" and people at the bottom as those "who are the worst off—who have the least money, least education, and the least respected jobs or no jobs." In the ladder anchored in community, respondents are given more open-ended instructions with no explicit reference points. They are told, "People define community in different ways; please define it in whatever way is most meaningful for you. At the top of the ladder are the people who have the highest standing in their community. At the bottom are the people who have the lowest standing in their community." In both versions, respondents are then asked to place themselves on the rung that best represents their own standing, mindful of how others regard them.

Contact with the criminal justice system is strongly related to where people place themselves on the ladder. Furthermore, contact is related in a gradient-like fashion. In one survey, respondents were arrayed according to whether they either (1) had committed no crime or been arrested and therefore had no correctional contact, (2) had committed a crime but had not

Table 4.1 Effects of Incarceration on the Subjective Status of Former Inmates

	Whites		African Americans	
	Community Status	US Status	Community Status	US Status
No Crime	0	0	0	0
Crime, but No Arrest	−0.014	−0.055	−0.479	−0.572
Arrest, but No Incarceration	−0.198	−0.199	−1.301*	−0.840*
Short Incarceration (<30 days)	−0.445*	−0.448*	−1.323*	−0.903*
Long Incarceration (30+ days)	−0.597*	−0.607*	−1.583*	−1.536*

* Effect statistically significant at $p < .05$.

Note: Estimates derived from Schnittker and Bacak (2013), Tables 2 and 3.

been arrested, (3) had been arrested but not incarcerated, (4) had been incarcerated for a short time (less than thirty days), or (5) had been incarcerated for a long time (thirty days or more). Table 4.1 presents how the last three groups viewed themselves, relative to those who had committed no crimes. The differences are broken according to the two versions of the ladder, as well as by race. At least two aspects of the ladder are important to discuss before moving on. First, the average person places themselves slightly above the ladder midpoint. Moreover, the average person is reluctant to move themselves too far in either direction. Few people place themselves at the bottom of the ladder or even much lower than the midpoint. Slightly more people place themselves at the very top than at the bottom of the ladder, but most people are reluctant to do this as well. In sum, the gravity that pulls people to "slightly above average" is strong. Among those with a history of incarceration, however, the situation is different. Increasing contact with the criminal justice system results in a progressively lower placement on the ladder. Those who have been arrested place themselves lower than those who have only committed a crime, and those who have been incarcerated place themselves even lower still. The largest declines are for those who have been incarcerated for thirty days or more. Those who have been incarcerated are well aware of the stigma of their status.

Stigma, Coping, and the Dilemmas of Reintegration

This evidence indicates that the stigma of incarceration is felt by people released from prison, but the stigma of incarceration involves even more facets that further potentiate its deleterious effect. For one, the stigma surrounding incarceration is complex, involving a variety of different beliefs and expectations. This makes incarceration salient across a range of encounters. Among the most prominent beliefs, for instance, is that individuals who have been incarcerated are dangerous. Policies that prevent people released from prison from living in certain areas and working in certain jobs are often rooted in this belief. But, for a different set of reasons, people released from prison are also regarded as poor employees and undependable spouses. Studies that ask individuals to describe the characteristics of "criminals" using open-ended responses—a research design that might ordinarily lead to layered and complex descriptions—find few positive characteristics (MacLin and Herrera 2006). Those people deemed "criminal" are often described in terms of their pervasively negative personalities, using terms such as aggressive, antisocial, manipulative, demanding, and hot-tempered. In addition, they are regarded as cold, dishonest, and incompetent. Because there are almost no positive stereotypes regarding people released from prison—and an ever-smaller number of people believe in the possibility of second chances—there is little space for those with a criminal record to achieve broad social acceptance. For the same reason, many of these negative stereotypes are difficult to contest. Precisely because so many opportunities are denied to people released from prison, and because they are often so isolated from other people, there are fewer situations that can afford individuals the opportunity to present themselves in a more flattering light or demonstrate their competence.

Stigma impacts health in at least two ways. In the first instance, stigma is the source of many of the disadvantages people face upon release, including difficulty in housing, employment, and social integration. Second, stigma is stressful in and of itself. In general, discrimination is bad for mental health, approximately doubling the odds of developing a mood or anxiety disorder, for instance (Kessler, Mickelson, and Williams 1999). For people released from prison, the consequences of discrimination for mental health may be even greater given that some coping resources that might be available to other people are not available to them. Discrimination is damaging to mental health because it is perceived as unfair and dehumanizing, not only because it results in reduced opportunities (though it does that too). Being denied a job is painful, for instance, but it is even more painful when it is seen as a result of prejudice. In the case of hiring people with a felony conviction, employers often have little reason to hide their prejudice. In many labor markets, for instance, applicants are still asked upfront about any criminal convictions, and the application itself frequently includes a check box to indicate a conviction (Holzer, Raphael, and Stoll 2004; Vuolo, Lageson, and Uggen 2017). People released from prison are expected to find employment, but the labor market provides routine reminders of their diminished status.

These psychological processes matter because they provide additional context to the stress people released from prison experience. Faced with numerous challenges, all of which are difficult to overcome, people released from prison risk wholesale disengagement. For most people, failure in one domain might do little damage if they are able to buttress their self-respect in another (Crocker and Major 1989). Yet the multidimensional negative stereotypes surrounding criminality make attainment in alternative areas difficult. Similarly, when faced with rejection, some stereotyped groups can still find support in other people. Among people released from prison, though, the likelihood of being rejected by others is high, even among family and friends. People released from prison are aware of this and hold strong expectations of rejection. One study found that those with prison records anticipate even more negative attitudes than are actually held against them by members of the community (Moore, Stuewig, and Tangney 2013). They believe, for example, that people in the community think all criminals are the same, that criminals are beyond rehabilitation, and that criminals are bad people. Even if a community is more tolerant than people returning from prison realize, the expectation of rejection almost certainly diminishes the motivation to persist in the face of rejection, discrimination, or difficulty. In this light, some long-term effects of incarceration on health are certainly possible, and indeed, evidence indicates that they are significant.

The Effects of Incarceration on the Health of People Released from Prison

Evidence for the long-term effects of incarceration on health are apparent in a variety of different studies. As before, though, it is important to be careful regarding claims of causality. When we argue that incarceration has an effect on health after release, we are, in part, claiming that people released from prison do poorly because of their criminal record or because of the lingering effects of their experiences in prison. But determining the long-term causal effects of prior incarceration is difficult for a variety of reasons, including the dynamics of prison and community: the apparent effect of current incarceration can reflect the effect of prior incarceration, and one apparent spell of incarceration can indicate multiple spells (Wildeman and Muller 2012). In addition, a prison record is rarely the only negative influence in the lives of people released from prison. Because of this, it is difficult to assign special significance to incarceration when the fact that people involved with the criminal justice system have worse health might just as easily be attributed to poverty, racism, low levels of education, a risk-prone personality, a disadvantaged childhood, or any number of other factors.

Even so, there is evidence that prior incarceration undermines health following release, and the long sinews of the process ultimately lead back to incarceration itself. Studies have adopted several strategies to gather evidence for causal effects of earlier incarceration. One strategy is to exploit timing—whether gradual changes or abrupt transitions—in a methodological fashion. In our own work, discussed more shortly, we follow people over time to see what changes when and if they are incarcerated, as well as what trajectory they follow after release. Still another strategy is to exploit differences between when incarceration occurs and the onset of disease, focusing on the specific character of the disease under consideration. In studying the effects of incarceration on psychiatric disorders, for example, it is possible to eliminate from consideration disorders that began *before* the age of first incarceration, a common situation given the early onset of many disorders, including those plausibly made worse by incarceration, such as anxiety. Other research has used a similar intuition for other diseases. One study, for instance, explored the effects of incarceration on HIV infection by using information on the timing of release relative to the latency period of an HIV infection (Johnson and Raphael 2009). A basic strategy employed by virtually all studies is simply to statistically control for as many factors as possible. In the case of incarceration, this usually involves, at a minimum, adjustments for socioeconomic status and basic features of childhood background, factors correlated with both the risk of incarceration and poor health. A related strategy is to make strategic and specific comparisons, referred to as matching. In studies of this sort, each person released from prison is compared to someone who is very similar but was never incarcerated, providing a type of counterfactual.

In considering research assessing the causal effects of incarceration among those released from prison, a useful place to start, as we did before, is with mortality. Several studies have explored mortality following release from prison. One study, conducted in Washington state, found a mortality rate among people released from prison that was 3.5 times higher than for residents of the state generally (Binswanger et al. 2007). The excess mortality was not, however, distributed evenly over time. The risk of death was highest during the first two weeks after release, at which point the risk was 13 times higher than for the general population. Other studies find significant variation in the risk of death depending on the amount of time the person served (Patterson 2013). A New York study estimated that each additional year in prison yielded a 15.6% increase in the odds of death, dramatically decreasing life expectancy for people serving longer sentences.

The specific causes of death also tell us something about the risks that people released from prison face. During the initial period after release, the most common cause of death is from drug overdoses (Binswanger et al. 2007; Møller et al. 2010). As discussed earlier, this partly reflects a gap in the continuity of care people released from prison receive. They may have received treatment in prison, but this treatment is unlikely to continue upon release. It also reflects the failure of a prison system that provides treatment with little appreciation of what happens following release. Even among those who are successfully weaned from drugs, their nominally successful treatment implies a substantially reduced tolerance upon release. When people return to the community, the opioid doses they tolerated before institutionalization are much more likely to be fatal. And the likelihood of a return to using drugs is especially acute among those who are not placed on maintenance therapy. The likelihood of an overdose is enhanced by other factors, also particular to the social circumstances surrounding release. People released from prison are, for instance, more likely to abuse multiple illicit and legal drugs, and the use of other drugs enhances the risks associated with opioids: each additional drug taken in tandem with an opioid nearly doubles the risk of death (Møller et al. 2010).

After a sufficient time following release, the elevated risk of mortality declines. But it does not disappear altogether, and the ongoing risk varies substantially by other characteristics, including sex and race. The elevated risk of death is much higher among white than Black releasees (Rosen, Schoenbach, and Wohl 2008; Spaulding et al. 2011). In addition, the long-term effects of incarceration are higher among women than men (Massoglia et al. 2014). The causes of death found among people released from prison point to long-term struggles, not simply tenuous recovery in the weeks immediately following release. In fact, several causes of death remain disproportionately high over the long term, including accidents, homicide, liver disease, and cirrhosis. People released from prison have a consistently elevated risk of suicide, one comparable to the risk among discharged psychiatric patients (Pratt et al. 2006). The suicide rate among recently released women is about thirty times higher than the general female population and among recently released men is about eight times higher.

Prior incarceration also increases the risk of poor health. Here too the patterns suggest that whatever health benefits were apparent in prison disappear after release and, as before, the patterns are disease specific (Massoglia 2008). Table 4.2 provides a summary. A positive relationship between incarceration

Table 4.2 Effects of Prior Incarceration on the Odds of Health Problems

	Increase in Odds of Problem among Former Inmates
Health Problems Related to Stress	
Hypertension	4.51*
Heart Problems	1.95*
Chronic Lung Disease	16.58*
Chest Pain	2.04*
Infectious Disease	
Urinary Tract Infection	11.31*
Hepatitis or Tuberculosis	6.25*
Health Problems Unrelated to Stress	
Arthritis	1.36
Cancer	1.35
Diabetes	1.44
Epilepsy	1.59
Anemia	1.29

* Effect statistically significant at $p < .05$.

Note: Estimates derived from Massoglia (2008), Tables 2 and 3.

and disease is expressed in terms of an increased odds. These odds are derived from a matching strategy—comparing the risk of disease among former inmates relative to the risk for the same disease among those who did not go to prison but are otherwise similar. For instance, former inmates report odds of hypertension 4.51 times higher than the odds among those who are socially and demographically similar but were never incarcerated. Although among people released from prison incarceration is generally bad for health, incarceration does not affect the risk of all diseases equally. The diseases most related to incarceration either involve stress or are infectious. Incarceration increases the risk of heart problems, lung disease, chest pain, and urinary tract infections. But incarceration is not significantly related to arthritis, cancer, diabetes, epilepsy, or anemia, conditions that are not generally caused by stress or an infection. The other pattern of note is simply the magnitude of the relationships. For those conditions significantly associated with incarceration, the odds of the condition more than double with exposure to prison. The size of these odds is perhaps even more remarkable because the matching approach already adjusts for many of the things that might plausibly be a consequence of incarceration and are known to affect health, such as marital status. In this sense the estimates are conservative.

A similar granularity applies to evaluating the effects of prior incarceration on psychiatric disorders. Table 4.3 shows the relationship between prior incarceration and the odds of a current psychiatric disorder. In the case of this relationship, it is important to attend to age-of-onset considerations, as well as the role of childhood background factors that contribute to both psychiatric disorders and incarceration. There is remarkable overlap between the two: those childhood factors that increase the risk of developing a psychiatric disorder in adulthood are remarkably similar to those that increase the risk of incarceration. Table 4.3 presents the relationship between incarceration and specific psychiatric disorders, represented again by the increase in the odds of developing the disorder. In addition, the table presents the percentage of the apparent incarceration effect that is attributable to influences prior to incarceration, including childhood background and the presence of psychiatric disorders that emerged before incarceration. In this case, the evidence indicates that most disorders apparent after incarceration were also apparent before. Of the eleven disorders, incarceration only appears to be causally related to four, that is, after adjustments for confounding influences. Based on this research, we can be most confident that incarceration is a cause

Table 4.3 Effects of Prior Incarceration on the Odds of a Current Psychiatric Disorder

Current Psychiatric Disorder	Increase in Odds of Disorder among Former Inmates (Percentage of Association Accounted for by Selection)
Anxiety Disorders	
Panic Disorder	1.66 (40%)
Agoraphobia	1.81 (19%)
Specific Phobia	1.82 (0%)*
Social Phobia	1.38 (56%)
Generalized Anxiety Disorder	1.45 (35%)
Posttraumatic Stress Disorder	1.78 (49%)
Adult Separation Anxiety	1.66 (34%)
Mood Disorders	
Major Depressive Disorder	1.48 (34%)*
Dysthymia	2.11 (22%)*
Bipolar Disorder	1.62 (31%)
Impulse Control Disorder	
Intermittent Explosive Disorder	1.88 (31%)*

* Effect statistically significant at $p < .05$.

Note: Estimates derived from Schnittker, Massoglia, and Uggen (2012), Table 2.

of mood disorders and less confident that incarceration is a cause of other disorders. To be sure, incarceration also increases the risk of developing a specific phobia, but specific phobia disorder is only one of seven possible anxiety disorders, suggesting no general relationship between incarceration and symptomatic fear. The disorders for which incarceration has the most consistent causal effects have a somewhat later age of onset. But even within these scope conditions, the impact of incarceration on mental health is considerable. Mood disorders are disabling conditions, much more so than anxiety disorders. And for former inmates, the challenges presented by major depression are likely to be even greater, given that successful reintegration requires considerable motivation, focus, and fortitude. To say that the long-term effects of incarceration are limited to depression does not limit those effects' scope or behavioral impact.

Synergy between Health Protections and Successful Reintegration

There are a variety of ways in which the experiences of reintegration can undermine health, especially when considered in terms of a long-term process. But it is also important to appreciate the synergistic relationship between health and reintegration—health lies at the center of many of the challenges facing people currently or formerly in prison. To this point, we have focused on the effects of incarceration on health and framed these effects in terms of ongoing social and psychological struggles. Another way to think about the same process is in terms of how health itself adds to the many challenges. A substance abuse problem, for example, can severely undermine someone's ability to sustain a supportive marriage or be a successful employee. Similarly, depression can undermine the motivation necessary to continue applying for jobs in the face of rejection. There is growing evidence that people released from prison struggle in no small part because they are in poor health, and mental health appears to be especially significant in this regard. One study, for instance, found that virtually *all* released individuals who were struggling with homelessness and economic instability were also struggling with drug and alcohol addiction (Harding et al. 2014). Another study found that nearly a third of people recently released from prison with a psychiatric disorder reported never receiving any support from family members, a critical resource for reintegration (Western et al. 2015).

In this sense, poor health becomes a source of disability, an impaired capacity to reintegrate. Disability refers to the inability or diminished ability to function in a person's normal social roles. We already know that physical and mental health problems contribute a great deal to disability, and for those released from prison, poor mental health might be especially disabling. Indeed, one of the most significant contributors to disability worldwide is major depression (Üstün et al. 2004). Depression is an especially significant contributor because its symptoms cut across a variety of domains and behaviors: depression undermines physical health, it impairs the ability to think and concentrate, it slows movement, and it diminishes motivation. If incarceration adversely impacts mental health, mental health might in turn help to explain the struggles experienced by people released from prison.

The concept of disability also encourages us to think comprehensively. The World Health Organization Disability Assessment Schedule (WHO-DAS) is a popular survey instrument for measuring disability in a multidimensional way (Rehm et al. 1999). It focuses on six dimensions: (1) role loss, defined as the number of days within the last thirty days in which the person was unable to complete normal activities; (2) self-care limitations, defined as difficulty with washing, getting dressed, and staying alone; (3) mobility limitations, defined as difficulty standing for thirty minutes, moving inside the house, and walking a long distance; (4) cognition, defined as difficulty concentrating for ten minutes, understanding what was going on, remembering to do important things, and learning a new task; (5) social functioning, defined as difficulty getting along with others, maintaining a conversation, dealing with people they did not know, maintaining friendships, making new friends, and controlling emotions around other people; and (6) social participation, defined as the amount of embarrassment and discrimination due to health problems. Table 4.4 presents the extent to which health problems explain the added disability people released from prison experience in each of these six dimensions. The percentages are calculated from nationally representative data that include, among other things, a comprehensive assessment of mental health. Relative to those who have not been incarcerated, people who have been incarcerated experience more disability on each of these dimensions (Schnittker, Massoglia, and Uggen 2012). They experience more social difficulties, more difficulties with cognition, and more difficulties with self-care. And, of the additional disability experienced by people released from prison, much of it is the result of health problems. For example,

Table 4.4 Percentage of Additional Disability among Former Inmates Explained by Health Problems and Psychiatric Disorders

Disability Dimension	Percentage of Incarceration Effect Explained by Health Problems and Psychiatric Disorders
Self-Care	44%
Cognitive	88%
Mobility	32%
Extent Out of Roles	39%
Social Integration	50%
Social Participation	48%

Note: Estimates derived from Schnittker, Massoglia, and Uggen (2012), Table 3.

health problems explain 88% of the added difficulty they experience with respect to cognition, and about half of the additional difficulty with respect to social integration. Health matters less for other dimensions of disability, especially those involving physical impairments, but even in the case of mobility limitations, health problems explain about a third of the additional disability. Of the psychiatric disorders involved, mood disorders are particularly relevant. Each additional mood disorder increases cognitive disability by about 2.3 units (on a 0 to 100 scale, where 0 is no disability and 100 is full disability). By contrast, each additional chronic physical condition increases disability by 0.64 units. Other dimensions of disability show a similar pattern. Each additional mood disorder increases disability in social participation by 3.82 units, whereas each additional physical disorder increases disability by only 1.2 units. In short, people released from prison are disabled largely because of their health problems, and, at that, psychiatric disorders are the major contributing factor.

* * *

There are many challenges to reintegration. People released from prison are tasked with reintegrating into society, forming new relationships, and finding work and housing. They are exposed to many new forms of stress, even as their resources for coping with that stress are diminished. The health care they might have received in prison is suddenly gone. For many, the parole system introduces additional obligations and expectations, with severe consequences for failing to meet them. Adjusting to all these transitions and challenges would be difficult for anyone, but they are especially difficult for people released from prison, and they form the foundation for their ongoing physical and mental health problems.

For many of these challenges, people released from prison are effectively going it alone, navigating a mix of social, emotional, and legal challenges with only the resources they are able to gather for themselves. There are few legal, cultural, or social resources for them to draw from; not least is a dignifying vision for what a person released from prison can be. Yet despite this situation, the problems experienced by people released from prison are not theirs alone. Their problems reverberate outward, affecting their loved ones, the people who depend on them, the families they might have begun prior to incarceration, the communities to which they return, and even the larger health care system, within which they are inextricably embedded. People released from prison are socially isolated, to be sure. They are, in many states, excluded from the ordinary rights of citizenship through felon disenfranchisement. But their problems are not sequestered or atomized. They resound to others, even those seemingly far removed from them. The remaining chapters trace these connections.

5

The Effects of Incarceration on Communities

Understanding the effects of incarceration on communities requires viewing health and incarceration from different angles and over multiple levels. We need to think about the social connections of people released from prison, starting with close friends and family. We also must consider the characteristics of people before and after prison, as we have throughout this book. But when considering community effects, we must adopt a somewhat different framework from what we adopted before. Although there are reasons to believe that prisons might improve some aspects of community health—if, for example, people who engage in repeated violent crime are removed from the community—a short-sighted ledger, one adopting a strict criminal justice frame, for instance, risks overlooking the many pathways through which incarceration can undermine community health. Incarceration can, for instance, diminish the mental health of the partners that men and women in prison leave behind. Incarceration can also undermine the health of families by creating unemployment and income loss. In pursuit of a comprehensive approach, we begin with close connections, before expanding outward to health care systems.

Incarceration and Sexual Markets

Incarceration can increase the risk of infectious disease in communities by changing the marriage and sexual market, particularly in the recent US context of large-scale, racialized mass incarceration. Although diverse types of people are incarcerated in the United States, this discussion will emphasize those groups most subject to incarceration, including especially Black men. Even if potential partners avoid men with a history of incarceration, the fact that in some communities a very large number of men are or have been in prison alters the marriage prospects of those who remain behind, as well as the types of men available to the marriage market. In some communities the sex ratio has, in fact, shifted. With fewer available men, the likelihood of marriage declines. Considering only people of the same race in a county, there are about eighty-five Black men per one hundred Black women, whereas the sex ratio is closer to one to one among whites (Pouget et al. 2010). Although rates of intermarriage have risen rapidly since the 1960s, interracial marriages only made up about 17% of all marriages in 2015 (Pew Research Center 2017). An immediate consequence of this imbalance is that Black women are much less likely to marry than white women. And indeed, Black women's retreat from marriage is long-standing and ongoing and has implications for health (Lichter et al. 1992). Although the benefits of marriage to life expectancy are stronger for men, they are still evident for women. The benefits of marriage may also be declining, even if social support generally remains strongly beneficial (Tumin 2018). The benefits of marriage are also complicated by race, but there is nonetheless evidence that marriage has health benefits among Black couples (Koball et al. 2010).

The effects of incarceration on marriage and sexual markets can also be subtle, suggesting that the impact may be more than simply the removal of eligible men. The forced removal of men from a neighborhood can also change the quality of the marriage unions that form. In high-incarceration neighborhoods, some women might be forced to "marry down" (Charles and Luoh 2010; Cohen and Pepin 2018). This shift decreases the household income women might ordinarily enjoy if they were able to marry men with approximately the same economic prospects as their own. Additionally, high-quality marriages—characterized simply by high levels of marital satisfaction—tend to have even more health-promoting consequences. Studies find that, among African Americans, a high-quality marriage protects couples from the distress of financial strain and racial discrimination (Lincoln and Chae 2010). In addition, a reduction in the number of eligible men increases the likelihood of having multiple sex partners (Pouget et al. 2010). When the sex ratio is between 81.1 and 83.7 men per 100 women— very low by traditional standards—Black men have 90% greater odds of having multiple sexual partners in a given year, and Black women have 30% greater odds (relative to a ratio at or near one to one). A similar pattern applies to white men and women, though fewer live in such conditions due, in part, to race disparities in incarceration: the average white person reports living in a county where the sex ratio is 99.5, compared to 84.8 for the average Black person.

Several social processes come together to partially explain these patterns. For one, a low sex ratio makes more female sex partners available, both because men are in prison and because prison tends to dissolve existing relationships. In addition, women who have a partner who is incarcerated are more likely to have concurrent partners, which facilitates the spread of infectious disease more rapidly than consecutive partnerships (Adimora et al. 2003). In addition to these changes in the structure of sexual networks, there is some evidence that neighborhood social cohesion also plays a role in the spread of infectious disease. In neighborhoods with a high level of incarceration, such cohesion tends to decline, which in turn makes people less likely to practice safe sex (Thomas, Torrone, and Browning 2010).

Effects on the Health of Mothers

The effects of incarceration described previously, though significant, are, in some sense, limited. A focus on sexual and marriage markets forces us to consider the sum total of people of all races and genders seeking partners, but in this focus the most adverse consequences operating in this fashion pertain to heterosexual women who are sexually active and unmarried. It is important to consider the effects of incarceration more broadly. Incarceration can also affect the health of mothers, albeit through a different set of processes. Many people currently or formerly in prison have children, but relationships among parents vary (Glaze and Maruschak 2008). In some cases, there is no relationship. In others, there is a relationship but not one conducive to good mental or physical health. Anecdotally, one could see how the removal of an abusive father could improve the well-being of a mother (as well as the child, which we discuss later). Yet, the evidence suggests that the incarceration of fathers adversely affects the health of mothers, almost irrespective of the quality of the relationship they had prior to incarceration.

Much of the research to date has focused on incarcerated fathers and nonincarcerated mothers. The best of these studies has followed mothers over time, allowing researchers to explore the relationship between changes in the mothers' mental health and changes in their relationship with their children's father (Turney, Schnittker, and Wildeman 2012; Wildeman, Schnittker, and Turney 2012). To a remarkable degree, the effects of incarceration on the mental health of nonincarcerated mothers parallels that of formerly incarcerated fathers, especially when a child is present. For example, the incarceration of a father increases the odds of a major depressive episode in the mother by about 50%. Furthermore, the incarceration of a father is consequential regardless of the quality of the relationship they had before the incarceration occurred. Even if the relationship had soured sometime earlier, mothers are at a minimum affected by the shock of a father's incarceration.

Spillovers of this sort happen for a variety of reasons. For one, a parent's incarceration impacts a nonincarcerated partner's socioeconomic situation. Nearly 70% of incarcerated fathers provide at least some financial support to their children prior to their incarceration, even if their contributions are occasionally financed by criminal activities (Edin 2000). Accordingly, a father's incarceration might increase the financial instability of mothers. A father's incarceration also appears to deteriorate the quality of the relationship he had with the mother, which could impact mental health. Even when fathers were not involved with their children on a daily basis prior to incarceration, they at least report frustration in missing key milestones while in prison, and most try to keep at least some contact with their children (Edin, Nelson, and Paranal 2004; Glaze and Maruschak 2008). The quality of the relationship among fathers, mothers, and children tends to decline during and after incarceration.

Although these influences are important, much of the spillover is driven by an increase in the stress of parenting. After a father is incarcerated, mothers are more likely to report feeling trapped by the responsibilities of being a parent, feeling that being a parent was more work than pleasure, and feeling worn out from raising a child. Mothers report many of these feelings under even optimal conditions, but when they stem from the incarceration of a father it reflects a lack of optimism: most incarcerated fathers are eventually released, but there is little evidence that parenting stress suddenly subsides when they return.

The criminal justice system disrupts relationships in other enduring ways too. Several studies have described how police have used personal relationships and family support services to serve arrest warrants (Goffman 2009; Gustafson 2011; Herring, Yarbrough, and Alatorre 2020; Weaver and Geller

2019). This practice can damage relationships in ways that are both subtle and significant. For instance, police can threaten the partners of people with outstanding warrants in an attempt to learn their location. Similarly, if police are aware of personal relationships between a person with a warrant and a mother, they can use milestones—such as birthdays—to locate a father. Even if the father fails to show for the event, the possibility of arrest can damage the social fabric of neighborhoods. Fearing arrest in public places or in tandem with major life events, individuals with warrants often avoid the very people and institutions that might elevate their circumstances (Gustafson 2011). People with criminal records might avoid, for instance, contacting other family members, applying for jobs, or applying for other social benefits, fearing that such contact makes their activities and location known. One police operation targeted people with arrest warrants who were receiving welfare benefits. They were notified that there was a problem with their benefits, they were told a time and place to show up to rectify the problem, and they were arrested when they arrived (Gustafson 2011). Although this was a police operation, the partners of people with records are sometimes complicit in these tactics. Goffman (2009), for instance, documents the ways in which some mothers use the threat of calling the police to encourage better parenting. Using nationally representative quantitative data, Brayne (2014) brings the strength of institutional avoidance into sharper relief. She finds that people who had any contact with the criminal justice system—whether stopped by police, arrested, convicted, or incarcerated—were much more likely to avoid institutions involved with any indirect surveillance, including educational, financial, and medical institutions. In particular, she shows that contact with the criminal justice system reduced the likelihood of visiting a hospital, opening a bank account, or participating in school or work (see also Haskins and Jacobsen 2017).

For many mothers, the risk of someone they know being incarcerated is certainly not limited to the fathers of their children. Parallel evidence shows that the incarceration of an adult son increases a mother's distress as well (Green et al. 2006; Sirois 2020; Wildeman, Schnittker, and Turney 2012). A child's incarceration diminishes a mother's health in middle age, especially if the mother has grandchildren (Goldman 2019). And, once again, the psychological damage operates through the filaments of familial obligation. When an adult son is incarcerated, mothers experience greater financial hardship, especially in low-income communities. Some mothers also experience an increased burden of grandparenting while a son is incarcerated. In this case, the stress of grandmothers abates more when their son is released than it does for mothers when a father is released. But these patterns nonetheless indicate that the burden of incarceration is borne across generations through the obligations apparent in nurturing families.

Incarceration and the Health of Children

All this raises a critical question: what happens to the health of children whose parents are incarcerated? Here too, there is more evidence on the incarceration of fathers than on the incarceration of mothers, in part because far more fathers are incarcerated. And, as before, when considering the effects of parental incarceration on the health of a child, it is necessary to weigh the characteristics of the father in a multifaceted way. Regardless of the reason it occurred, when a parent leaves the household, their absence is disruptive to the child. For instance, the children of divorced parents tend to have lower well-being than the children of intact families (Amato and Keith 1991). In addition, children whose parents have been deployed for military service report lower well-being when their parent is away than when they are not (Chandra et al. 2010).

One of the most comprehensive studies of its kind is the Fragile Families and Child Wellbeing Study, referred to simply as Fragile Families. Befitting its name the study focused on families, but it followed individuals even if the family split. These twin aspects of the study's design have been useful for researchers interested in understanding the effects of confinement. In particular, its design has allowed researchers to study the consequences of incarceration over multiple parties and follow people over long periods as their health, circumstances, and relationships change. Research using Fragile Families has demonstrated that the incarceration of a father undermines the health and well-being of a child, though the impact is conditioned by the characteristics of the father (Wakefield and Wildeman 2013). In general, the children of incarcerated fathers are more likely to be physically aggressive, depressed, anxious, and impulsive. In many cases, these behavioral problems are long-standing, but the incarceration of a father tends to both create new problems and deepen existing ones.

When evaluated over the entire life course, incarceration has more systematic effects on families. Some studies estimate that 3% to 4% of women are pregnant at the time they enter prison, and about 6% of children born in custody will be preterm and one-third will be cesarean (Glaze and Maruschak 2008; Sufrin et al. 2019). Although studies of the effects of incarceration on families focus on the complex dynamics of moving in and out of prison and relationships, incarceration can lead to more permanent dissolution. One study found a relationship between the rise of female incarceration and the growth of the foster care system (Swann and Sheran 2006). Between 1985 and 2000, foster care caseloads more than doubled, and about 30% of this increase can be explained by female incarceration. Studies have also demonstrated a relationship between incarceration and infant mortality. Parental incarceration increases the odds of infant mortality by about 40% (Wakefield and Wildeman 2013). This difference is approximately as large as the Black-white difference in infant mortality, and comparable in impact to maternal smoking. Furthermore, this difference is net of a variety of other risk factors related to infant mortality, including whether the mother was married, whether she smoked during pregnancy, whether prenatal care was adequate, and child birthweight.

One way to think synthetically about the effects of incarceration on families is in terms of how incarceration is experienced by different people. Incarcerated women may be shackled during the birth and postpartum period (Shlafer, Hardeman, and Carlson 2019). For a child with an incarcerated father, his absence is registered as the loss of a person who used to be in their life. If that father was abusive, the child's well-being might improve. But even the loss of a negligent father is still experienced as the loss of someone who cared while he was around. For mothers, the loss of a partner reverberates in different ways. In addition to the loss of a companion, mothers lose a regular source of financial support or, at a minimum, a person to draw on in case of an emergency. Although many mothers are able to successfully shield their children from the stress of an incarcerated father, they might be able to do so only because they are managing the episode assiduously, by keeping their finances as stable as possible, by seeking resources from friends, and by enlisting the assistance of grandparents. Parenting stress might be absorbed to serve the needs of a child, even if it is detrimental to the well-being of a mother.

The Spread of Stigma

Although those released from prison carry the bulk of the stigma of incarceration, there is considerable evidence that stigma can spread to others. The stigma of incarceration is sticky, adhering to those who come in contact with it, and has become stickier with the advent of electronic criminal records (Braman 2004; Lageson 2016; Uggen and Blahnik 2016). In households affected by incarceration usually only one family member has ever been incarcerated, but there is evidence that stigma spreads quickly and thoroughly within households. In his study, Donald Braman (2004) found that female members of virtually every family he interviewed reported feeling shame and humiliation because of the incarceration of a father, husband, or partner. Recognizing the damage that stigma can do, these women worked hard to conceal the fact of incarceration, though they were mostly unsuccessful, as the reputations of incarcerated men were usually well known and durable. The losses associated with incarceration are experienced as both long-term disruptions and smaller everyday absences, long after a prison sentence has been served. To take one small but telling example, Sarah Lageson (2016) describes a father who could not accompany his daughter on a hockey trip to Canada, fearing that his old criminal record would cause problems at the border.

The stigma of incarceration adheres in more direct ways as well. Those visiting someone in prison are subject to much of the same scrutiny as inmates (Comfort 2003). A standard procedure, for instance, involves the presentation of proper identification, a search of personal belongings, and a metal detector test. Even more extreme, some visitors are searched physically. Visitors can of course leave at the end of their visit, but this added scrutiny is not inconsequential. Some scholars have interpreted it in terms of "secondary prisonization," leaving visitors feeling as though they have the same status and must adjust accordingly (Comfort 2007). One way to think about the mental health consequences of secondary stigma is to compare the mental health of those whose partners have been incarcerated with those whose partners are prisoners of war. In both circumstances, the partners are held captive. But in the case of incarceration the captivity is stigmatized for being punishment, whereas in the case of wartime captivity the captivity is honorable for being service to country. Evidence indicates that the partners of incarcerated people are more likely to experience grief, in part because their experience is more demoralizing (Daniel and Barrett 1981).

Incarceration and the Health of Communities

Many of the consequences described previously are sticky but still proximate: they describe what incarceration does to the reputation of close family members. If we move our analysis a step further and think about entire communities, the effects of incarceration become somewhat more challenging to evaluate, though stigma is still a relevant consideration. A 2014 National Research Council report concludes that incarceration imposes high financial, social, and human costs on already disadvantaged communities (National Research Council 2014). Accounting for the full range of community health effects, however, involves a consideration of the potential positive consequences of the penal system. The stated purpose of prisons is to control crime through some combination of retribution, incapacitation, deterrence, and rehabilitation. To the extent that incarceration succeeds in some of these goals, certain dimensions of health might improve if, for instance, violent crime is prevented.

Most of the evidence suggests that incarceration does reduce crime, albeit at a great cost to individuals and society. Furthermore, to the extent that it does reduce crime, it does so only in a mechanistic way and mostly for crimes that have no direct relationship with health (e.g., homicide is directly related to mortality) (Donohue 2009). While estimates can vary, the overall association between incarceration rates and crime rates appears to be somewhere between $-.2$ and $-.4$, meaning a 1% increase in incarceration leads to between a 0.2% to 0.4% decrease in crime. The effects vary greatly, however, depending on the type of crime considered. Some of the largest effects are for robbery and burglary (Johnson and Raphael 2012; Levitt 1996). In many studies, the relationship between incarceration and violent crime is statistically insignificant, including the effect of incarceration on homicide (Besci 1999; Levitt 1996; Marvell and Moody 1994).

Another way to think about the relationship between incarceration and crime reduction is in terms of the correspondence of one trend with another. In the past two decades there has been an increase in incarceration and a decrease in crime, but the two trends are not in sync. Incarceration increased rapidly in the mid-1970s, but crime decreased much later, starting in the early 1990s. Prior to the 1990s the crime rate was relatively flat, even as incarceration was growing rapidly (Clear and Frost 2014). Beyond a lack of correspondence in their timing, trends in incarceration and crime are incommensurate in their magnitude. Between 1993 and 2001, imprisonment increased by 66%, but crime decreased by only 2% to 5% (Western 2006). In fact, there is some evidence that the effect of incarceration on crime, though perhaps once significant, has decreased (Liedka, Piehl, and Useem 2006; Roeder, Eisen, and Bowling 2015). This reflects the shifting composition of the prison population. Incarceration has a bigger impact on crime when it incapacitates active and high-frequency offenders, those who would be committing serious crimes in the community were it not for the fact that they were incarcerated. Although prisons continue to house some people of this sort, the sheer volume of the prison system in the twenty-first century, as well as the aging of the incarcerated population, suggests the prison system incapacitates many inactive offenders as well. As of 2020, more than one in seven US prisoners were serving a life sentence, and 30% of these prisoners were age fifty-five or older (Nellis 2021).

Even if incarceration does little to improve community health by way of crime reduction, it might still make communities *feel* safer. Such consequences should not be neglected, but again, the evidence does not indicate that incarceration improves perceived safety. There are at least three reasons incarceration does not change perceptions of safety in a community. First, a high rate of incarceration can undermine the informal social relationships that are mobilized when residents feel besieged (Rose and Clear 1998). Second, the presence of a large police force can itself increase anxiety, particularly in the context of racialized police violence, such as the George Floyd police killing in 2020. Third, the experience of prison and the subsequent stigma of a criminal record can lead individuals to commit more crime after they are released. As deterrence researcher Daniel Nagin and colleagues concluded in a 2009 review, "Compared to non-custodial sanctions, incarceration has a null or mildly criminogenic effect on future criminal involvement" (Nagin et al. 2009, p. 115).

A Synthetic Approach to Community Effects

The relationship between incarceration and community health involves several considerations. Incarceration might reduce certain crimes, but not in ways that produce large improvements in public health. The prison system treats particular ailments, including infectious diseases, but perhaps not at a scale that could affect community outcomes. *Estelle* mandates certain treatments but leaves significant gaps, especially regarding the many diseases that are not considered serious. One way to consider community effects in a more encompassing fashion is to think about incarceration in two ways at once: at a much higher level of aggregation (moving away from the individuals affected by incarceration directly) and with respect to a variety of specific diseases (especially diseases that vary in how prisons might treat them).

Along these lines, one strategy is to study the effects of state-level incarceration rates on state-level infectious disease rates. Infectious disease serves as an especially useful test of community effects because infectious disease lies at the center of the many influences discussed in this and other chapters. On the one hand, prisons might be instrumental in the spread of infectious disease, in the sense that people in prison live in close quarters and have sexual contact with each other. And most people are sexually active after release, allowing for the possibility of continued transmission. On the other hand, prisons focus much of their health care resources on the detection and treatment of infectious disease. Furthermore, people in prison are likely to be medically underserved prior to incarceration. From this perspective, prisons might help curtail certain treatable infectious diseases, like tuberculosis, perhaps performing even better than conventional health care providers.

Table 5.1 presents a summary of statistical models that estimate the annual incidence of specific infectious diseases between the years 1987 and 2010 in US states, showing how incarceration might impact state-level community health. For each infectious disease, incidence was estimated as a function of the percentage of residents in the state who were once incarcerated, along with a variety of control variables. We generated estimates for men and women separately (except for tuberculosis). Human immunodeficiency virus (HIV) was assessed through deaths from HIV/acquired immunodeficiency syndrome (AIDS), rather than from the incidence of HIV infections. Table 5.1 shows separate models predicting incidence among men and women, which allows us to glimpse additional features of the underlying process linking incarceration and state-level health outcomes. Incarceration is, of course, much more common among men. If the effects of incarceration are larger for men than women, it would suggest that prisons are the focal point of infection. Incarceration affects men in the first instance, and some infected men go on to infect women as well. In contrast, if the effects of incarceration are as large for women as men, it would suggest that social processes after release are more significant.

Table 5.1 Effects of Incarceration on Incident Infectious Disease in US States

Disease	Sex	Direction of Effect	Magnitude
Tuberculosis	Both	Decrease	8%
Chlamydia	Male	Increase	40%
	Female	Increase	58%
Gonorrhea	Male	No change	0%
	Female	Increase	13%
Syphilis	Male	Decrease	11%
	Female	No change	0%
HIV Deaths	Male	Increase, but declining	17% in 2003
	Female	Increase	27%

The evidence points to contingent effects, as expected given the uncertain legal mandate of prison care, as discussed previously. Although for most infectious diseases incarceration increases the state-wide incidence, an increase in the number of released inmates decreases the incidence of several infections, including tuberculosis. The number of formerly incarcerated people in a state is also linked to the spread of HIV, but its impact on HIV deaths among men is declining, suggesting improvements in monitoring and treatment. For other infectious diseases, however, an increase in the incarceration rate is associated with an increase in the spread of infectious disease. This is especially apparent with respect to chlamydia. One caveat is important: this increase could be an artifact of improvements in *detecting* chlamydia rather than an increase in the actual incidence of the disease. The detection of chlamydia has improved substantially over time, but most of these improvements pertain to detection in women, and it is unclear whether prisons alone are at the vanguard of chlamydia testing. For instance, far fewer prisons test for chlamydia than test for syphilis, HIV, and certainly tuberculosis. For this reason, the positive relationship between incarceration and chlamydia among men is unlikely to be driven entirely by prisons simply detecting previously undiagnosed conditions.

Interpreting the set of relationships in Table 5.1 brings several patterns to light. For one, the results suggest incarceration disrupts sexual networks in ways that can promote the spread of infectious disease in communities. With the exception of tuberculosis, all the infections presented in the table are sexually transmitted. For those diseases in which incarceration is positively related to the spread of infections, incarceration is usually associated with the spread of infections in women and men. In fact, the impact of incarceration on HIV deaths is stronger among women than men, as is the relationship between incarceration and gonorrhea. In addition, the role of incarceration in the spread of infection is greater for those infections that prisons generally overlook. Both gonorrhea and chlamydia involve significant complications, though these complications tend to be worse among women. Perhaps for this reason—and given the emphasis on providing treatment for serious medical needs in prison, as set in *Estelle*—testing for these conditions is less common in prison than is testing for other infections. HIV and syphilis, by contrast, are serious in both men and women alike, and prisons more uniformly test for both conditions.

Another facet to these patterns pertains to the gap filled by prison health care relative to community care. Many people who have tuberculosis, for instance, will pass through the prison system at some point. But many will not be aware of their symptoms and are unlikely to receive care or testing in other settings. Because prisons routinely test for tuberculosis—and, indeed, they test more routinely than is done in regular ambulatory care settings— prisons can play a crucial role in treating and, thereby, preventing the spread of tuberculosis. The same applies to syphilis, which has long been a focus of prison testing regimes. For both diseases, those states that incarcerate more people see declines in the incidence of infectious disease. We view these findings more as a reflection of the availability and quality of care *outside* prisons—where there is no constitutional mandate to care—than an endorsement of prisons or prison services.

In a somewhat different way, these patterns reveal the ambiguous health care mandate of prisons, apart from the parameters of *Estelle*. It is perhaps not surprising that prisons do better in addressing the spread of airborne infections than sexually transmitted ones. Historically prisons have minimized or neglected problems regarding sexual contact among people in prison, stating first and foremost that sexual contact between incarcerated people is illegal (Borchert 2016; Najdowski 2011). In this light, it is perhaps not surprising that prisons would do more to promote the spread of chlamydia than the spread of tuberculosis, given that the spread of chlamydia cannot be dealt with as readily by a policy targeting behavior. Addressing sexually transmitted infections would require that prisons grapple with the issue of sexuality, whereas addressing the spread of tuberculosis requires merely that prisons acknowledge that tuberculosis can be spread in confined spaces. In a different way, the declining relationship between incarceration and HIV infections also reflects the demands of legal reform. In the current legal climate, prisoners are much more effective in litigating around specific aspects of care, including specific serious conditions, rather than around the general quality-of-care issues. In part through legal efforts, the treatment of HIV in prison has improved over time, redressing previous deficiencies. With these efforts, the relationship between incarceration and the spread of HIV has declined, even if incarceration continues to play a role in the spread of other infections. If inmates were able to successfully sue for better detection and treatment of chlamydia, the positive effects of incarceration on its spread would likely decrease as well. Such a possibility is remote, however, given the prevailing legal climate and the demonstrably worse consequences of HIV than chlamydia.

The COVID-19 Pandemic

The COVID-19 pandemic provides another illustration of uncertain mandate of prison care. In a later chapter we turn to the role of COVID-19 in compassionate release—that is, the early release of people at risk of infection while incarcerated—but apart from health-motivated decarceration of this sort, it is important to note that prisons are implicated in the community spread of COVID-19. Prison outbreaks of COVID-19 have been common, and the outbreaks are not limited to those in custody. By virtue of their large staffs, who are entering, exiting, and commuting, prison outbreaks have spread to neighboring communities. During the summer of 2020, COVID-19 cases grew more quickly in nonmetropolitan counties with large prisons relative to similar areas without prisons (Schwartzapfel, Park, and Demillo 2020). In Texas, California, and Florida, the prison system is estimated to have contributed over 250,000 total new cases between May and August. COVID-19 also arrived sooner in counties with a large number of people in prison, setting the stage for an earlier peak in high-incarceration locations. Furthermore, these outbreaks exacerbated many pre-existing inequalities, especially as they spread outward. Black Americans are much more likely to be incarcerated. They are also more likely to be infected and hospitalized with COVID-19. And they are more likely to know someone who died of COVID-19.

Prisons did not respond quickly to the pandemic, or in a manner proportional to the threat, reflecting a system that cannot respond nimbly to emergent health problems. One response of prisons was to relax compassionate release standards, which to some extent they did (as we discuss later). Although laudable from the standpoint of decarceration and a tool that can ostensibly work quickly, this response also serves to highlight the difficulty of providing care in a policy and legal environment not well suited for doing so. The response operationally led to decarceration, but it also betrayed an admission on the part of prison officials that there was little they were able or willing to do to reduce risk among those still in their care. Jails have also been ill-prepared for the pandemic, though facets of jailing exacerbate the problem, especially the high volume and daily turnover. One study found that for every person who cycles through a jail, just over two new COVID-19 cases emerge three to four weeks later (Reinhart and Chen 2020). With rapid turnover of the jail population, seemingly small correlations of this sort lead to especially large outbreaks in highly policed neighborhoods. In this particular study, jail cycling accounted for 60% of cases of COVID-19 in Chicago, most of them in majority-Black zip codes, consistent with jailing practices.

The role of prisons and jails in the transmission of COVID-19 has produced a good deal of legal action, much of it focused on reducing the size of the incarcerated population rather than mandating testing or treatment. Even so, these rulings have reduced overcrowding and in principle the risk of infection. Rulings have specified, for instance, that jails reduce their capacity by 20% to 50% to allow for social distancing, that bail be reduced to zero to prevent admissions among those unable to pay, that weekend sentences be eliminated, that those with pre-existing conditions or over the age of sixty be released or not jailed if arrested, that people held for low-level nonviolent crimes be released, that courts avoid issuing bench warrants, and that people held on technical violations be released (Prison Policy Initiative 2021). These rulings are crafted in various ways, though they all share the intent of situational decarceration. The breadth of the criteria for release suggests general recognition that jails incarcerate too many low-risk people.

* * *

The effects of incarceration on community health reflect both the size of the US prison system and the specific policies and procedures that govern the provision of care inside prison and out. To this point we have emphasized the sharp difference between the care people in prison receive while they are incarcerated and what they are likely to receive after release. Yet there are other connections between prison health care and the functioning of the broader health care system. In the next chapter we turn to spillovers between the functioning of the prison system and the functioning of regional health care systems. In no small measure, the inadequacies of prison care redound to the capacity of health care systems to deliver effective care to everyone.

6

The Effects of Incarceration on Health Care Systems

Incarceration affects the health of families and communities in both direct and indirect ways. But the foregoing discussion, even if demonstrating the broad scope of incarceration's impact, might still suggest that much of the damage of incarceration is concentrated in a relatively small number of communities, particularly lower-income communities of color. By virtue of racial, economic, and geographic segregation, those who are least likely to be incarcerated are also least likely to have family members or neighbors who are incarcerated. For many people, the expansion of the prison system seems far removed from their personal experience, and some communities are effectively shielded, even in high-incarceration regions, by virtue of a highly unequal criminal justice system. But it would be a mistake to imagine that the effects of incarceration are limited to a narrow segment of the population or that incarceration only has an impact on those who are already disadvantaged. Under some conditions incarceration can impact an entire health care system, particularly a health care system that is as multifaceted and entwined as in the United States. The US health care system is interwoven with other institutions, reflecting existing inequalities even as it effectively serves wide segments of the public. Understanding spillovers from incarceration to health care requires moving beyond the mechanisms discussed earlier to thinking about how prisons and those who move through them can change the market for health services. Understanding spillovers also requires an appreciation of the relationship between incarceration, insurance, and uncompensated care.

The closest parallel to the spillover effects of incarceration pertains to the spillover effects of community uninsurance. Such effects begin with the behavior of uninsured individuals and propagate outward to impact other health care consumers. For those who are uninsured, just under 10% of the US population in 2020, their lack of insurance presents a major barrier to care (Cohen et al. 2021). The uninsured are much more likely to report an unmet need for care, even for care they know is essential. Uninsured people with diabetes, for instance, are more likely to forego regular exams, including eye and foot exams, necessary to prevent vascular complications. They are also less likely to receive preventive care, such as flu shots.

Yet a lack of insurance does not prevent people from receiving care altogether. By law, hospitals cannot deny service to individuals in the emergency room (ER) based on their ability to pay (Fields et al. 2001). Congress passed the Emergency Medical Treatment and Labor Act in 1986 with a narrow focus—the goal was to prevent the denial of emergency care—but its implications have grown more pronounced as the number of uninsured has increased. With few other options available to them, the uninsured are more likely than the insured to use ERs as a regular source of care. ER care is particularly expensive, and much of the care patients receive in an ER setting remains uncompensated. Given the patchwork nature of the health insurance market, combined with laws regarding the right to urgent care, former prisoners must often rely on emergency department visits for medical care. For example, one Rhode Island study followed a cohort of released prisoners and found that 32% had three or more ER visits in the first year after release and 25% had a first ER visit within a month of release (Frank et al. 2013). The situation would likely be very different if former inmates were provided with more adequate care.

This situation is also consequential. When the burden of uncompensated care is beyond what a hospital can absorb, hospitals are forced to adapt, either by reducing the availability of services, reducing the quality of services, or raising the price of services. These changes affect everyone who consumes care, and, from an administrative perspective, there are few strategies for preventing uncompensated care altogether. A hospital could, for instance, cut back on those services that result in the most uncompensated care. They might also decide to cut services that are unprofitable, including, for instance, addiction treatment. But when facing budget shortfalls, hospitals tend to cut services in a blunt fashion, impacting consumers with a range of needs. They cut, for instance, hospital beds, surgical capacity, psychiatric services, trauma centers, burn units, community outreach transportation, and programs such as Meals on Wheels (Institute of Medicine 2003). Hospitals operate on very narrow margins, with little room to shift expenses, and this is especially the case in hospitals that disproportionately treat the poor and uninsured.

Furthermore, problems of revenue and capacity can compound. Hospitals faced with significant financial pressures can cut primary care services, paradoxically shifting patients from appropriate sources of routine care to overcrowded and more expensive ERs. In addition, because hospitals with high levels of uncompensated care tend to have fewer privately insured patients, there is little opportunity to derive additional revenue from more generously insured consumers. The contributions of physicians' philanthropic efforts alleviate only a small part of the burden. To be sure, the burden of uncompensated care is not assumed by hospitals alone. In fact, most uncompensated care is eventually paid through public sources, including Medicare and Medicaid, which make general payments to assist hospitals in care for the uninsured (Hadley and Holahan 2003). But these supplementary sources are funded through tax revenues, and absent diverting funds from other parts of the budget, revenue must be increased to maintain the viability of public insurance programs, including through higher taxes. State and local governments pay for uncompensated care too and face similar budget problems, with even more political reluctance to raise taxes.

Spillovers can be demonstrated by tracing connections from regional and market characteristics to individual health behavior. Research has explored whether individuals report any unmet need for care in the preceding year (Pauly and Pagán 2007). Although reporting an "unmet need" first requires recognizing a need for care, subjective reports of unmet need are generally accurate. Studies using these reports show that people living in communities with a large number of uninsured people are more likely to report an unmet need for care, even after statistically controlling for whether they personally have health insurance. Aspects of the spillover process can also be demonstrated using aggregate data. Some studies, for instance, have shown that as the size of the uninsured population increases, the capacity of hospitals declines, as measured by hospital beds per capita and other indicators (Institute of Medicine 2003).

Before thinking about the role of incarceration in catalyzing spillovers, it is useful to think about the specific kinds of patients that contribute to uncompensated care. Although frequent ER users are few in number, they are large in impact. They account for about a third of all patients and more than 60% of visits to the ER (Cook et al. 2004). Even apart from their potential contributions to uncompensated care, their limited health care options and consumption patterns create problems, both for providers and for the patients themselves. For one, frequent ER users consume health care in ways that are ineffective, relying on a delivery setting that is not suitable for long-term care. For these patients, though, a lack of insurance is the critical issue, not an ill-informed strategy for health care consumption. When the state of Massachusetts enacted a precursor version of the Affordable Care Act and expanded health insurance coverage considerably, ER use dropped by 5% to 8%, as consumers who might ordinarily have gone to the ER went elsewhere (Miller 2012). Furthermore, frequent ER users are costly to treat, not only because of where they receive care, but also because of the nature of their health problems. Frequent ER users tend to have worse health, higher levels of stress, lower levels of social support, and higher rates of depression, a portfolio of comorbidity that is difficult to treat well (Sandoval et al. 2010). In many ways, the characteristics of frequent ER users resemble those of people released from prison, and there is, in fact, evidence linking incarceration to spillovers similar to those produced by uninsurance. Because people in prison have limited access to care, they frequently rely on the ER as their primary source of medical care, resulting in more frequent and costly emergency visits for needs that might be better addressed in other settings.

Incarceration as a Catalyst for Spillovers

Incarceration and the resulting stigma of a criminal record increase the likelihood that a person released from prison will be uninsured. In part this is because the dominant source of health insurance in the United States is through employer-sponsored plans. People released from prison are more likely to be unemployed, and even when they can find a job, it is rarely the kind that provides health benefits. Similarly, a large number of Americans are insured through the policies of their spouse. People released from prison, though, are less likely to be married and so must rely on their own employment. But they also struggle with securing Medicaid benefits, a program that historically has not been widely available to childless men. For these reasons, incarceration moves hand in hand with uninsurance. Figure 6.1 shows two maps of the United States. The first shows the percentage of people who are former inmates by state. The second shows the percentage of people who are uninsured. Many high incarceration states, especially in the south, also tend

Panel A. Percent Former Inmates

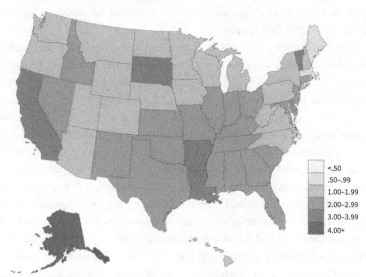

	<.50
	.50–.99
	1.00–1.99
	2.00–2.99
	3.00–3.99
	4.00+

Panel B. Percent Uninsured

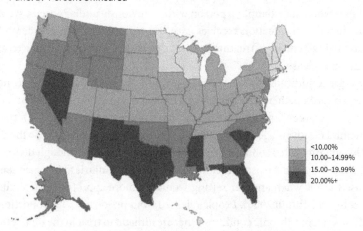

	<10.00%
	10.00–14.99%
	15.00–19.99%
	20.00%+

Figure 6.1 Percentage of Former Inmates and Uninsured by State, United States 2010. **A.** Percent Former Inmates. **B.** Percent Uninsured.

to have high levels of uninsurance. If incarceration increases the number of people in a state who are uninsured, it also increases the potential for spill-overs to the health care system.

Yet the spillovers associated with incarceration stretch beyond a lack of insurance. Americans lose their insurance for a variety of reasons, including through the loss of a job, a divorce, or losing eligibility for public insur-ance because of a higher income. For most, this spell of being uninsured does not correspond to a period in which their need for insurance or care is necessarily greater, but for people released from prison the situation is more of a confluence. The loss of insurance is often directly tied to an in-crease in their need for care. As discussed earlier, people are provided with health care while they are incarcerated, and on average, they use more serv-ices in prison than they did prior to admission. If people continue to use appropriate services after release, incarceration will have simultaneously increased their demand for care and reduced their access. The demand for care can be increased in other ways as well. The intraprison transmission of infectious disease, as discussed earlier, increases the need for services among at least some people in prison. Newly diagnosed conditions do the same, as when, for example, a person with a previously undiagnosed psychi-atric disorder or infection receives care and treatment while incarcerated. Recognizing benefits of treatment, they are likely to want to continue treat-ment after release.

Evidence indicates that, after release from prison, most people do not forego care altogether, consistent with a high demand for care. But when they do seek care, they tend to do so in cost-intensive ways, consistent with their structural disadvantages. As noted earlier, former inmates tend to use the ER with regularity, often soon after release (Frank et al. 2013). Although they can use the ER for good reason, including for traumatic injuries, they also tend to use the ER when another setting would be more appropriate (Conklin, Lincoln, and Tuthill 2000). People released from prison also disproportion-ately suffer from chronic conditions that are difficult to treat in the long term. Hepatitis B/C and human immunodeficiency virus (HIV), for instance, re-quire ongoing medication and frequent physician visits. When treatment is foregone or delayed, whether because of negligence on the part of the patient or difficulty providing the right services, even costlier treatments can re-sult. The total size of the US former prison population is roughly five million people, with an additional ten million having felony-level criminal records that typically include jail time (Shannon et al. 2017). A large percentage of these individuals will be uninsured. Although this group likely makes up a small percentage of the estimated thirty million Americans who did not have health insurance in 2019, it takes few patients with complex disorders and suboptimal utilization patterns to dramatically increase the burden of uncompensated care (Keisler-Starkey and Bunch 2020).

There are reasons to expect unevenness in the spillovers from incarceration to health care. Because a large number of incarcerated people return to a few communities, spillovers might affect hospitals serving high-incarceration places but have less impact on other hospital systems. Consistent with this, there is overlap between neighborhood segregation and hospital segregation. Hospital care for African Americans, for instance, is concentrated in a relatively small number of hospitals (Jha et al. 2007). Nearly half of all elderly Black patients are seen in the 5% of hospitals that serve the highest volume of Black patients. Furthermore, the burden of uncompensated care has become more concentrated over time, suggesting growing spatial inequality (Cunningham and Tu 1997).

Yet evidence suggests a relationship between state-level incarceration rates and the likelihood of reporting an unmet need for care (Schnittker et al. 2015). This evidence also suggests these spillover effects are demographically broad, affecting those far removed from the prison system. Table 6.1 presents the relationship between the percentage of former inmates within a state and the odds of reporting an unmet need for care. The data are drawn from a nationally representative survey of adults, which includes people with and without a history of incarceration. The outcomes presented in Table 6.1 represent different dimensions of health care consumption and quality. If spillovers from incarceration are sufficiently powerful, they should affect not only basic access to care but also the quality of services received. The models control for a variety of factors related to the propensity to seek care and the characteristics of the health care market individuals reside in, including insurance type, health, age, race, marital status, sex, and socioeconomic status. The models also control for state-level characteristics, including the average income in the state, the percent below poverty, the percent unemployed, the percent African American, and, crucially, the percent uninsured. The numbers in the table correspond to the percent increase or decrease in the odds of a given experience for each additional 1% increase in formerly incarcerated individuals within a state.

Table 6.1 Relationship between Percentage of Former Inmates in State and Health Care Consumption among Individuals

Health Care Use	
Reported an Unmet Need for Care	+6%
Visited a Doctor	−5%
Visited a Hospital	−11%
Had Surgery	−6%
Had Mammogram	−5%
Received Psychiatric Care	−2%
Quality of Care	
Have Usual Place for Care	−8%
Satisfied with Care	−9%
Satisfied with Choice of Doctor	−9%
Satisfied with Choice of Specialist	−12%
Do Not Trust Personal Physician	+10%

Note: Derived from estimates presented in Schnittker et al. (2015).

People living in states with more former inmates are more likely to report an unmet need for care. They are also less likely to visit a doctor, to have surgery, and to receive mammography. Other indicators suggest that health care quality is diminished as well. People in high-incarceration states are less likely to have a usual place for care and to be satisfied with their care and are more likely to say they do not trust their physician. To evaluate the breadth of these spillovers, Table 6.2 presents the same quantities and outcomes but over two select subpopulations, chosen to reflect groups ostensibly far removed from the correctional system through social distance. The first column presents the same relationships presented earlier but among those who are insured, while the second presents the relationship among those whose income is at least twice the federal poverty line. The same relationships that were apparent in the overall sample are also apparent among those who are most socially distant from people formerly in prison. Indeed, many of the relationships are larger among the insured than they are overall, which is not unexpected if the health care consumption of people with fewer resources is determined more by their personal situation than by the market for services generally. None of these spillovers from incarceration suggests other influences are unimportant. Indeed, when evaluated from a strictly

Table 6.2 Relationship between Percentage of Former Inmates in State and Health Care Consumption among the Insured and the Nonpoor

	Among the Insured	Among Those with Incomes at Least Twice the Poverty Line
Health Care Use		
Reported an Unmet Need for Care	+17%	+18%
Visited a Doctor	−7%	−8%
Visited a Hospital	−10%	−8%
Had Surgery	−5%	−5%
Had Mammogram	−8%	−10%
Received Psychiatric Care	−4%	−1%
Quality of Care		
Have Usual Place for Care	−15%	−15%
Satisfied with Care	−13%	−11%
Satisfied with Choice of Doctor	−15%	−15%
Satisfied with Choice of Specialist	−21%	−18%
Do Not Trust Personal Physician	+18%	+20%

Note: Derived from estimates presented in Schnittker et al. (2015).

quantitative perspective, other influences are more important. Those who are uninsured, for instance, are much more likely to report an unmet need for care than are those who are insured, as are those with poor health relative to those in excellent health. Yet the fact that the experience of people formerly in prison can affect access to care among even well-resourced health care consumers suggests that the spillover effects of incarceration, much like the spillover effects of community uninsurance, are both broad and meaningful. As before, the connections between criminal justice and health are deep and multifaceted.

The Blending of Health Care and Criminal Justice

Although these patterns provide an especially vivid illustration of spillover effects, incarceration affects the health care system in other ways too. Studies of ERs, in particular, show how physicians are on the front line of many criminal justice issues, whether they are prepared for it or not (Lara-Millán 2014). Prisons are obligated to provide health care, as discussed earlier, but they need not provide it on their own premises. Some jail systems work in collaboration with local ERs to provide intake services. If a police officer determines that a person in custody requires medical aid, the person can be taken to an ER prior to booking in a jail. This arrangement has consequences for what ERs are able to provide for other patients seeking services. Lara-Millán (2014) studied an urban ER that actively collaborated with a local jail. He documented several patterns. For one, he showed that people who have been arrested are often moved to the front of the ER line by police, forcing other patients to wait longer. This occurs irrespective of the person's need for services, and indeed, many people are brought in by police for relatively simple treatments. In such cases, ER staff accept people brought by the police as a matter of professional courtesy, although they recognize that doing so interferes with the care they are able to provide others. The presence of police officers in the ER can also heighten tensions in the waiting room, blending the mission of criminal justice and care. When hospital staff begin to suspect that some patients in the ER are seeking prescription narcotics, they are, in effect, trained to think in terms of crime and crime control. In addition, they implicitly align some patients as closer to the criminal justice system than others. Even absent a strong police presence, hospital staff might very well act in a similar fashion, but Lara-Millán's study shows that the mission of criminal justice and the mission of an ER are resolved in complex ways when the two collide. When hospital staff are thinking about which patients to admit first, they primarily use medical criteria, but they also involve criminal justice considerations, including whether a patient was brought in by the police and the likelihood that the patient was involved in a crime. In this way, hospital staff think like police offers, discriminating between the sick and well partly based on inferences about criminality.

More generally, the rise of the prison system increases the burdens of those working in an ER. ER overcrowding is a major crisis, affecting hospitals around the country (Hoot and Aronsky 2008). Incarceration and policing are not to blame for this crisis, but they have certainly not alleviated the pressure. Arrangements between local jails and ERs are appropriate and even desirable in the sense that those who have been arrested or incarcerated need health care, and ERs provide a good setting for triage and the delivery of some of the care they need. Arresting officers in doubt about the mental health of an arrestee, for instance, are much better off referring the case to a physician than admitting the person to a jail without any professional evaluation. Yet the intersection of incarceration and health care has made it even more difficult to manage ER overcrowding. Furthermore, arrangements between jails and ERs introduce ethical dilemmas for physicians, beyond the dual-loyalty considerations discussed earlier (Dubler 2014). For instance, arrestees in an ER are supervised by police officers, raising questions about confidentiality. The American Medical Association instructs physicians to avoid any situation where another person present in the room could affect the delivery of care, but it is difficult to imagine a physician being entirely unaffected by the presence of a police officer or the circumstances surrounding an arrest (Defilippis 2016). In addition, people who have been arrested are almost always restrained while in the ER, a violation of a patient's right to refusal. Physicians are not explicitly trained to deal with these challenges, and those not practicing in jails or prisons might have little incentive to seek out such specialized training (Tuite, Browne, and O'Neill 2006).

* * *

The criminal justice system intersects with the health system in numerous ways. These intersections present a challenge for those who wish to minimize the impact of the criminal justice system on health and health care. In the next chapter we evaluate these institutional, political, and cultural challenges directly. The collision of the criminal justice system with the health care system has been facilitated by the numerous forces that conceal the significance of these problems and diffuse responsibility over different sectors. The connections between incarceration and health take root in the cracks in the system.

7

The Policy Challenges
of Incarceration and Health

In a society that incarcerates a significant share of its population, mitigating the health effects of incarceration will not be easy, in part because there are so many facets to the relationship. Some policies related to criminal justice certainly intersect with health, but they do not address it head-on. Reducing prison populations by 50%, for instance, would reduce the number of people who are at risk of incarceration-related health problems, but it would do little for those who have already been released. By the same token, improving prison care would help to reduce some of the risks of intraprison transmission, but there are legal barriers to wholesale improvements in care. Some otherwise ambitious health care policies fail to address the needs of those who come into contact with the correctional system. The Affordable Care Act (ACA), for instance, does much for the uninsured and even for certain released individuals. Yet it leaves gaps in coverage and the act itself remains vulnerable to political factors, especially at the state level.

These challenges reflect the dilemmas this book has sought to uncover. The relationship between incarceration and health is sustained by a broad set of political, legal, and cultural forces—the same forces that compel prisons to only partially address the needs of those in its care, that obscure the significance of the prison system as a public health institution, and that force a blending in the missions of care and punishment—but the remedies available to policymakers usually apply to only a narrow window of influence. These challenges are exacerbated by the many jurisdictions involved with incarceration and health, and the limited capacity of the federal government to mandate and implement change in state prisons and municipal jails. Federal, state, and local prisons and jails are all subject to different constraints and opportunities, rendering policies that might be effective in federal prisons inadequate in jails. Providing a bridge for former inmates between prison health care and health care in the community is critical to reintegration, but it is fundamentally a local challenge, where there is no easy handoff from one institution to the other. This chapter reviews the political, legal, and cultural challenges to addressing incarceration and health.

Private Prisons and the Political Challenge of Mitigating the Damage of Incarceration

One option for mitigating the impact of incarceration is to reduce the number of people who are incarcerated. There are many reasons to believe the United States incarcerates too many people, and the fact that incarceration undermines health is just one among many reasons for reform. A related option, pursued by several Scandinavian nations, is to shorten prison sentences or restrict prison to only the most active or violent offenders (Uggen, Stewart, and Horowitz 2018). Some of the evidence discussed earlier indicates this alone would mitigate harm. The relationship between incarceration and infant mortality, for instance, is driven by the incarceration of nonviolent offenders, as they make up the bulk of incarcerated individuals and ordinarily can provide some support for children (Wakefield and Wildeman 2013).

There are numerous political barriers to reform, but traditional political axes are not a major one. There is widespread support for shrinking the prison system, spanning the political spectrum. From a left-leaning and racial justice perspective, advocates emphasize prison's damaging and disparate impact. Recognizing that racial/ethnic minorities are much more likely to be incarcerated, and that incarceration is especially damaging for minority communities, some emphasize alternative forms of punishment and more discretionary sentencing guidelines. From a right-leaning and small government perspective, advocates emphasize the same goal, albeit from a different set of concerns. Some have emphasized government overreach, individual rights and liberties, and the high cost of the prison system (Levin 2018; Miron and Waldock 2010). Arguments related to the financial burden of prisons have become increasingly popular as more and more states face budget shortfalls. With the COVID-19 pandemic, releasing older nonviolent inmates has become an even more attractive option.

There are significant signs of change, with political coalitions increasing the momentum. After four decades of increase, the long wave of racialized mass incarceration has begun to recede. From 2009 to 2019, the overall US imprisonment rate dropped by about 17% and the Black imprisonment rate declined by 29% (though significant racial disparities remain) (Carson 2020b). In addition, the coronavirus pandemic has accelerated some of these downward trends. In the first few months of the COVID-19 pandemic, the US prison and jail populations fell by about 9% and 24%, respectively (Kang-Brown, Montagnet, and Heiss 2021).

Yet there are reasons to doubt the longevity of this ad hoc coalition as well as the durability of the situational factors now pushing reform. Moreover, there are reasons to doubt whether reducing the size or costs of the prison system will coincide with efforts to improve health outcomes for people released from prison. For one, reducing the costs of prisons is, in fact, difficult. Most prison costs are fixed and stem from the costs of human resources, such that reducing the number of incarcerated people has a minimal impact on system costs (Gottschalk 2014). For the same reason, the costs of prisons can grow much faster than the size of the populations they hold. Between 1985 and 2010, for instance, the state prison population grew by 205%, but spending on corrections grew by 674% (Vera Institute of Justice 2010). The Great Recession from 2007 to 2009 occasioned some declines in the size of the prison population. For the first time in almost forty years, the state prison population decreased in 2009 (Pew Center on the States 2010). Yet these overall trends mask great differences across the states. In fact, the overall decline following the recession was largely been driven by a handful of states, such as California and New York, that have historically incarcerated the most people. Furthermore, even though many states have reduced the amount they spend on prisons, these cuts are often directed toward staff (Vera Institute of Justice 2010). Many states cut salaries, benefits, or overtime—human resources are a major component of the fixed costs of prisons—while other states cut programming or food services. Still other states have not cut prison costs or populations at all (Clear 2021; Ghandnoosh 2019). Of the eleven states with the highest incarceration rates, six rank in the top ten for lowest per-prisoner costs (Alexander 2008). Moreover, in 2010 and 2011, when state budgets were particularly strained, a significant number of states *increased* their appropriations for corrections.

In general, the fiscal imperative for reform is weak. There is little evidence that states feel particularly compelled to reduce the number of inmates they house, even when faced with a diminished budget. On this point, Marie Gottschalk (2014) reviews the various ways in which a recession can *increase* the size of prisons. As an example, she highlights aspects of the American Recovery and Reinvestment Act of 2009, the so-called stimulus package. With a quick recovery in mind, the Obama administration sought projects that were ready to hire workers and could begin immediately. State and local authorities responded to the call for shovel-ready projects with a variety of proposals, many of which were related to criminal justice. In some places, the stimulus was used to expand and support prisons, including funding for policing programs. Beyond shaping the targets of stimulus, a slowing economy can feed some of the same cultural responses that gave rise to mass incarceration in the first place. Recessions, for instance, can foment the social anxiety and uncertainty that encourage tough-on-crime policies.

Even if it results in decarceration, concerns over fiscal considerations can undermine prison conditions in ways that damage the health and well-being of incarcerated people. Hiring fewer correctional officers might ease state budgets given the high fixed costs of personnel, but it risks creating a more violent prison environment. Overcrowding allows prisons to house more people without significantly increasing costs, but it is also associated with prison violence. In addition, health care can be a tempting place to cut a prison's budget, especially given the dominant mandate of prisons to punish and protect. In an environment focused on austerity, politicians generally favor cutting prison budgets only insofar as the cuts do not compromise public safety. Prison health care has implications for public health, as we have shown, though its benefits for public health are less clearly understood by policymakers and easy to overlook when politicians hold the mindset that those in prison are not part of the public. Although mental health treatment prevents recidivism—a point we return to later—it is harder to document the public safety benefit of enhanced disease screening. In addition, even though health care represents a relatively small part of the correctional budget in most states, that part has grown faster than others, making it more visible. Some legal rulings exacerbate these problems. In *Wilson v. Seiter*, the court entertained the relevance of cost considerations when it came to evaluating cruel and unusual punishment and did not explicitly reject the argument that prison officials could defend themselves against claims of deliberate indifference by appealing to fiscal considerations (Alexander 2008). But the Eighth Amendment itself provides little guidance for institutions, as we argued earlier. Claims of cruel and unusual punishment rest more on culpable individuals as opposed to ill-funded organizations.

There are, of course, other ways to reduce costs, and a focus on fiscal considerations can increase the appeal of private sector solutions. A long-standing premise of conservative economic thought is that the private sector operates with much more efficiency than the public sector. Although the Biden administration's Department of Justice and many states have begun to move away from private prisons (after renewed interest under Trump), privatization continues to hold considerable appeal, including in corrections. The overall number and proportion of privately held US prisoners peaked in 2012 at approximately 8.7% of all people in prison, before falling back to about 8% by 2019 (Carson 2020b; Gaes 2019). States that have moved in the direction of privatizing corrections have generally done so under the assumption that private prisons can perform the same functions at lower costs. Overall, about 7% of state prisoners and about 16% of federal prisoners are held in private institutions (Carson 2020b; Kirchoff 2010).

There is considerable cross-state variation in the use of private prisons, as well as how contracts with private prisons are structured. Many states have no prisoners in private facilities, even though other states have moved decisively in the direction of privatization (Kirchoff 2010; Sabol, West, and Cooper 2009). Despite the allure of cost savings, research on private prisons suggests that savings are minimal (Lundahl et al. 2009). Whatever savings come through privatization are usually realized through reductions in labor costs (Austin and Coventry 2001). On average, private prisons pay correctional officers less than public prisons and have higher inmate-to-staff ratios (Blakely and Bumphus 2004). If public prisons have a difficult time recruiting qualified staff (e.g., Buble 2021), private prisons struggle even more. It is unclear too whether private prisons can provide the same quality of services as public prisons. Accurate comparisons between public and private institutions are difficult. Private prisons can appear higher quality than public prisons, not because they are better at delivering services, but rather because they tend to house people who require only minimal security (Perrone and Pratt 2003). In effect, private prisons can strategically select people who present the fewest challenges for staff. Studies that attempt more accurate apples-to-apples comparisons usually find more problems at private prisons than public ones. Studies focusing only on medium- or minimum-security facilities, for instance, find that private facilities have more inmate-on-inmate assaults: private prisons have 33.5 assaults per 1,000 inmates, whereas public prisons have 20.2 (Austin and Coventry 2001).

Although they might not offer much in the way of cost savings, private prisons have nonetheless positioned themselves for growth in the twenty-first century (Gottschalk 2014). Moreover, they positioned themselves in ways that could further circumvent oversight. Contractual arrangements between states and private prisons have shifted over time. In the past, private prison companies were constrained in at least one important respect: they usually only managed the institution, while the state maintained ownership of the prison. This arrangement allowed states a good deal of power in that they could replace providers if necessary. Over time, though, private companies have built more prison facilities, and states rely more on private companies both for the management of their prisons and for the brick-and-mortar facilities. Adding to the challenge is the difficulty of replacing staff. To ensure accountability—especially in a high-stakes and fraught industry like corrections—states need leverage. They must have the capacity, for instance, to replace officers quickly if the officers at a private facility are found unacceptable (Aman 2005). Recruitment and retention of correctional officers is structurally difficult: quality staff cannot be hired and adequately trained en masse in a short time. Furthermore, the ability of a state to step in deteriorates the longer and more completely they cede prisons to private entities. To allow for more routine review, some states have limited their contracts to a finite period, usually two or three years. Many states, though, do not restrict their contacts in this fashion. Furthermore, the market for private prisons has grown less competitive. Two companies, Corrections Corporation of America and the Geo Group, now control the bulk of the private prison industry, crowding out opportunities for competitors.

Yet even a more flexible contract or a more competitive environment would not ensure accountability, and the health of people in prison can easily be overlooked. Private prisons are not governed by the same administrative laws as public prisons (Aman 2005; Burkhardt 2019). They are not required, for example, to abide by the Administrative Procedure Act (APA), which governs how agencies interact with the public. The APA encompasses, among other things, the Freedom of Information Act. Courts and prisons are subject to scrutiny when they are open about what they do. Many private prisons, however, withhold information that state and federal prisons are required to reveal. To be sure, states are increasingly writing contracts that encourage or demand that private companies release such information, but there are no rules requiring them to do so, and states often write rather abbreviated contacts (Burkhardt 2019). In many states, the decision to privatize prisons has been hasty, especially when made in the face of budgetary crises. Fearing the spread of inadequate contracts, some have pushed for the development of a model manual or "code" for privatizing prisons. Such a code would, in effect, provide states with a template for ensuring better oversight (Aman 2005). Yet templates of this sort are difficult to craft, in part because of the peculiar mission of prisons, an issue that looms over this entire book. Perfectly comprehensive codes are difficult to articulate given that prisons are responsible for every aspect of a prisoner's life, including discipline, health care, food, recreation, and environmental quality (Dolovich 2005). Writing comprehensive standards would also require a consideration of all the complexities of prison life, which involves numerous procedural contingencies. This is especially the case with respect to institutional discipline. In both public and private prisons, the appropriate use of force remains a flashpoint for prison litigation (Dolovich 2009b). Yet, as a contractual matter, it is difficult to outline a priori standards for determining when the use of force is appropriate. Most states do require private prisons to meet the certification requirements set by the American Correctional Association, but these standards are relatively easy to meet and largely regulate matters of process. In general, they involve simply whether policies are in place at all rather than standards regarding actual practices or procedures.

The administrative pitfalls of private prisons are magnified in the prevailing legal environment. As discussed earlier, the courts have historically deferred to prison administrators. Even in cases such as *Estelle*, where the courts have been more forceful, they have ruled narrowly and in an only modestly prescriptive fashion. In *Estelle*, the court ruled against the plaintiff even as it established the conditions under which the treatment of people in prison might violate the Eighth Amendment. If this precedent continues to inform jurisprudence, the court's deference could accentuate the divide between public and private prisons. Dolovich (2005) provides a useful example with respect to the use of force (pp. 482–483). In the past, the Supreme Court has ruled that for an inmate to have a viable Eighth Amendment claim, they must demonstrate that the correctional officer acted with the intent to cause harm rather than to preserve order. Practically, this means officers can defend themselves by arguing that the use of force—even excessive force resulting in injury—was necessary for disciplinary purposes. However, what is necessary in matters of discipline is not well established, as a matter of either law or administration. Furthermore, some officers receive more training in appropriate disciplinary techniques than do others. For this reason, poorly trained officers could have even wider latitude in making an argument that excessive force was necessary: they could credibly claim to be unaware of less severe methods for diffusing conflict or preserving order. A similar possibility pertains to health care. The standard of deliberate indifference requires that a prison official knew of a health risk and intentionally disregarded it. The standard thus centers on the state of mind of the official, and any actions on the part of a prisoner that prevented or delayed care diminishes the likelihood of a successful claim. Relative to public prisons, private prisons appear more intent on limiting health care consumption. For-profit prison health care providers often create care-denying policies and onerous procedures, requiring, for instance, prompt notification and diligence at every stage (Hylton 2003; Weiss 2015). Barriers of this sort move the onus to inmates. Moreover, the way courts have focused on discerning the indifference of parties provides a disincentive for hiring or training the most professional medical staff, as poorly trained staff can deflect the responsibility of the institution.

Apart from some especially notable examples of recklessness on the part of for-profit companies, private and public prisons face different incentives related to health (Aman 2005). Although correctional officers and their unions have lobbied for prison expansion, public prison officials are also motivated to reduce the number of people they house, especially given the burden of overcrowding (Page 2011). Prison administrators are well aware that they are operating above capacity and they recognize the problems overcrowding can cause, most notably for staff and incarcerated individuals themselves. Furthermore, as discussed earlier, the budget for public prisons consists largely of fixed personnel and facility costs, which are more responsive to change in the number of staff than the number of prisoners. In this context, certain instruments for reducing the size of the prison population have appeal. In particular, increasing "good time" credit, "earned time" credit, and pathways to compassionate release can be attractive because they accelerate release (Demleitner 2017). Private prisons, however, are usually paid on the basis of daily occupancy, which can encourage private prisons to hold people for longer, especially if those people are less costly because they are well behaved or healthy. Until recently, this possibility has been mostly speculative, but research has demonstrated it empirically (Mukherjee 2016).

Studies suggest that, relative to comparable people housed in a public prison, people in a private prison serve an additional sixty to ninety days, corresponding to an additional 4% to 7% of their sentence. In addition, those held in private prisons are 15% more likely to receive a conduct violation, which is often used by administrators to justify longer stays. There is no evidence, however, that private prisons are truly housing more dangerous people: the recidivism rate among people released from private or public prisons is approximately the same (Powers, Kaukinen, and Jeanis 2017).

The Costs and Benefits of Providing Better Health Care in Prison

At this point, it is useful to take a step back and consider the value of prison expenditures. For all the concern over slashing budgets and rising costs, and the particular concern over rising health care costs, there is evidence that providing health care to people in prison can eventually yield significant cost savings. The explanation for these savings rests with the particular health conditions people currently and formerly in prison have, as well as how those conditions combine. Treating psychiatric and substance use disorders is especially significant in this regard. One study compared the growth of medical costs between two groups, adults who needed substance abuse treatment and adults who did not (Bechelli et al. 2014). In general, medical costs increased for both groups, but this study compared differences in the rate of growth over a period in which coverage for substance abuse treatment was expanded. Assuming new benefits increase costs, growth in expenses should be higher in the group receiving new substance abuse treatments. Remarkably, though, growth was *lower* when treatment was expanded. Prior to the expansion, expenses for adults needing substance abuse treatment increased 10.8% per year, whereas after the expansion expenses increased only 1.4% per year. Even more remarkable, expenses increased more for those *not* needing substance abuse treatment than for those needing it (3.8% versus 1.4%). The relatively slow rate of growth among those with substance abuse problems was largely driven by avoiding inpatient hospital costs. These cost savings are short term, but the cost savings of substance abuse treatment can be even greater in the long term if treatment prevents the onset of other more costly problems, including organ failure. Moreover, substance abuse treatment can yield especially large cost savings in criminal justice settings by reducing the risk of drug-related spells of incarceration. Though the average cost of substance abuse treatment is just over $6,000, the value per treated patient with respect to criminal justice is over $18,000 (including avoiding the costs incurred to crime victims). Effects of this magnitude are large but not implausible, especially in light of research showing that people using drugs and involved with the criminal justice system commit considerably more crime during periods of active use. One study found that illegal earnings rose by $500 to $700 per month during periods of active cocaine and heroin use, relative to periods of abstinence from these substances (Uggen and Thompson 2003). Where effective treatment can be provided, it is justified on economic as well as humanitarian grounds.

Although the medical conditions of people in prison are unique in some respects—with especially high levels of substance abuse, infectious disease, and comorbidity—their utilization patterns are not dissimilar from other patients suffering from similar problems. There are lessons from other populations that can be applied to people in prison. Health homes, for instance, are designed to improve care coordination through a network of providers with expertise in comorbid problems, including behavioral disorders, developmental disabilities, and other chronic conditions. When people released from prison are provided with a health home, they tend to use the emergency room less and have better outcomes (Bechelli et al. 2014). A related challenge among people released from prison is navigating the health care system. The health care system is layered and complicated, especially for those suffering from multiple problems, but health care navigation services are relatively inexpensive and cost-effective. One study found that the average expense for a health care navigation service was $174 per person on parole but resulted in annual savings of $31,000 (Muskegon Community Health Project 2007).

There are other examples of cost-effective programs for formerly incarcerated people, but their clear benefits suggest that the most significant barriers to reform reflect a failure of imagination more than any financial considerations. It is difficult to appreciate the full range of benefits derived from robust health care when people released from prison are viewed primarily through the lens of criminal justice. This reflects not only a clash between a hospital's mission of providing care and a prison's mission of meting out punishment; it is also a matter of the range of treatments deemed appropriate in a prison setting. The lens of criminal justice distorts the meaning of health.

Mental health again provides a useful example. Prisons are undeniably in the business of providing mental health care. And there is abundant evidence that prisons do, in fact, provide treatment to most of those who need it. Yet prisons often approach psychiatric disorders using the treatments that are easiest for them to administer, especially pharmaceuticals. This approach is not necessarily wrong or out of step with modern medical practice—pharmaceuticals are effective treatments that can provide substantial relief. Nonetheless, many incarcerated individuals face challenges that could be treated as well using cognitive-behavioral therapy (CBT), especially because CBT can be used to treat both psychiatric disorders and some of the behaviors implicated in offending. CBT attempts to improve mental health by focusing on faulty thought processes. In the case of depression, for instance, an individual undergoing CBT is encouraged to avoid making automatic negative associations and to appraise situations in more positive and less generalized ways (e.g., avoid inferring "I'm not good at anything"). When applied in criminal justice settings, CBT is often modified and supplemented in constructive ways. CBT in prison, for instance, often includes a focus on the thought processes that lead to anger or criminal behavior (Milkman and Wanberg 2007). There is good evidence that CBT is effective in treating psychiatric disorders, and there is growing evidence that CBT can prevent some types of criminal behavior as well. In an especially notable evaluation, school-aged boys were randomly assigned to one of two groups (Heller et al. 2015). The first group—the treatment group—participated in a weekly session wherein they were encouraged to think less instinctively or automatically and, instead, to reflect on their decisions in a slow and deliberate fashion. The second group—the control group—did not receive this training and they were treated as usual. The results were remarkable: the treatment group did, in fact, end up thinking more about their decisions. They also changed their behavior: they committed 44% fewer violent crimes and were more engaged in their schoolwork, which resulted in improved grades. Treatment programs of this sort can be further fine-tuned in criminal justice settings to produce an even stronger impact. Other studies find especially large effects of CBT programs administered among those at high risk of reoffending. Studies of this sort find especially large effects when CBT programs are focused on other skills, like anger control and interpersonal problem solving. Indeed, meta-analyses find that skills of this sort—involving both emotion management and social acumen—are more effective than programs that focus narrowly on behavior modification or understanding how one's behavior affects victims or communities (Landenberger and Lipsey 2005).

These findings are counterintuitive in the sense that they do not align with the prevailing philosophy of corrections, which generally focuses on encouraging personal responsibility and appreciating the impact of crime on victims. Victim impact interventions, for instance, are designed to encourage people to recognize the effects of their behavior on others, something they may or may not have done before. Yet such interventions are less effective in preventing recidivism than is teaching people more general cognitive skills and habits. Similarly, efforts to improve moral reasoning focus on improving the capacity to reflect on right and wrong. Yet efforts to promote moral reasoning are much less effective than simply promoting better anger management (Landenberger and Lipsey 2005, Table 6). The value of mental health treatment is apparent even in the personnel who are best at providing mental health services in prison. The most effective providers of CBT are those with a mental health background, rather than those with a criminal justice background. Findings of this sort suggest prisons should focus on general behavioral health and care rather than the moral dimensions of crime and punishment.

The relevance of considering mental health over moral failings is also apparent in studies of the effectiveness of drug courts and other forms of therapeutic jurisprudence (Brown 2010). Although evidence surrounding the effectiveness of therapeutic jurisprudence is mixed, the weak evidence partly reflects the operational difficulty of blending a thoroughgoing medical approach with the mandates of a criminal justice system. Drug courts are designed to treat an underlying illness more than punish people. There are nearly 3,000 drug court programs in the United States, and their appeal has grown given the poor record of standard criminal justice processing (National Drug Court Resource Center 2014). In the abstract, drug courts have the potential to curb crime, incarceration, and substance abuse. Many people are incarcerated directly for drug- and alcohol-related offenses, and many nondrug crimes involve drug or alcohol dependence as a contributing factor. In addition, drug courts are a useful mechanism for delivering services. They have the benefit of retaining individuals in treatment for longer than they would otherwise, much like the treatment of some infectious diseases in a prison setting. Overall, the empirical evidence regarding the effectiveness of drug courts remains mixed. Some of the evidence suggests the benefits vary by the characteristics of participants. Some meta-analyses, for instance, find lower recidivism among adult drug court participants but less impact among youth participants (Mitchell et al. 2012). One complication in assessing the impact of drug courts pertains to the type of individual most likely to enter such courts. Eligibility for a drug court is strongly influenced by the decisions of prosecutors, who are often reluctant to refer people they do not think can be treated successfully or those whose crimes they believe are too severe for a "lesser" punishment. In addition to the discretion of prosecutors, drug courts have strict eligibility criteria. Participants generally cannot have a history of violent convictions or have used a weapon in their offense, a restrictive condition. In some states, drug crimes are themselves classified as violent offenses (Minnesota Statutes §609.1095). Studies that compare people who enter drug court with similar people sentenced in more typical ways find that drug courts may reduce incarceration and substance abuse, but the effects are not uniform. Drug courts do not, for instance, reduce rearrests (Brown 2010).

If drug courts aim to improve health outcomes, a challenge they face is in delivering truly appropriate services, given their simultaneous mission in health and criminal justice. A related challenge pertains to what falls under the purview of such courts. Despite comorbidity between substance abuse and other psychiatric disorders, a remarkable number of drug courts have eligibility criteria that eliminate those with a past history of mental health treatment. Some courts even narrow the definition of a "drug" offense and exclude individuals who abuse alcohol (Bhati, Roman, and Chalfin 2008; see especially Table 3.1). The Cincinnati Drug Court, for instance, stipulates that to qualify for the court an individual must not suffer from another mental illness and that their behavior must be largely drug driven (Listwan et al. 2003). It is difficult to imagine a large number of drug-involved defendants who are entirely free of other psychiatric disorders, including disorders that are commonly treated with psychiatric medications. Studies screening drug court participants find rates of moderate anxiety or depression, for instance, as high as 35% and 42%, respectively (Hagedorn and Willenbring 2003). Strict eligibility criteria of this sort likely shape the apparent effectiveness of drug courts. Indeed, one way to interpret the mixed evidence surrounding drug courts is that they serve only a very particular subset of justice-involved people who are struggling with substance use disorders. And, among those they do serve, drug courts vary in their capacity to address the full range of psychiatric and behavioral issues people may be confronting. Successful drug courts may treat people with relatively uncomplicated disorders, whereas seemingly failing drug courts may neglect the full spectrum of issues that are apparent in their patients. An early study found that about 42% of drug courts lacked access to specialized mental health care (apart from substance abuse), and about the same percent lacked even a liaison to such services (Cooper 1997).

Evidence from mental health courts—which are ostensibly better positioned to fill these gaps—is also mixed. Those who participate in such courts tend to have lower rearrest rates than similar individuals who do not. Yet even here the apparent success of mental health courts varies according to the clinical characteristics of those who enter and the thoroughness of the court's approach (Steadman et al. 2011). Individuals suffering from a mental illness but not using illegal substances are less likely to be rearrested. In addition, those who received treatment before they participated in a mental health court have better outcomes, suggesting continuity of care is critical. Mental health courts that adopt a comprehensive and long-term approach— involving intensive case management integrated with addiction treatment— perform better than others, though such programs are rare (Loveland and Boyle 2007).

Just as prisons are constrained by their ability to provide care in a carceral setting, the effectiveness of drug and mental health courts is constrained by the fact that they are, in the end, courts. Their responsibility stems from society's reaction to *crime* rather than to robust medical considerations. As noted, some drug courts explicitly limit eligibility to individuals whose behavior stems only from drug or alcohol use, but even mental health courts— despite their seemingly broader remit—focus largely on those disorders that are plainly related to criminal behavior. The large number of people with depressive disorders, for instance, are less well served by mental health courts than the few with bipolar disorder. At the same time, some otherwise effective treatments that are administered in clinical settings are off-limits in drug courts. Many drug courts do not use treatments such as methadone or buprenorphine, for instance, because they are themselves narcotics and controlled substances (Matusow et al. 2013; see Tables 3, 4, and 6). Surveys of drug court administrators are informative on this point. Virtually all drug courts serve some defendants with opioid dependence, but only 56% use any medication-assisted treatment for dependence. About 50% of courts do not permit the use of agonists under any circumstances, including pregnancy, or even the continuation of therapy an individual was already receiving. Other forms of treatment are strongly preferred. About 92% of courts, for instance, use some form of counseling. Studies also reveal a good deal of misinformation among drug court administrators regarding the effectiveness of addiction medications. Contrary to current best practice, many administrators believe that nonpharmacological treatments are more effective than pharmacological ones. Many administrators also report that treatment medications merely substitute one addiction for another, though empirical studies usually provide a different interpretation, indicating that prolonged medication-assisted treatment decreases the likelihood of relapse (Magura and Rosenblum 2001). A striking number of administrators are also simply unfamiliar with the range of treatments available to treat addiction and so default to simple abstinence or moralizing "strong-arm rehab" (Gowan and Whetstone 2012). The reach of the crime and justice mentality is broad.

Legal Challenges to Improving Prison Health Care

Some of the challenges to improving prison health care pertain to the cross-purposes of punishment and treatment and the infusion of the clinical with the moral, but others are legal in nature. Even here, though, the deeper issue is the ambiguous intersection of health care and corrections. As discussed earlier, the Eighth Amendment has been the driving force behind much of the improvement in prison care. Without the foundation of *Estelle*, many of the positive effects of incarceration discussed earlier in this book, such as the role of prisons in reducing the spread of tuberculosis, would not be possible. Yet there are clear limits to the provision of care based on avoiding cruel and unusual punishment. Among the most important limitations of *Estelle* is that it focused on individuals rather than institutions. The law does not so much provide an affirmative obligation to care or uphold a certain standard of treatment as provide a mandate to hold some individuals accountable for certain outcomes. At present there are few legal tools for safeguarding practices. In contrast to many other nations, the United States lacks an independent national agency empowered to monitor the conditions of prisons, including their health care (Human Rights Watch 2009).

Short of a different philosophy or better oversight, there are ways the law might be supplemented to impose a more affirmative obligation. Sharon Dolovich (2009a), for instance, proposes several enhancements to the concept of cruel and unusual punishment. The first pertains to negligence. Based on the standard of negligence currently in place, the obligations of prisons regarding health care are mostly episodic and reactive—prisons are obligated to treat only when they notice threats to an inmate's physical or mental health. But correctional officers are not required to have much foresight in such matters or even to be particularly vigilant (Dolovich 2009a, p. 945). They cannot be held liable, for instance, for failing to treat medical conditions about which they were unaware, as discussed earlier. *Estelle* mandates the treatment of existing conditions, to be sure, but as a framework for delivering health care, it departs from standard medical practice— it may result in secondary or tertiary care but rarely preventive care. Prisons must not be cruel, according to *Estelle*, but it is far easier to attribute cruelty to individuals rather than to entire institutions. In this light, Dolovich recommends an enhanced liability standard, based on the idea that prisons are cruel in root and branch. She argues that there is abundant evidence that the prison environment itself presents a risk to health and could therefore be regarded as cruel. An enhanced liability standard cast in light of the risks stemming from the prison environment—premised on what prison officials *should* have known if they accepted that the prison environment is hazardous—would demand more diligence, both in officials' day-to-day interactions with people and in their responsibility for the larger conditions of the facility. Courts have not been completely opposed to this sort of reasoning. Indeed, Dolovich bases her proposal on Justice John Paul Stevens's original dissent in *Estelle*. In his dissent, Stevens highlighted the importance of system-wide deficiencies in understanding Gamble's mistreatment, juxtaposing those deficiencies against the court's framing of the case as mere medical malpractice. Stevens highlighted, for instance, how medical staff at the prison were overworked in an overcrowded prison with substandard medical facilities (concerns that have only grown more pronounced since the decision). In the same light, Dolovich advocates for a negligence standard that spreads outward from the premise that prisons are essentially health-degrading environments. Such an enhanced standard could apply to correctional officers who fail to prevent violence or who fail to act when people show signs of suicidality.

A related legal problem for reform stems from premising health care on the concept of a *right*, as attractive as that might be. This is perhaps ironic: although the provision of health care in prisons is properly regarded as a right in the sense that it is mandated by law, this framing of correctional care contrasts uncomfortably with how health care is regarded in the United States generally. In law, policy, and public opinion, the United States has wavered between regarding health care as an entitlement or a privilege, but it has never seriously regarded care as a right to be guaranteed by the state. Even the ACA—the most significant reform package since Medicare and Medicaid—falls short of explicitly casting health care as a right. Befitting its name, the ACA mainly aims to keep health care *affordable* and, in doing so, maintains a market-based approach and casts insurance as a regulated commodity (Levitsky 2013). The ACA is not unique in stopping short of a guarantee. The Emergency Medical Treatment and Active Labor Act prohibited hospitals from refusing to treat patients based on their ability to pay, but it went no further than that. The act only required that patients be stabilized; it did not grant a right to ongoing care, and hospitals certainly still seek reimbursement even from those they know cannot pay.

Public beliefs about health care sit at this nexus of rights and privileges, which almost certainly dilutes the political will to improve prison care. Historically, public support for entitlement programs has waxed and waned. It has also been sharply divided along political party and demographic lines (Schlesinger and Lee 1993). To be sure, health care is seen as somewhat different from other entitlements. Support for health care reform has grown, even as support for other programs has declined. According to the Kaiser Health Tracking Poll, as of February 2021, 54% of American adults viewed the ACA favorably, relative to 39% who had unfavorable views (Kaiser Family Foundation 2021). The areas where Americans have most accepted the language of rights are those where the issue can be cast in terms of shared risk. Medicare, for example, is successful—albeit not without some initial resistance—because most Americans recognize that they will eventually need health insurance, and that securing insurance in later life is very difficult so long as it is not guaranteed. Similarly, the success of Social Security stems from the idea that everyone will benefit from greater financial security in their retirement years. The challenge with respect to prison health care is convincing other people of the risks, and perhaps the moral shortcomings, of not providing care to incarcerated Americans.

As we have shown, nonprisoners and communities also benefit when prisoners receive care, so there are public health as well as humanitarian reasons for the public to support such care. For example, incarceration is linked to the spread of sexually transmitted disease, and health care in prisons can prevent some infections. Still, spillovers of this sort are unlikely to resonate with people who view people in prison as "others" held apart from the public and feel no personal risk of, say, contracting syphilis or tuberculosis. Recall also the persistent "principle of less eligibility" concerns regarding providing services inside prisons that might exceed those available to the least advantaged people outside prisons. Without a firm health care guarantee to people outside prison, it is difficult to allay concerns about providing prison health care beyond that required by law. The fates of incarcerated and nonincarcerated people are thus intertwined with regard to the provision of care and health outcomes.

Indirect Policies for Improving Health and Health Care among Former Inmates

There are many challenges to directly improving prison health care, but there are policies that will at least indirectly improve the situation of people currently or formerly in prison (Marks and Turner 2014). Prior to the passage of the ACA, insurance from Medicaid was rare among childless men who were healthy enough to work. In this way, Medicaid eligibility criteria effectively restricted benefits among men involved with the criminal justice system. The ACA, however, has allowed the extension of benefits to low-income adults regardless of whether they have children or are disabled. The impact of this expansion for people released from prison is considerable. One study, for instance, estimated that about one in six people expected to enroll under Medicaid expansion will have spent some time in a jail in the last year (Regenstein and Rosenbaum 2014). The rate of uninsurance declined significantly from 2009 to 2017 among recently incarcerated men (Gutierrez and Pettit 2020). In addition, the ACA expanded eligibility to include those with incomes up to 138% of the federal poverty level. About 60% of jail inmates are at or below this income level. The ACA has additional provisions, including premium subsidies, that help those above the limit (Somers et al. 2014).

The ACA also benefits those involved with the criminal justice system by improving the treatment of psychiatric disorders. The establishment of equal benefits for mental and physical health, referred to as parity, is among the most important reforms associated with the ACA. Because of parity, many existing insurance policies will provide improved coverage for mental health and substance use disorders. Parity was largely implemented in 2014, ahead of some of the ACA's other provisions, though the scope of parity was expanded with an additional mandate that all insurance policies provide ten essential benefits, including but not limited to treatment for mental health and substance abuse disorders (Mechanic and Olfson 2016). Though many insurance policies already included benefits for the items on this list, the expansion of mental health benefits is estimated to have provided new and additional coverage for over sixty million people (Beronio et al. 2013). In addition, the ACA encourages more collaborative efforts among treatment providers, something useful for serving those who might fall through the cracks. The ultimate impact of these provisions is unclear, but they are likely to be especially important for mental health treatment, which often suffers from a lack of coordination. The provisions could, for instance, ensure that conditions such as depression and anxiety—which loom large in primary care settings—are not neglected in favor of seemingly more pressing acute problems.

Other elements of the ACA are also likely to be of indirect benefit to justice-involved people. Medicaid cannot be used to pay for services provided in prison, but states have long been permitted to suspend rather than terminate Medicaid benefits for those entering prison. Suspension is far less onerous than termination, but some states have adopted the more severe option of termination for fear that Medicaid might be used improperly, as discussed earlier. The ACA attempts to ease the transition between prison and Medicaid by, for instance, increasing federal funding for the development of new systems to determine Medicaid eligibility (Somers et al. 2014). In addition, the ACA allows people who have been incarcerated prior to conviction to maintain (or even enroll in) health insurance plans available on the marketplace. This provision is especially consequential for county jails, wherein about six in ten inmates are awaiting adjudication and have not been convicted (Minton 2013).

Although many current and formerly incarcerated individuals are eligible for Medicaid under the ACA, this does not necessarily guarantee they will receive better care. There are numerous remaining challenges to providing services to former inmates (Boutwell and Freedman 2014). For one, they often present different needs than the women and children who make up the bulk of Medicaid recipients. In light of their existing caseload, Medicaid plans usually reflect some familiarity with obstetrics and pediatrics, and policies are crafted accordingly. By contrast, Medicaid plans usually have much less experience with young men, who have different needs in the area of sexual and reproductive health and exposure to violence (Pastuszak et al. 2016). In addition, Medicaid recipients are often highly engaged with their providers, creating an environment of patient-driven care coordination. People released from prison are typically less engaged and require more intervention to participate fully. Other problems pertain to the administration of care. Community health care providers might have a more difficult time accessing their health care records of released individuals, especially if those records are housed in the prison system rather than the local hospital. The rise of health information technology provides an opportunity to bridge this divide, though sharing information still requires cooperation among prisons, correction officials, and hospitals (Butler and Murphy 2014).

Tensions between Federal, State, and Local Reform

The importance of coordination points to another barrier to reform. Improving prison health care requires straddling disparate jurisdictions, each with its own needs, procedures, and political pressures. Prisons and jails are distinct in this regard, and the public health potential of jails is probably higher than that of prisons, given that jails process more people (Freudenberg 2001). Jails admit over 11 million people per year, whereas state and federal prisons admit under 700,000 (Carson 2015; Minton and Zeng 2015). Weekly turnover in jails is around 60% and is even higher in smaller jurisdictions, which helps explain why jails were able to release people so much faster than prisons during the COVID-19 pandemic (Kang-Brown, Montagnet, and Heiss 2021). Most jail admissions do not result in a prison stay, and most people in jail are returned directly to the community (Sabol, West, and Cooper 2009). Jails could provide a mechanism for quickly reaching some underserved populations, but given the short time frame most individuals are in jail, jails are less attuned to the health of people than are prisons, precisely because their responsibilities are more truncated. Jails tend to focus on acute symptoms, if they focus on health at all. Medications for already diagnosed conditions are usually continued in jails, but new conditions are rarely detected, especially if they require expensive diagnostic tests. In general, the adequacy of institutional care can be arrayed on a gradient, from federal prisons, to state prisons, to jails, an order that, not coincidentally, corresponds to the average length of stay.

If state correctional budgets are strained, county correctional budgets are strained even more. In response to budget costs, many county jails have begun to charge inmates for elements of their stay, especially medical care. One survey found that 90% of the jails charged fees of some kind, and the most common fees were for services related to health care (Harner, Wyant, and Da Silva 2016; Krauth and Stayton 2005). Of the jails charging any fees, most (59%) charged for prescriptions and physician visits. In addition, about a quarter of jails charged for substance use testing, with fees ranging from $4 to $6. Other jails employ cost sharing through copays. Jail fees of this sort have been challenged under the Eighth Amendment, which prohibits "excessive fines" (in addition to cruel and unusual punishment). To date, these challenges have been largely unsuccessful, mostly because they are novel. In contrast to the extensive case law regarding what constitutes cruel and unusual punishment, there is very little case law regarding what constitutes an excessive fine. As with cruel and unusual punishment, much hinges on the various elements in the text of the amendment. In the case of excessive fines, courts must decide what is *excessive* and even what a *fine* is. Courts have generally ruled that fines must be proportionate to the offense, but when fines are assessed to offset the cost of a service, as in the case of health care, courts have been uncertain about whether they should be regarded as "fines" so much as "fees," a critical distinction that can prevent consideration of a case on Eighth Amendment grounds (Colgan 2021; Eisen 2015).

The strategies jails use to offset the costs of care vary greatly from locale to locale. The adequacy of these efforts depends a great deal on the potential for collaboration in that location. Some county jail systems, for instance, allay health care costs by coordinating with other entities, much like some state prison systems (Henrichson, Rinaldi, and Delaney 2015). In some larger counties, medical costs in jail are paid through health departments and other municipal agencies outside of corrections. In still others, jails have coordinated with other institutions or agencies to deliver care. In the Bernalillo County Metropolitan Detention Center, for instance, the University of New Mexico provides hospital care. In New York City jails, the New York City Department of Health and Mental Hygiene provides services. Although many of these collaborations have been successful, they reflect the patchy and idiosyncratic nature of jail administration. In places where high-quality care is made available to people in jail, the situation was one that either was forced by a court ruling or was made by jail administrators who recognized that health care was best provided by an agency with expertise. In addition, the most successful efforts often involve coordination among multiple sectors, including health insurers, Medicaid, jail administrators, and health care providers (Patel et al. 2014). The value of collaboration only reinforces how the cultural, legal, and political silos surrounding the criminal justice system prevent a thorough focus on health.

As the coronavirus pandemic has illustrated, both the financial pressure on jails and the extent of their health care responsibilities are likely to increase. Although the ACA has expanded access to care for justice-involved people, it has also increased pressure on local governments to control costs. A lesser-known provision of the ACA decreases federal funds to offset the costs of uncompensated care, referred to as disproportionate-share hospital allotments (Somers et al. 2014). These allotments were designed to assist hospitals that treat low-income patients. The payments were considerable, amounting to over $11 billion a year (Neuhausen et al. 2014). The ACA reduces these payments, based on the assumption that more Americans will have insurance under the ACA and the burden of uncompensated care will, therefore, decrease. The ACA has, in fact, resulted in more Americans being insured, but hospital revenue might still decline, particularly revenue for safety-net hospitals. One study of California public hospitals, for instance, estimated a shortfall of over $1 billion resulting from a drop in disproportionate-share payments (Neuhausen et al. 2014). In response to these shortfalls, the state of California has created an incentive pool, providing funds for hospitals that create innovative programs to reduce costs.

The fact that only some states are responding to the opportunities of the ACA points to another issue. When it comes to improving the health of incarcerated and formerly incarcerated people, there is a sharp distinction between the decisions states make with respect to incarceration and the decisions they make with respect to health care. Indeed, many high-incarceration states have made important strides in addressing the health care needs of inmates. Mississippi, for instance, incarcerates many people, but it has substantially improved mental health care in its prisons (Kupers et al. 2009). To be sure, Mississippi did so in response to a court order. Following a suit brought by the American Civil Liberties Union, the Mississippi Department of Corrections was forced to improve the conditions of its high-security facility. The state was required to, among other things, remove individuals with serious mental illness from the facility, provide them with treatment, and rethink their institutional classification system and standards for administrative segregation. Although spurred by a court order, the state eventually responded in a serious way. Mississippi implemented a more objective system of inmate classification, which effectively set a higher bar for the use of solitary confinement. It also established separate mental health treatment units for people with serious mental health problems. The unit was designed to deliver intensive and professional services but also encouraged greater cooperation through a team-based approach to treatment. The program reduced misconduct on the part of inmates and the use of force on the part of correctional officers.

Systems Integration as Opportunity and Barrier

The jurisdictional complications of prison health care reform operate at other levels as well. Several scholars have advocated for better system integration (Freudenberg and Heller 2016). Successful programs of this sort involve collaboration across sectors, including health care systems, public health departments, and correctional systems. But there are few mechanisms for promoting broad integration of this sort, apart from efforts explicitly designed to better serve those in prison. The expansion of Medicaid, for instance, will help many people who were incarcerated, but to serve the needs of this population well there should be supplementary efforts to help people released from prison secure benefits and find appropriate providers. In addition, effective programs solicit the input of those affected by the prison system prior to implementation (Freudenberg and Heller 2016). The marginalization and silencing of people released from prison renders even this task difficult.

Recognizing that many people released from prison return to a relatively small number of communities, some agencies have adopted targeted place-based strategies, wherein local corrections and law enforcement professionals, in tandem with community-based organizations, share information and resources to prevent recidivism and improve integration across regional agencies (Clement, Schwarzfeld, and Thompson 2011). Even here, though, coordination is difficult and trust is in short supply. Different groups have different motivations and incentives for targeting particular neighborhoods, which can lead to conflicting philosophies and policy initiatives. Law enforcement might regard a neighborhood as a hot spot for crime, whereas a public health department might regard the same place as a hot spot for infection. In areas where a place-based strategy has worked, collaborations have been brokered or negotiated by a different overarching organization. One such example is the Community Safety Initiative, a large community development organization providing assistance to Kansas City neighborhoods (Clement, Schwarzfeld, and Thompson 2011).

A related problem pertains to appreciating cost savings when expenditures and savings are realized across systems in discontinuous ways. Expenditures in one system are often only realized in another system or they are realized only in the long term. Spending more on public health might eventually save costs on corrections, but savings will not happen overnight. Efforts to realize cost savings require a bird's-eye view and considerable foresight. When states and municipalities are focused on discrete parts of the budget, they generally seek immediate savings rather than future savings based on reinvestment. This dilemma is made even sharper by policymakers' lack of access to detailed cost-savings calculations related to corrections. Analyses of this sort are particularly difficult given the lack of data on individuals who are no longer under correctional supervision, combined with staffing cuts in the research divisions of many state corrections departments (Clement, Schwarzfeld, and Thompson 2011). Prisons continue to spend less on staff (Mai and Subramanian 2017).

Perhaps the greatest jurisdictional barrier is simply the fact that the responsibilities of the prison system formally end when a person is released. Efforts focused on a single sector tend to fail precisely at the point where one sector's responsibilities end and another's begins, once an inmate is released, for instance, or when a patient enters prison. To be sure, people are often released from prison conditionally on parole, and so remain under close supervision. Furthermore, some prisons are forward thinking in the sense that they provide robust discharge planning related to health care. Yet efforts to rethink how prisons provide health care and consider the long-term health of those in their care will usually stop short of the period after release.

As with much else at the intersection of incarceration and health, these issues ultimately reflect the collision of two systems, governed by very different responsibilities and guiding philosophies. Mass incarceration enhanced these tensions and has laid bare the social, legal, and cultural conditions that link incarceration and health. The next chapter turns to the future of this nexus. There are substantial signs of decarceration across the US states, but this alone will almost certainly not break the connection between incarceration and health, nor the need for serious reform.

8
The Collision of Prisons and Health

Many of the basic parameters of mass incarceration are well understood. It is understood, for instance, that the United States is a world leader in incarceration. Many of the historical and political processes that got us to this point are also well known. In addition, we know a great deal about the relationship between incarceration and crime prevention. Yet some aspects of the relationship between incarceration and population health remains obscured, though they are essential for understanding what mass incarceration has wrought. For those focused on reducing mass incarceration, the effects of incarceration on health might seem like an afterthought, as only one of many reasons to reduce the size of our prison system or to abolish the system altogether. Others might argue that the relatively poor mental and physical health of the incarcerated is simply one of many disadvantages they face. People in prison are much more likely to be born into poverty, to suffer abuse, to drop out of high school, and to use drugs and alcohol. The fact that incarceration adds to these problems by undermining health and health care might seem incidental.

But the sinews that connect incarceration and health are deep, powerful, and systematic. They are sustained by policies that put people into prison, by a legal environment that fails to ensure adequate care, by procedures that diminish the safety of the prison environment, and by an environment that undermines the capacity of people to fully reintegrate when they are released. Throughout this book, we have shown the deep and multifaceted connections between incarceration and health. Yet for all the evidence tying the two institutions together, policymakers and the public fail to grapple with a central fact: that prisons are squarely in the business of providing health care. Appreciating this fact is, to be sure, not easy: to do so would require acknowledging several other uncomfortable facts, about the scale of mass incarceration, about its contribution to inequality, about the paucity of health care available to many nonincarcerated citizens, and about the long neglect of basic human rights in America.

Furthermore, there are barriers to reform. One is simply that health and health care delivery among the currently and formerly incarcerated are clouded by other considerations. The symptoms of many psychiatric disorders, for instance, involve impulsive and threatening behavior. These symptoms can be framed in different ways, and a prison setting leaves ample room for disagreement about their nature and significance, leading to conflict and neglect. Medical staff focused on delivering services, for instance, might interpret these behaviors through the lens of disease and treat the symptoms according to a medical model and an ethic of care. Correctional officers concerned with maintaining order might interpret these behaviors as a threat, requiring disciplinary action, restraint, and further punishment. For one group, the behavior stems from a disorder, whereas for the other it stems from criminality. While both might see the behavior as a problem, each has its own approach to solving it.

Similarly, there is a tendency to regard chronic disease among incarcerated people through the lens of criminal justice. This is limiting. Prisons tend to focus on diseases for which a direct line can be drawn from the prison environment to the disease. These include infections and, to some extent, psychiatric disorders, although in both cases they focus on a limited subset of infections and disorders. Sick inmates are generally treated and quarantined, albeit unevenly across prisons, as the varying responses to COVID-19 make clear. The best prisons have special facilities for those with mental illness. Yet people who are or have been incarcerated suffer from a wide range of chronic conditions at higher rates. Indeed, virtually any disease that can be related to stress is related to incarceration.

A related complication pertains to the social invisibility of people involved with the criminal justice system, especially relative to the prominence of their health problems. Prisons and the people within them are often hidden from view. This is true in a literal sense in that prisons are often located in remote and inaccessible areas. But it is also true in the sense that those in the correctional system are not enumerated in conventional measures of social well-being (Pettit 2012). People who are incarcerated are not included in official unemployment statistics. If they were, reported unemployment would be higher than it is. They are also lost in more informal ways. By systematically ignoring those currently and formerly in prison, we risk overlooking their particular needs. People who are incarcerated are drawn from a relatively small number of communities, but upon release they often move to a different community, where they are in the company of strangers and easy to disregard. In addition, relatively little consideration is given to the quality or continuity of health care among those involved with the criminal justice system, especially in the course of movement between prison and community. When it comes to addressing the needs of formerly incarcerated people, medicine mostly derives guidance from similarly situated patients, including patients with comorbid conditions and psychiatric disorders. Efforts to think of justice-involved people as a special population have grown in recent years, as have the professional support systems of prison medical staff, but a great deal more could be done. At a basic level, medical records rarely travel with individuals upon release. For this reason, care is segregated and cumbersome: physicians on the outside will have a difficult time apprehending the problems of those with a history of incarceration relative to other patients with more complete records.

In the end, many of these issues are practical and procedural. More comprehensive testing and treatment could improve the health of those currently incarcerated. Better protocols for dealing with mental illness could stem abuse at the hands of other confined individuals and correctional staff. But larger issues still loom. Fully addressing the health care needs of the correctional population involves thinking about much bigger questions: What is the role of prisons in contemporary American society? What purpose do they serve? And who do they serve? Answers to these questions are rarely settled (Tonry 2001). Some see prisons primarily in terms of preventing crime and detaining offenders. Others see prisons in terms of administering punishment and extracting retribution. Still others see prisons as a vehicle for the systematic oppression and exclusion of racialized and marginalized communities, both in prison and by stripping people of their rights when they are released. Depending on one's philosophy, the health care mission of prisons can appear essential, incidental, or irrelevant. For those who see prisons in terms of preventing crime, it might appear natural to provide better mental health services, recognizing the role of mental illness in further offending. For those who see prisons in terms of punishment, the adverse effects of incarceration on health might appear irrelevant or perhaps something to foster, as injury can be construed as a penalty. For those who see prisons through an abolitionist lens, even humanitarian reforms are problematic because they legitimate further incarceration and prison expansion. Historically no one perspective on the proper role of prisons has remained dominant for an extended period. Because it is difficult to disentangle the delivery of health care from all the other functions of a prison, what is regarded as the proper function of prison health care is likely to shift too.

When it comes to health and incarceration, though, there as many hidden complementarities as sharp contradictions. A serious approach to improving the health of correctional populations would focus on all the psychiatric disorders incarcerated people are more likely to experience. Such a broad focus can, in fact, also improve the treatment of disorders that lie closer to the mission of criminal justice. Treating depression and anxiety, for instance, can increase the effectiveness of interventions designed to address substance abuse. They can also ease reintegration, preventing recidivism. At the same time, even if one primarily regards prison in terms of punishment, the health effects of incarceration and formal sentencing are not synchronous. The time individuals serve in prison is often more limited than the chronicity of depression, for instance. Once depression emerges it tends to cycle— with flare-ups and periods of remission—over long periods. In this sense, the punishment of prison endures well beyond the time served. Moreover, simply treating depression does not necessarily make other aspects of life in prison any less punitive. Time in prison is punishment for many reasons, including that it involves forced separation from others and a serious disruption in liberty. It is punishment because it involves long periods of isolation and boredom. Treating major depression among those in prison does not eliminate any of these elements and does not diminish the essence of incarceration as punishment.

In Norway and elsewhere, a "principle of normality" offers an alternative vision of punishment that is more fully consonant with prison health care (Uggen, Stewart, and Horowitz 2018). In its website and public-facing documents (http://www.kriminalomsorgen.no/informationin-english.265199. no.html), the Norwegian Correctional Service specifies that "punishment is the restriction of liberty; no other rights have been removed"; that "no one shall serve their sentences under stricter circumstances than necessary for security in the community"; and that "during the serving of a sentence, life inside will resemble life outside as much as possible." Medical and psychiatric services in this system are provided using an "import model," in which local and municipal service providers (rather than prison staff) care for incarcerated patients. Other countries have realized the complementarities available between health and criminal justice.

There are also complementarities that are perhaps closer to the concerns of US prison administrators. One of the most widely cited reasons for using solitary confinement is to increase safety. Those suffering from psychiatric disorders disproportionately serve time in administrative segregation. But evidence regarding the effectiveness of administrative segregation on institutional safety is weak. The opening of supermax prisons, for instance, does little to reduce aggregate levels of assault in a prison system (Briggs, Sundt, and Castellano 2003), nor does a decline in the use of solitary confinement correspond to a decline in assaults (Shames, Wilcox, and Subramanian 2015).

Indeed, it is no stretch to argue that providing better health care to those currently and formerly incarcerated can lead to a more efficient administration of justice. When a judge renders a sentence, the decision is based on several things. It is tied to the nature of the offense and characteristics of the defendant, such as their criminal history. A sentence is ostensibly proportional to the crime, and there is an expectation on the part of the judge that the bulk of the sentence will be served (or all of it, in jurisdictions bound by truth-in-sentencing laws). A sentence must also conform to the standards set in the Constitution. In short, a sentence must be accountable, reasoned, and judicious. In this formulation, health muddies the waters considerably, and as more than simply an extenuating circumstance. Poor health can introduce considerations that even staunch law-and-order advocates might find troubling. The justification for compassionate release, for instance, is often framed in terms of the dollars potentially saved by releasing sick individuals who require expensive care. In addition, several states allow advanced age as a mitigating circumstance in sentencing (Mueller-Johnson and Dhami 2009). This consideration appears to be based not on the idea that individuals over the age of thirty are well on their way to aging out of active offending—which, in any case, is true—but rather on the idea that many people in prison over the age of fifty are infirmed. The number of such middle-aged and older prisoners has risen dramatically in recent years. As noted in Chapter 4, more than one in seven people in US prisons are now serving life sentences, and 30% of these "lifers" are fifty-five or older (Nellis 2021).

This mindset is also apparent in the public at large, though sometimes in subtle ways. In one experiment, for instance, research participants were asked to serve as mock judges evaluating a series of fictional vignettes. The vignettes depicted a person who had committed a crime and randomly varied the defendant's health. Regardless of the nature of the crime—whether it was violent or sexual in nature—vignettes depicting a defendant in poor health resulted in shorter sentences (Mueller-Johnson and Dhami 2009). A judge concerned with eliminating such extralegal considerations—with sentencing entirely on the basis of guilt and the nature of the crime—might benefit from being assured that any health problem in a defendant could be addressed in a way that would allow the sentence to be served as intended. In the absence of such reassurance, concerns about the cost of care increase the salience of health in charging and sentencing decisions. Knowing that a county jail might have a difficult time providing dialysis, for instance, a judge might be reluctant to sentence a person with renal failure to jail, even for a short amount of time.

Beyond these sentencing and charging decisions, health is related to the concision of punishment, a particular concern among prison administrators. Prison administrators might feel more confident if they could segregate unruly individuals, for instance, without fear that segregation would make a psychiatric disorder worse, either by knowing that someone was not psychologically vulnerable in the first place or, even better, knowing that the conditions of administrative segregation were not conducive to even worse health. Health is also related to the total amount of a sentence that a person serves. Those with serious mental illness, for instance, might be more likely to serve the entirety of their sentence compared to those without mental illness, effectively creating a de facto two-tiered sentencing structure (Human Rights Watch 2003). Ordinarily incarcerated people can accumulate credit for good behavior, which can be put toward early release. But any accumulated credit is diminished by disciplinary infractions, which are much more common among those with psychiatric disorders. Similarly, parole determinations are often based on the likelihood of future offending, and the presence of a serious mental illness can complicate a parole board's evaluation. It would not be entirely incorrect for a parole board to infer that an individual with a certain active mental illness is more likely to commit a technical violation or even a new crime if released, but treatment greatly reduces that risk or even eliminates it insofar as the risk is related to the disorder. Treating mental illness in prison, and ensuring treatment continues after release, would allow for a better and more just decision. It would allow the parole board to consider factors that are traditionally more pertinent to their deliberations, such as character, attitude, history, and plans for release.

Confronting the relationship between incarceration and health also involves seriously considering what prisons do well, not just what they do poorly. Although this book has focused on the latter, it has also presented evidence that prison can be beneficial to some dimensions of health. Properly interpreting these benefits is, however, critical. The fact that some states see reductions in the spread of infectious disease that correspond to increases in incarceration speaks to many issues, not least the ongoing inability of the US health care system to reach medically underserved populations. The fact that prisons may provide an avenue for delivering care that might be unavailable to some patients on the outside speaks to the value and importance of improving access to care for everyone. Similarly, the fact that deaths from acquired immunodeficiency syndrome (AIDS) have declined precipitously in prisons reveals not only the effectiveness of prison health care but also gaps in the health care safety net outside of prison. Relying on the prison system to address these gaps is not a sustainable long-term solution. Absent other changes to the health care system, efforts to reduce correctional populations might even have the perverse effect of increasing the spread of diseases such as tuberculosis.

Confronting the relationship between incarceration and health also involves an appreciation of the scale of the prison system. This book has cast its net broadly, with respect to its consideration of both health and the prison system. It has been about the consequences of incarceration for the health of individuals, families, communities, and health care systems. In the first instance, improving health care in prison would improve the health of the millions of Americans currently behind bars. It would also improve the health of families and communities, at no real cost to other aspects of public safety. Children suffer when a parent or partner is incarcerated. Partners struggle to maintain households when a breadwinner is gone. Health care systems also struggle to serve patients who need care but are unable to pay. Many of these ramifications fall outside the immediate responsibilities of prison administrators—and, indeed, outside the recognized responsibilities of the criminal justice system—but they are surely part of the cost of incarcerating millions of people.

One important sign of change is the gradual trend in decarceration (Maruschak and Minton 2020). The total correctional population—those in prison, in jail, or on probation or parole—peaked in 2007 and has been declining since. By the end of 2018, the United States had reached a twenty-six-year low in the supervision rate with about one in forty adults under some form of correctional supervision. The population in prison or jail declined from 2,310,300 in 2008 to 2,123,100 in 2018. These changes are significant and meaningful, especially relative to the increases realized in the decades prior. In short, the United States appears to be turning a corner. These trends are especially important given real limits to remediation in the relationship between incarceration and health. Some of the more detrimental effects of incarceration on health can probably never be eliminated, short of eliminating prisons. Even the most humane and best-run prisons in the world do things that are detrimental to health. All prisons forcefully separate individuals from loved ones and communities. Institutions force individuals to serve time under conditions they would never choose of their own volition. These facts should remind us that a prison sentence is *always* a form of punishment, one that can certainly be enhanced, as in the case of solitary confinement, but never eliminated.

Reform within prisons is likely to be more consequential. Despite a decrease in the correlational population in recent years, the size of the prison population remains large. Furthermore, the reach of the correctional system remains expansive. During the same 2008 to 2018 period, the number on parole increased. Furthermore, the largest contributor to the overall decline in the population under correctional supervision during the period was not a decline in the prison or jail population so much as a large decline in the number on probation. Addressing incarceration and health cannot be limited to thinking only about the size of the prison system.

Whatever else, the connection between incarceration and health cannot be ignored. Prisons simply affect too many people, particularly in the United States. A variety of institutions and constituencies would benefit from improving the health of those who are or were institutionalized. There is a strong case for national action, but there is also a case for working from the ground up. Many innovative programs and partnerships in local jails and communities are available for adoption in other settings. Furthermore, the case for action has no necessary political valence. One could argue that punishment itself is best levied on an even playing field of health. Any effort to improve the health of the incarcerated also must recognize that the consequences of incarceration radiate outward and over time. Although many states are now rolling back their prison populations, the processes that link incarceration to health have a long memory and a deep structure. Real change will require a serious, simultaneous, and sustained commitment to redressing the inequalities that characterize both prisons and health care, elevating the relevance of health across all facets of criminal justice.

References

1974a. "Newman v. Alabama." P. 1321, vol. 503: U.S. Court of Appeals, Fifth Circuit.

1974b. "Procunier v. Martinez." P. 396, vol. 416: U.S. Supreme Court.

1976a. "Estelle v. Gamble." P. 97, vol. 429: U.S. Supreme Court.

1976b. "Gregg v. Georgia." P. 153, vol. 428: U.S. Supreme Court.

1991. "Wilson v. Seiter." P. 294, vol. 501: U.S. Supreme Court.

1996. "Niece v. Fitzner." P. 1497, vol. 941: U.S. District Court, E.D. Michigan, Southern Division.

1998. "Pennsylvania Department of Corrections v. Yeskey." P. 206, vol. 524: U.S. Supreme Court.

2006. "Woodford v. Ngo." P. 81, vol. 548: U.S. Supreme Court.

2010. "Brown v. Plata." P. 493, vol. 563: U.S. Supreme Court.

Adimora, Adaora A., Victor J. Schoenbach, Francis E. A. Martinson, Kathryn H. Donaldson, Tonya R. Stancil, and Robert E. Fullilove. 2003. "Concurrent Partnerships among Rural African Americans with Recently Reported Heterosexually Transmitted HIV Infection." *JAIDS Journal of Acquired Immune Deficiency Syndromes* 34(4):423–429.

Adler, Nancy E., Elissa S. Epel, Grace Castellazzo, and Jeannette R. Ickovics. 2000. "Relationship of Subjective and Objective Social Status with Psychological and Physiological Functioning: Preliminary Data in Healthy, White Women." *Health Psychology* 19(6):586–592.

Alexander, Elizabeth. 2008. "Prison Health Care, Political Choice, and the Accidental Death Penalty." *Journal of Constitutional Law* 11:1–22.

Aman, Alfred C. 2005. "Privatization, Prisons, Democracy, and Human Rights: The Need to Extend the Province of Administrative Law." *Indiana Journal of Global Legal Studies* 12(2):511–550.

Amato, Paul R., and Bruce Keith. 1991. "Parental Divorce and the Well-Being of Children: A Meta-Analysis." *Psychological Bulletin* 110(1):26–46.

Apel, Robert, Arjan A. J. Blokland, Paul Nieuwbeerta, and Marieke van Schellen. 2010. "The Impact of Imprisonment on Marriage and Divorce: A Risk Set Matching Approach." *Journal of Quantitative Criminology* 26(2):269–300.

Appelbaum, Kenneth L., Judith A. Savageau, Robert L. Trestman, Jeffrey L. Metzner, and Jacques Baillargeon. 2011. "A National Survey of Self-Injurious Behavior in American Prisons." *Psychiatric Services* 62(3):285–290.

Arrigo, Bruce A., and Jennifer Leslie Bullock. 2008. "The Psychological Effects of Solitary Confinement on Prisoners in Supermax Units: Reviewing What We Know and Recommending What Should Change." *International Journal of Offender Therapy and Comparative Criminology* 52(6):622–640.

162   References

Austin, James, and Garry Coventry. 2001. *Emerging Issues on Privatized Prisons.* Washington, DC: Department of Justice, Bureau of Justice Assistance.

Baćak, Valerio, Lars H. Andersen, and Jason Schnittker. 2019. "The Effect of Timing of Incarceration on Mental Health: Evidence from a Natural Experiment." *Social Forces* 98(1):303–328.

Baillargeon, J., T. P. Giordano, J. D. Rich, et al. 2009. "Accessing Antiretroviral Therapy Following Release from Prison." *JAMA* 301(8):848–857.

Bainbridge, Andrea A. 2012. *The Affordable Care Act and Criminal Justice: Intersections and Implications.* Washington, DC: Bureau of Justice Assistance, US Department of Justice.

Barnes, J. C., Tony Dukes, Richard Tewksbury, and Timothy M. De Troye. 2009. "Analyzing the Impact of a Statewide Residence Restriction Law on South Carolina Sex Offenders." *Criminal Justice Policy Review* 20(1):21–43.

Bechelli, Matthew J., Michael Caudy, Tracie M. Gardner, Alice Huber, David Mancuso, Paul Samuels, Tanya Shah, and Homer D. Venters. 2014. "Case Studies from Three States: Breaking Down Silos between Health Care and Criminal Justice." *Health Affairs* 33(3):474–481.

Beck, Allen J. 2015. *Use of Restrictive Housing in US Prisons and Jails, 2011–2012.* Washington, DC: US Department of Justice, Office of Justice Programs, Bureau of Justice Statistics.

Beck, Allen J., Marcus Berzofsky, Rachel Caspar, and Christopher Krebs. 2013. *Sexual Victimization in Prisons and Jails Reported by Inmates, 2011–2012 (NCJ 241399).* Washington, DC: Bureau of Justice Statistics.

Beck, Allen J., and A. Blumstein. 2012. *Trends in Incarceration Rates: 1980–2010.* Washington, DC: National Research Council Committee on the Causes and Consequences of High Rates of Incarceration.

Beck, John A. 1999. "Compassionate Release from New York State Prisons: Why Are So Few Getting Out?" *Journal of Law, Medicine & Ethics* 27(3):216–233.

Begier, Elizabeth M., Yussef Bennani, Lisa Forgione, Amado Punsalang, David B. Hanna, Jeffrey Herrera, Lucia Torian, Maria Gbur, Kent A. Sepkowitz, and Farah Parvez. 2010. "Undiagnosed HIV Infection among New York City Jail Entrants, 2006: Results of a Blinded Serosurvey." *JAIDS Journal of Acquired Immune Deficiency Syndromes* 54(1):93–101.

Beronio, Kirsten, Rosa Po, Laura Skopec, and Sherry Glied. 2013. *Affordable Care Act Expands Mental Health and Substance Use Disorder Benefits and Federal Parity Protections for 62 Million Americans.* Washington, DC: US Department of Health and Human Services, Office of the Assistant Secretary for Planning and Evaluation.

Besci, Zsolt. 1999. "Economics and Crime in the States." *Economic Review* 84(1):38–56.

Bhati, Avinash Singh, John K. Roman, and Aaron Chalfin. 2008. *To Treat or Not to Treat: Evidence on the Prospects of Expanding Treatment to Drug-Involved Offenders.* Washington, DC: Justice Policy Center, the Urban Institute.

Binswanger, Ingrid A., Marc F. Stern, Richard A. Deyo, Patrick J. Heagerty, Allen Cheadle, Joann G. Elmore, and Thomas D. Koepsell. 2007. "Release from

Prison—A High Risk of Death for Former Inmates." *New England Journal of Medicine* 356(2):157–165.

Blakely, Curtis R., and Vic W. Bumphus. 2004. "Private and Public Sector Prisons: A Comparison of Select Characteristics." *Federal Probation* 68:27–31.

Blakinger, Keri, and Joseph Neff. October 7, 2020. "Thousands of Sick Federal Prisoners Sought Compassionate Release. 98 Percent Were Denied." Marshall Project. https://www.themarshallproject.org/2020/10/07/thousands-of-sick-fede ral-prisoners-sought-compassionate-release-98-percent-were-denied.

Bock, Naomi N., Millie Reeves, Madie LaMarre, and Beverly DeVoe. 1998. "Tuberculosis Case Detection in a State Prison System." *Public Health Reports* 113(4):359–364.

Bonta, James, and Paul Gendreau. 1990. "Reexamining the Cruel and Unusual Punishment of Prison Life." *Law and Human Behavior* 14:347–372.

Borchert, Jay W. 2016. "Controlling Consensual Sex among Prisoners." *Law & Social Inquiry* 41(3):595–615.

Boutwell, Amy E., and Jonathan Freedman. 2014. "Coverage Expansion and the Criminal Justice–Involved Population: Implications for Plans and Service Connectivity." *Health Affairs* 33(3):482–486.

Braman, Donald. 2004. *Doing Time on the Outside: Incarceration and Family Life in Urban America*. Ann Arbor: University of Michigan.

Brayne, Sarah. 2014. "Surveillance and System Avoidance: Criminal Justice Contact and Institutional Attachment." *American Sociological Review* 79(3):367–391.

Brewer, T. Fordham, David Vlahov, Ellen Taylor, Drusilla Hall, Alvaro Munoz, and B. Frank Polk. 1988. "Transmission of HIV-1 within a Statewide Prison System." *AIDS* 2(5):363–368.

Briggs, Chad S., Jody L. Sundt, and Thomas C. Castellano. 2003. "The Effect of Supermaximum Security Prisons on Aggregate Levels of Institutional Violence." *Criminology* 41(4):1341–1376.

Britton, Dana M. 1997. "Gendered Organizational Logic: Policy and Practice in Men's and Women's Prisons." *Gender & Society* 11(6):796–818.

Brown, Randall T. 2010. "Systematic Review of the Impact of Adult Drug Treatment Courts." *Translational Research: Journal of Laboratory and Clinical Medicine* 155(6):263–274.

Buble, Courtney. February 11, 2021. "Federal Bureau of Prisons Launches New Hiring Effort." *Government Executive*. https://www.govexec.com/management/2021/02/federal-bureau-prisons-launches-new-hiring-effort/172016/.

Burkhardt, Brett C. 2019. "The Politics of Correctional Privatization in the United States." *Criminology & Public Policy* 18(2):401–418.

Butler, Ben, and Judy Murphy. 2014. "The Impact of Policies Promoting Health Information Technology on Health Care Delivery in Jails and Local Communities." *Health Affairs* 33(3):487–492.

Callahan, Lisa A., and Eric Silver. 1998. "Revocation of Conditional Release: A Comparison of Individual and Program Characteristics across Four U.S. States." *International Journal of Law and Psychiatry* 21(2):177–186.

Carson, E. Ann. 2015. *Prisoners in 2014*. Washington, DC: US Department of Justice, Office of Justice Programs, Bureau of Justice Statistics.

Carson, E. Ann. 2020a. *Prisoners in 2018*. Washington, DC: [NCJ 253516] US Department of Justice, Bureau of Justice Statistics.

Carson, E. Ann. 2020b. *Prisoners in 2019*. Washington, DC: US Department of Justice, Bureau of Justice Statistics.

Carson, E. Ann, and Mary P. Cowhig. 2020. *Mortality in State and Federal Prisons, 2001-2016—Statistical Tables*. Washington, DC: [NCJ 251920] US Department of Justice, Bureau of Justice Statistics.

Carson, E. Ann, and Daniela Golinelli. 2013. *Prisoners in 2012: Trends in Admissions and Releases, 1991-2012*. Washington, DC: US Department of Justice.

Centers for Disease Control and Prevention. 2001. "Hepatitis B Outbreak in a State Correctional Facility, 2000." *Morbidity and Mortality Weekly Report* 50:529–532.

Centers for Disease Control and Prevention. 2004. "Tuberculosis Transmission in Multiple Correctional Facilities—Kansas, 2002-2003." *Morbidity and Mortality Weekly Report* 53:734–738.

Centers for Disease Control and Prevention. 2006. "Prevention and Control of Tuberculosis in Correctional and Detention Facilities." *Morbidity and Mortality Weekly Report* 55:1–44.

Centers for Disease Control and Prevention. 2015. "2015 Sexually Transmitted Diseases Treatment Guidelines: Syphilis." https://www.cdc.gov/std/tg2015/syphilis.htm.

Chammah, Maurice, and Tom Meagher. 2015. "Why Jails Have More Suicides Than Prisons." Marshall Project. https://www.themarshallproject.org/2015/08/04/why-jails-have-more-suicides-than-prisons.

Chandra, Anita, Sandraluz Lara-Cinisomo, Lisa H. Jaycox, Terri Tanielian, Rachel M. Burns, Teague Ruder, and Bing Han. 2010. "Children on the Homefront: The Experience of Children from Military Families." *Pediatrics* 125(1):16–25.

Charles, Kerwin Kofi, and Ming Ching Luoh. 2010. "Male Incarceration, the Marriage Market, and Female Outcomes." *Review of Economics and Statistics* 92(3):614–627.

Christakis, Nicholas A. 1999. *Death Foretold: Prophecy and Prognosis in Medical Care*. Chicago, IL: University of Chicago.

Clarke, Jennifer G., and Eli Y. Adashi. 2011. "Perinatal Care for Incarcerated Patients: A 25-Year-Old Woman Pregnant in Jail." *JAMA* 305(9):923–929.

Clear, Todd R. 2021. "Decarceration Problems and Prospects." *Annual Review of Criminology* 4(1):239–260.

Clear, Todd R., and Natasha A. Frost. 2014. *The Punishment Imperative: The Rise and Failure of Mass Incarceration in America*. New York: New York University.

Clement, Marshall, Matthew Schwarzfeld, and Michael Thompson. 2011. *National Summit on Justice Reinvestment and Public Safety: Addressing Recidivism, Crime, and Corrections Spending*. New York: Council of State Governments Justice Center.

Cohen, Philip N., and Joanna R. Pepin. 2018. "Unequal Marriage Markets: Sex Ratios and First Marriage among Black and White Women." *Socius* 4:1–10.

Cohen, Robin A., Emily P. Terlizzi, Amy E. Cha, and Michael E. Martinez. 2021. "Health Insurance Coverage: Early Release of Estimates from the National Health Interview Survey, January–June 2020." National Center for Health Statistics.

Colgan, Beth A. 2021. "The Burdens of Excessive Fines Clause." *William & Mary Law Review* 63:407–496.

Comfort, Megan. 2003. "In the Tube at San Quentin: The 'Secondary Prisonization' of Women Visiting Inmates." *Journal of Contemporary Ethnography* 32:77–107.

Comfort, Megan. 2007. "Punishment beyond the Legal Offender." *Annual Review of Law and Social Science* 3(1):271–296.

Conklin, T. J., T. Lincoln, and R. W. Tuthill. 2000. "Self-Reported Health and Prior Health Behaviors of Newly Admitted Correctional Inmates." *American Journal of Public Health* 90(12):1939–1941.

Cook, Lawrence J., Stacey Knight, Edward P. Junkins, N. Clay Mann, J. Michael Dean, and Lenora M. Olson. 2004. "Repeat Patients to the Emergency Department in a Statewide Database." *Academic Emergency Medicine* 11(3):256–263.

Cooper, Caroline S. 1997. *1997 Drug Court Survey Report: Executive Summary.* Washington, DC: Drug Court Clearinghouse and Technical Assistance Project, US Department of Justice.

Copeland, William E., Shari Miller-Johnson, Gordon Keeler, Adrian Angold, and E. Jane Costello. 2007. "Childhood Psychiatric Disorders and Young Adult Crime: A Prospective, Population-Based Study." *American Journal of Psychiatry* 164(11):1668–1675.

Couloute, Lucius. 2018. *Nowhere to Go: Homelessness among Formerly Incarcerated People.* Northampton, MA: Prison Policy Initiative.

Cox, Verne C., Paul B. Paulus, and Garvin McGain. 1984. "Prison Crowding Research: The Relevance for Prison Housing Standards and a General Approach Regarding Crowding Phenomena." *American Psychologist* 39:1148–1160.

Cozad, Stacy Lancaster. 1995–1996. "Cruel but Not So Unusual: Farmer v. Brennan and the Devolving Standards of Decency." *Pepperdine Law Review* 23:175–204.

Crocker, Jennifer, and Brenda Major. 1989. "Social Stigma and Self-Esteem: The Self-Protective Properties of Stigma." *Psychological Review* 96:608–630.

Cullen, Francis T., B. S. Fisher, and B. K. Applegate. 2000. "Public Opinion about Punishment and Corrections." Pp. 1–79 in *Crime and Justice: A Review of Research,* vol. 27, edited by M. Tonry. Chicago, IL: University of Chicago.

Cunningham, Peter J., and Ha T. Tu. 1997. "A Changing Picture of Uncompensated Care." *Health Affairs* 16(4):167–175.

Daniel, Sally W., and Carol J. Barrett. 1981. "The Needs of Prisoners' Wives: A Challenge for the Mental Health Professions." *Community Mental Health Journal* 17(4):310–322.

Defilippis, Ersilia M. May 5, 2016. "When Hospital Rooms Become Prisons." *New York Times.* https://well.blogs.nytimes.com/2016/05/05/when-hospital-rooms-become-prisons/.

Deitch, Michele. 2010. "Independent Correctional Oversight Mechanisms across the United States: A 50-State Inventory." *Pace Law Review* 30(5):1754–1930.

Deitch, Michele. 2012. "The Need for Independent Prison Oversight in a Post-PLRA World." *Federal Sentencing Reporter* 24:236–244.

Demleitner, Nora V. 2017. "Time Off for Good Behavior." Pp. 1–4 in *The Encyclopedia of Corrections*, edited by K. R. Kerley. New York: Wiley.

Department of Homeland Security. 2019. *U.S. Immigration and Customs Enforcement: Budget Overview*. Washington, DC: Department of Homeland Security.

Dolovich, Sharon. 2005. "State Punishment and Private Prisons." *Duke Law Journal* 55:437–546.

Dolovich, Sharon. 2009a. "Cruelty, Prison Conditions, and the Eighth Amendment." *New York University Law Review* 84:881–979.

Dolovich, Sharon. 2009b. "How Privatization Thinks: The Case of Prisons." Pp. 128–147 in *Government by Contract: Outsourcing and American Democracy*, edited by J. Freeman and M. Minow. Cambridge, MA: Harvard University Press.

Donohue, John J. 2009. "Assessing the Relative Benefits of Incarceration: Overall Changes and the Benefits on the Margin." Pp. 269–341 in *Do Prisons Make Us Safer?*, edited by S. Raphael and M. A. Stoll. New York: Russell Sage Foundation.

Dubler, Nancy. 2014. "Ethical Dilemmas in Prison and Jail Health Care." *Health Affairs Blog*, vol. 2016. Health Affairs, Project Hope.

Edin, Kathryn. 2000. "Few Good Men: Why Poor Mothers Don't Marry or Remarry." *American Prospect* 11:26–31.

Edin, Kathryn, Timothy J. Nelson, and Rechelle Paranal. 2004. "Fatherhood and Incarceration as Potential Turning Points in the Criminal Careers of Unskilled Men." Pp. 46–75 in *Imprisoning America: The Social Effects of Mass Incarceration*, edited by M. Patillo, D. Weiman, and B. Western. New York: Russell Sage Foundation.

Eisen, Lauren-Brooke. 2015. *Charging Inmates Perpetuates Mass Incarceration*. New York: Brennan Center for Justice, New York University School of Law.

Ellwood, John W., and Joshua Guetzkow. 2009. "Footing the Bill: Causes and Budgetary Consequences of State Spending on Corrections." Pp. 207–238 in *Do Prisons Make Us Safer?: The Benefits and Costs of the Prison Boom*, edited by S. Raphael and M. A. Stoll. New York: Russell Sage Foundation.

Ewald, Alec, and Christopher Uggen. 2012. "The Collateral Effects of Imprisonment on Prisoners, Their Families, and Communities." Pp. 83–103 in *The Oxford Handbook on Sentencing and Corrections*, edited by J. Petersilia and K. Reitz. New York: Oxford University Press.

Faiver, Kenneth L. 2005. "Health Care." Pp. 399–404 in *Encyclopedia of Prisons & Correctional Facilities*, edited by M. Bosworth. Thousand Oaks, CA: SAGE Publications.

Fazel, Seena, and John Danesh. 2002. "Serious Mental Disorder in 23 000 Prisoners: A Systematic Review of 62 Surveys." *The Lancet* 359(9306):545–550.

Fazel, Seena, and Martin Grann. 2006. "The Population Impact of Severe Mental Illness on Violent Crime." *American Journal of Psychiatry* 163(8):1397–1403.

Feeley, Malcolm M., and Jonathan Simon. 1992. "The New Penology: Notes on the Emerging Strategy of Corrections and Its Implications." *Criminology* 30:449–474.

Fellner, Jamie. 2006. "A Corrections Quandary: Mental Illness and Prison Rules." *Harvard Civil Rights-Civil Liberties Law Review* 41(2):391–412.

Fields, W. Wesley, Brent R. Asplin, Gregory L. Larkin, Catherine A. Marco, Loren A. Johnson, Charlotte Yeh, Keith T. Ghezzi, and Michael Rapp. 2001. "The Emergency Medical Treatment and Labor Act as a Federal Health Care Safety Net Program." *Academic Emergency Medicine* 8(11):1064–1069.

Ford, Matt. June 8, 2015. "America's Largest Mental Hospital Is a Jail." *The Atlantic.* http://www.theatlantic.com/politics/archive/2015/06/americas-largest-mental-hospital-is-a-jail/395012/.

Frank, Joseph W., Christina M. Andrews, Traci C. Green, Aaron M. Samuels, T. Tony Trinh, and Peter D. Friedmann. 2013. "Emergency Department Utilization among Recently Released Prisoners: A Retrospective Cohort Study." *BMC Emergency Medicine* 13(1):16.

Freudenberg, Nicholas. 2001. "Jails, Prisons, and the Health of Urban Populations: A Review of the Impact of the Correctional System on Community Health." *Journal of Urban Health* 78(2):214–235.

Freudenberg, Nicholas, and Daliah Heller. 2016. "A Review of Opportunities to Improve the Health of People Involved in the Criminal Justice System in the United States." *Annual Review of Public Health* 37(1):313–333.

Fu, Jeannia J., Nickolas D. Zaller, Michael A. Yokell, Alexander R. Bazazi, and Josiah D. Rich. 2013. "Forced Withdrawal from Methadone Maintenance Therapy in Criminal Justice Settings: A Critical Treatment Barrier in the United States." *Journal of Substance Abuse Treatment* 44(5):502–505.

Furnham, Adrian. 1994. "Explaining Health and Illness: Lay Beliefs on the Nature of Health." *Personality and Individual Differences* 17(4):455–466.

Gaes, Gerald G. 2019. "Current Status of Prison Privatization Research on American Prisons and Jails." *Criminology & Public Policy* 18(2):269–293.

Genty, Philip M. 1996. "Confusing Punishment with Custodial Care: The Troublesome Legacy of *Estelle v. Gamble.*" *Vermont Law Review* 21:379–407.

Getahun, Haileyesus, Alberto Matteelli, Richard E. Chaisson, and Mario Raviglione. 2015. "Latent Mycobacterium Tuberculosis Infection." *New England Journal of Medicine* 372(22):2127–2135.

Ghandnoosh, Nicole. 2019. *U.S. Prison Population Trends: Massive Buildup and Modest Decline.* Washington, DC: Sentencing Project.

Glaze, Lauren E., and Thomas P. Bonczar. 2011. *Probation and Parole in the United States, 2010.* Washington, DC: US Department of Justice, Bureau of Justice Statistics.

Glaze, Lauren E., and Erinn J. Heberman. 2013. *Correctional Populations in the United States, 2012.* Washington, DC: US Department of Justice, Bureau of Justice Statistics.

Glaze, Lauren E., and Laura M. Maruschak. 2008. *Parents in Prison and Their Minor Children.* Washington, DC: Bureau of Justice Statistics.

Glowa-Kollisch, Sarah, Jasmine Graves, Nathaniel Dickey, Ross MacDonald, Zachary Rosner, Anthony Waters, and Homer Venters. 2015. "Data-Driven Human Rights:

Using Dual Loyalty Trainings to Promote the Care of Vulnerable Patients in Jail." *Health and Human Rights* 17(1):124–135.

Goffman, Alice. 2009. "On the Run: Wanted Men in a Philadelphia Ghetto." *American Sociological Review* 74:339–357.

Goldman, Alyssa W. 2019. "Linked Lives in Double Jeopardy: Child Incarceration and Maternal Health at Midlife." *Journal of Health and Social Behavior* 60(4):398–415.

Gottschalk, Marie. 2014. *Caught*. Princeton, NJ: Princeton University Press.

Gowan, Teresa, and Sarah Whetstone. 2012. "Making the Criminal Addict: Subjectivity and Social Control in a Strong-Arm Rehab." *Punishment & Society* 14(1):69–93.

Grassian, Stuart. 1983. "Psychopathological Effects of Solitary Confinement." *American Journal of Psychiatry* 140(11):1450–1454.

Grassian, Stuart. 1986. "Effects of Sensory Deprivation in Psychiatric Seclusion and Solitary Confinement." *International Journal of Law and Psychiatry* 8(1):49–65.

Green, Kerry M., Margaret E. Ensminger, Judith A. Robertson, and Hee-Soon Juon. 2006. "Impact of Adult Sons' Incarceration on African American Mothers' Psychological Distress." *Journal of Marriage and Family* 68(2):430–441.

Greene, Judith, and Marc Mauer. 2010. *Downscaling Prisons: Lessons from Four States*. Washington, DC: Sentencing Project.

Gustafson, Kaaryn. 2011. *Cheating Welfare: Public Assistance and the Criminalization of Poverty*. New York: NYU Press.

Gutierrez, Carmen M., and Becky Pettit. 2020. "Employment and Health among Recently Incarcerated Men before and after the Affordable Care Act (2009–2017)." *American Journal of Public Health* 110(S1):S123–S129.

Hadley, Jack, and John Holahan. 2003. "How Much Medical Care Do the Uninsured Use, and Who Pays for It?" *Health Affairs* 22(Supplement 1):W3–66–W3–81.

Hagedorn, Hildi, and Mark L. Willenbring. 2003. "Psychiatric Illness among Drug Court Probationers." *American Journal of Drug and Alcohol Abuse* 29(4):775–788.

Hammett, Theodore M., Sofia Kennedy, and Sarah Kuck. 2007. "National Survey of Infectious Diseases in Correctional Facilities: HIV and Sexually Transmitted Diseases." Washington, DC: US Department of Justice.

Haney, Craig. 2003. "Mental Health Issues in Long-Term Solitary and 'Supermax' Confinement." *Crime & Delinquency* 49(1):124–156.

Haney, Craig. 2006. *Reforming Punishment: Psychological Limits to the Pains of Imprisonment*. Washington, DC: American Psychological Association.

Harcourt, Bernard E. 2006. "From the Asylum to the Prison: Rethinking the Incarceration Revolution." *Texas Law Review* 84:1751–1786.

Harding, David J., Jeffrey D. Morenoff, and Jessica B. Wyse. 2019. *On the Outside: Prisoner Reentry and Reintegration*. Chicago, IL: University of Chicago.

Harding, David J., Jessica J. B. Wyse, Cheyney Dobson, and Jeffrey D. Morenoff. 2014. "Making Ends Meet after Prison." *Journal of Policy Analysis and Management* 33(2):440–470.

Harner, Holly M., Brian R. Wyant, and Fernanda Da Silva. 2016. "'Prison Ain't Free Like Everyone Thinks': Financial Stressors Faced by Incarcerated Women." *Qualitative Health Research* 27(5):688–699.

Harzke, Amy J., Jacques G. Baillargeon, Michael F. Kelley, Sandi L. Pruitt, John S. Pulvino, and David P. Paar. 2011. "Leading Medical Causes of Mortality among Male Prisoners in Texas, 1992–2003." *Journal of Correctional Health Care* 17(3):241–253.

Haskins, Anna R., and Wade C. Jacobsen. 2017. "Schools as Surveilling Institutions? Paternal Incarceration, System Avoidance, and Parental Involvement in Schooling." *American Sociological Review* 82(4):657–684.

Heller, Sara B., Anuj K. Shah, Jonathan Guryan, Jens Ludwig, Sendhil Mullainathan, and Harold A. Pollack. 2015. *Thinking, Fast and Slow? Some Field Experiments to Reduce Crime and Dropout in Chicago*. Cambridge, MA: National Bureau of Economic Research.

Henrichson, Christian, Joshua Rinaldi, and Ruth Delaney. 2015. *The Price of Jails: Measuring the Taxpayer Cost of Local Incarceration*. New York: Vera Institute of Justice.

Herring, Chris, Dilara Yarbrough, and Lisa Marie Alatorre. 2020. "Pervasive Penality: How the Criminalization of Poverty Perpetuates Homelessness." *Social Problems* 67(1):131–149.

Holzer, Harry J., Stephen Raphael, and Michael A. Stoll. 2004. "Will Employers Hire Former Offenders? Employer Preferences, Background Checks, and Their Determinants." Pp. 205–243 in *Imprisoning America: The Social Effects of Mass Incarceration*, edited by M. Pattillo, D. Weiman, and B. Wester. New York: Russell Sage Foundation.

Hoot, Nathan R., and Dominik Aronsky. 2008. "Systematic Review of Emergency Department Crowding: Causes, Effects, and Solutions." *Annals of Emergency Medicine* 52(2):126–136.e1.

House, James S., Karl R. Landis, and Debra Umberson. 1988. "Social Relationships and Health." *Science* 241(4865):540–545.

Howell, Benjamin A., Lisa Puglisi, Katie Clark, Carmen Albizu-Garcia, Evan Ashkin, Tyler Booth, Lauren Brinkley-Rubinstein, David A. Fiellin, Aaron D. Fox, Kathleen F. Maurer, Hsiu-Ju Lin, Kathryn McCollister, Sean Murphy, Diane S. Morse, Shira Shavit, Karen Wang, Tyler Winkelman, and Emily A. Wang. 2021. "The Transitions Clinic Network: Post Incarceration Addiction Treatment, Healthcare, and Social Support (TCN-PATHS): A Hybrid Type-1 Effectiveness Trial of Enhanced Primary Care to Improve Opioid Use Disorder Treatment Outcomes Following Release from Jail." *Journal of Substance Abuse Treatment* 128:108315.

Huebner, Beth M. 2005. "The Effect of Incarceration on Marriage and Work over the Life Course." *Justice Quarterly* 22(3):281–303.

Human Rights Watch. 2003. *Ill-Equipped: US Prisons and Offenders with Mental Illness*. New York: Human Rights Watch.

Human Rights Watch. 2009. *No Equal Justice: The Prison Litigation Reform Act in the United States*. New York: Human Rights Watch.

Human Rights Watch. 2015. *Callous and Cruel: Use of Force against Inmates with Mental Disabilities in US Jails and Prisons*. New York: Human Rights Watch.

Hummer, Robert A., and Elaine M. Hernandez. 2013. "The Effects of Educational Attainment on Adult Mortality in the United States." *Population Bulletin* 68(1):1–16.

Hylton, Wil S. 2003. "Sick on the Inside: Correctional HMOs and the Coming Prison Plague." *Harper's Magazine* August:43–54.

Innes, C. A. 1993. "Recent Public Opinion in the United States toward Punishment and Corrections." *Prison Journal* 73:220–236.

Institute of Medicine. 2003. *A Shared Destiny: Community Effects of Uninsurance.* Washington, DC: National Academies Press.

Iroh, Princess A., Helen Mayo, and Ank E. Nijhawan. 2015. "The HIV Care Cascade before, during, and after Incarceration: A Systematic Review and Data Synthesis." *American Journal of Public Health* 105(7):e5–e16.

Jacobs, James B. 1977. *Stateville: The Penitentiary in Mass Society.* Chicago, IL: University of Chicago Press.

James, Doris J., and Lauren E. Glaze. 2006. *Mental Health Problems of Prison and Jail Inmates.* Washington, DC: Bureau of Justice Statistics, US Department of Justice.

Jha, Ashish, John Orav, Zhonghe Li, and Arnold M. Epstein. 2007. "Concentration and Quality of Hospitals That Care for Elderly Black Patients." *Archives of Internal Medicine* 167(11):1177–1182.

Johnson, Rucker C., and Steven Raphael. 2009. "The Effects of Male Incarceration Dynamics on AIDS Infection Rates among African-American Women and Men." *Journal of Law & Economics* 52:251–293.

Johnson, Rucker, and Steven Raphael. 2012. "How Much Crime Reduction Does the Marginal Prisoner Buy?" *Journal of Law & Economics* 55(2):275–310.

Kaba, Fatos, Andrea Lewis, Sarah Glowa-Kollisch, James Hadler, David Lee, Howard Alper, Daniel Selling, Ross MacDonald, Angela Solimo, Amanda Parsons, and Homer Venters. 2014. "Solitary Confinement and Risk of Self-Harm among Jail Inmates." *American Journal of Public Health* 104(3):442–447.

Kaeble, Danielle. 2020. *Probation and Parole in the United States, 2017–2018.* Washington, DC: [NCJ 252072] US Department of Justice, Bureau of Justice Statistics.

Kaeble, Danielle, and Mariel Alper. 2020. *Probation and Parole in the United States, 2017–2018.* Washington, DC: [NCJ 252072] US Department of Justice, Bureau of Justice Statistics.

Kahn, Richard H., Daniel T. Scholl, Simon M. Shane, Anne L. Lemoine, and Thomas A. Farley. 2002. "Screening for Syphilis in Arrestees: Usefulness for Community-Wide Syphilis Surveillance and Control." *Sexually Transmitted Diseases* 29(3):150–156.

Kaiser Family Foundation. 2021. "More Than a Third of Americans Say They've Struggled to Pay Living Expenses since December; 6 in 10 Families Hit by Covid Have Lost a Job or Income." Accessed March 19, 2021. https://www.kff.org/coro navirus-covid-19/press-release/kff-tracking-poll-more-than-a-third-of-americ ans-say-theyve-struggled-to-pay-living-expenses-since-december-6-in-10-famil ies-hit-by-covid-have-lost-a-job-or-income/.

Kang-Brown, Jacob, Chase Montagnet, and Jasmine Heiss. 2021. *People in Jail and Prison in 2020.* New York: Vera Institute of Justice.

Kapoor, Reena. 2014. "Taking the Solitary Confinement Debate out of Isolation." *Journal of the American Academy of Psychiatry and the Law Online* 42(1):2–6.

Keisler-Starkey, Katherine, and Lisa N. Bunch. 2020. *Health Insurance Coverage in the United States: 2019.* Washington, DC: US Government Publishing Office.

Kessler, Ronald C., Wai Tat Chiu, Olga Demler, and Ellen E. Walters. 2005. "Prevalence, Severity, and Comorbidity of 12-Month DSM-IV Disorders in the National Comorbidity Survey Replication." *Archives of General Psychiatry* 62(6):617–627.

Kessler, Ronald C., Kristin D. Mickelson, and David R. Williams. 1999. "The Prevalence, Distribution, and Mental Health Correlates of Perceived Discrimination in the United States." *Journal of Health and Social Behavior* 40(3):208–230.

Kim, KiDeuk, and Bryce Peterson. 2014. *Aging Behind Bars: Trends and Implications of Graying Prisoners in the Federal Prison System* Washington, DC: Urban Institute.

Kirchoff, Suzanne M. 2010. *Economic Impacts of Prison Growth.* Washington, DC: Congressional Research Service.

Kling, Jeffrey R. 2006. "Incarceration Length, Employment, and Earnings." *American Economic Review* 96:863–876.

Koball, Heather L., Emily Moiduddin, Jamila Henderson, Brian Goesling, and Melanie Besculides. 2010. "What Do We Know about the Link between Marriage and Health?" *Journal of Family Issues* 31(8):1019–1040.

Krauth, Barbara, and Karin Stayton. 2005. *Fees Paid by Jail Inmates: Fee Categories, Revenues, and Management Perspectives in a Sample of U.S. Jails,* edited by C. Clem. Washington, DC: US Department of Justice, National Institute of Corrections Information Center.

Krebs, Christopher P., and Melanie Simmons. 2002. "Intraprison HIV Transmission: An Assessment of Whether It Occurs, How It Occurs, and Who Is at Risk." *AIDS Education and Prevention* 14:53–64.

Krelstein, Michael S. 2002. "The Role of Mental Health in the Inmate Disciplinary Process: A National Survey." *Journal of the American Academy of Psychiatry and the Law Online* 30(4):488–496.

Kruttschnitt, Candace, and R. Gartner. 2005. *Marking Time in the Golden State: Women's Imprisonment in California.* New York: Cambridge University Press.

Kupers, Terry A., Theresa Dronet, Margaret Winter, James Austin, Lawrence Kelly, William Cartier, Timothy J. Morris, Stephen F. Hanlon, Emmitt L. Sparkman, Parveen Kumar, Leonard C. Vincent, Jim Norris, Kim Nagel, and Jennifer McBride. 2009. "Beyond Supermax Administrative Segregation: Mississippi's Experience Rethinking Prison Classification and Creating Alternative Mental Health Programs." *Criminal Justice and Behavior* 36(10):1037–1050.

Lageson, Sarah. 2020. *Digital Punishment: Privacy, Stigma, and the Harms of Data-Driven Criminal Justice.* New York: Oxford University.

Lageson, Sarah Esther. 2016. "Found Out and Opting Out: The Consequences of Online Criminal Records for Families." *Annals of the American Academy of Political and Social Science* 665(1):127–141.

Lamb, H. Richard, and Linda E. Weinberger. 1998. "Persons with Severe Mental Illness in Jails and Prison: A Review." *Psychiatric Services* 49:483–492.

Landenberger, Nana A., and Mark W. Lipsey. 2005. "The Positive Effects of Cognitive-Behavioral Programs for Offenders: A Meta-Analysis of Factors Associated with Effective Treatment." *Journal of Experimental Criminology* 1(4):451–476.

Lara-Millán, Armando. 2014. "Public Emergency Room Overcrowding in the Era of Mass Imprisonment." *American Sociological Review* 79(5):866–887.

Lawrence, Claire, and Kathryn Andrews. 2004. "The Influence of Perceived Prison Crowding on Male Inmates' Perception of Aggressive Events." *Aggressive Behavior* 30(4):273–283.

Levin, Marc. 2018. "Finding Smart Ways to Be Tough on Crime: A Perspective on Federal Criminal-Justice Reform 2018 Federalist Society Texas Chapters Conference." *Texas Review of Law and Politics* 23(2):327–334.

Levitsky, Sandra R. 2013. "Integrating Law and Health Policy." *Annual Review of Law and Social Science* 9(1):33–50.

Levitt, Steven D. 1996. "The Effect of Prison Population Size on Crime Rates: Evidence from Prison Overcrowding Litigation." *Quarterly Journal of Economics* 111:319–351.

Lichter, Daniel T., Diane K. McLaughlin, George Kephart, and David J. Landry. 1992. "Race and the Retreat from Marriage: A Shortage of Marriageable Men?" *American Sociological Review* 57(6):781–799.

Liedka, Raymond V., Anne Morrison Piehl, and Bert Useem. 2006. "The Crime-Control Effect of Incarceration: Does Scale Matter?" *Criminology & Public Policy* 5(2):245–276.

Lincoln, Karen D., and David H. Chae. 2010. "Stress, Marital Satisfaction, and Psychological Distress among African Americans." *Journal of Family Issues* 31(8):1081–1105.

Link, Bruce G., John Monahan, Ann Stueve, and Francis T. Cullen. 1999. "Real in Their Consequences: A Sociological Approach to Understanding the Association between Psychotic Symptoms and Violence." *American Sociological Review* 64(2):316–332.

Listwan, Shelley Johnson, Jody L. Sundt, Alexander M. Holsinger, and Edward J. Latessa. 2003. "The Effect of Drug Court Programming on Recidivism: The Cincinnati Experience." *Crime & Delinquency* 49(3):389–411.

Lobato, Mark N., Linda S. Leary, and Patricia M. Simone. 2003. "Treatment for Latent TB in Correctional Facilities: A Challenge for TB Elimination." *American Journal of Preventive Medicine* 24(3):249–253.

Loveland, David, and Michael Boyle. 2007. "Intensive Case Management as a Jail Diversion Program for People with a Serious Mental Illness: A Review of the Literature." *International Journal of Offender Therapy and Comparative Criminology* 51(2):130–150.

Lundahl, Brad W., Chelsea Kunz, Cyndi Brownell, Norma Harris, and Russ Van Vleet. 2009. "Prison Privatization: A Meta-Analysis of Cost and Quality of Confinement Indicators." *Research on Social Work Practice* 19(4):383–394.

Lundquist, Jennifer Hickes, Devah Pager, and Eiko Strader. 2018. "Does a Criminal Past Predict Worker Performance? Evidence from One of America's Largest Employers." *Social Forces* 96(3):1039–1068.

Macalino, Grace E., David Vlahoc, Stephanie Sanford-Colby, Sarju Patel, Keith Sabin, Christopher Salas, and Josiah D. Rich. 2004. "Prevalence and Incidence of HIV, Hepatitis B Virus, and Hepatitis C Virus Infections among Males in Rhode Island Prisons." *American Journal of Public Health* 94:1218–1223.

MacLin, M. Kimberly, and Vivian Herrera. 2006. "The Criminal Stereotype." *North American Journal of Psychology* 8(2):197–207.

Magura, S., and A. Rosenblum. 2001. "Leaving Methadone Treatment: Lessons Learned, Lessons Forgotten, Lessons Ignored." *Mount Sinai Journal of Medicine* 68:62–74.

Mai, Chris, and Ram Subramanian. 2017. *The Price of Prisons: Examining State Spending Trends, 2010–2015*. New York: Vera Institute of Justice.

Mallik-Kane, Kamala. 2005. *Returning Home Illinois Policy Brief: Health and Prisoner Reentry*. Washington, DC: Urban Institute Justice Policy Center.

Mallik-Kane, Kamala, and Christy A. Visher. 2008. *Health and Prisoner Reentry: How Physical, Mental, and Substance Abuse Conditions Shape the Process of Reintegration*. Washington, DC: Urban Institute.

Manderscheid, Ronald W., Joanne E. Atay, and Raquel A. Crider. 2009. "Changing Trends in State Psychiatric Hospital Use from 2002 to 2005." *Psychiatric Services* 60(1):29–34.

Marks, James S., and Nicholas Turner. 2014. "The Critical Link between Health Care and Jails." *Health Affairs* 33(3):443–447.

Marshall Project. 2021. "A State-by-State Look at Coronavirus in Prisons." Accessed February 18, 2021. https://www.themarshallproject.org/2020/05/01/a-state-by-state-look-at-coronavirus-in-prisons.

Martin, Michael S., Katie Hynes, Simon Hatcher, and Ian Colman. 2016. "Diagnostic Error in Correctional Mental Health: Prevalence, Causes, and Consequences." *Journal of Correctional Health Care* 22(2):109–117.

Martin, S. L., R. H. Rieger, L. L. Kupper, R. E. Meyer, and B. F. Qaqish. 1997. "The Effect of Incarceration during Pregnancy on Birth Outcomes." *Public Health Reports (Washington, DC: 1974)* 112(4):340–346.

Maruschak, Laura M., and Todd D. Minton. 2020. *Correctional Populations in the United States, 2017–2018*. Washington, DC: US Department of Justice, Bureau of Justice Statistics.

Marvell, Thomas B., and Carlisle E. Moody. 1994. "Prison Population Growth and Crime Reduction." *Journal of Quantitative Criminology* 10(2):109–140.

Massoglia, Michael. 2008. "Incarceration as Exposure: The Prison, Stress, and Infectious Disease." *Journal of Health and Social Behavior* 49:56–71.

Massoglia, Michael, Glenn Firebaugh, and Cody Warner. 2013. "Racial Variation in the Effect of Incarceration on Neighborhood Attainment." *American Sociological Review* 78:142–165.

Massoglia, Michael, Paul-Philippe Pare, Jason Schnittker, and Alain Gagnon. 2014. "The Relationship between Incarceration and Premature Adult Mortality: Gender Specific Evidence." *Social Science Research* 46:142–154.

Massoglia, Michael, Brianna Remster, and Ryan D. King. 2011. "Stigma or Separation? Understanding the Incarceration-Divorce Relationship." *Social Forces* 90(1):133–155.

Matusow, Harlan, Samuel L. Dickman, Josiah D. Rich, Chunki Fong, Dora M. Dumont, Carolyn Hardin, Douglas Marlowe, and Andrew Rosenblum. 2013. "Medication Assisted Treatment in US Drug Courts: Results from a Nationwide Survey of Availability, Barriers and Attitudes." *Journal of Substance Abuse Treatment* 44(5):473–480.

McGuire, Kathleen, and Ann Pastore. 1993. *Sourcebook of Criminal Justice Statistics, 1992*, vol. 634. Washington, DC: US Government Printing Office.

Mechanic, David, and Mark Olfson. 2016. "The Relevance of the Affordable Care Act for Improving Mental Health Care." *Annual Review of Clinical Psychology* 12(1):515–542.

Metraux, Stephen, and Dennis P. Culhane. 2004. "Homeless Shelter Use and Reincarceration Following Prison Release." *Criminology and Public Policy* 3:139–160.

Milkman, Harvey, and Kenneth Wanberg. 2007. *Cognitive-Behavioral Treatment: A Review and Discussion for Corrections Professionals*. Washington, DC: US Department of Justice, National Institute of Corrections.

Miller, Sarah. 2012. "The Effect of Insurance on Emergency Room Visits: An Analysis of the 2006 Massachusetts Health Reform." *Journal of Public Economics* 96(11–12):893–908.

Minton, Todd D. 2013. *Jail Inmates at Midyear 2012*. Washington, DC: US Department of Justice, Bureau of Justice Statistics.

Minton, Todd D., and Zhen Zeng. 2015. *Jail Inmates at Midyear 2014*. Washington, DC: US Department of Justice, Office of Justice Programs, Bureau of Justice Statistics.

Miron, Jeffrey A., and Katherine Waldock. 2010. *The Budgetary Impact of Ending Drug Prohibition*. Washington, DC: Cato Institute.

Mitchell, Ojmarrh, David B. Wilson, Amy Eggers, and Doris L. MacKenzie. 2012. "Assessing the Effectiveness of Drug Courts on Recidivism: A Meta-Analytic Review of Traditional and Non-Traditional Drug Courts." *Journal of Criminal Justice* 40(1):60–71.

Møller, L. F., S. Matic, B. J. van den Bergh, K. Moloney, P. Hayton, and A. Gatherer. 2010. "Acute Drug-Related Mortality of People Recently Released from Prisons." *Public Health* 124(11):637–639.

Moore, Kelly, Jeffrey Stuewig, and June Tangney. 2013. "Jail Inmates' Perceived and Anticipated Stigma: Implications for Post-Release Functioning." *Self and Identity: Journal of the International Society for Self and Identity* 12(5):527–547.

Morgan, Robert D., Jarrod Steffan, Lucas B. Shaw, and Scott Wilson. 2007. "Needs for and Barriers to Correctional Mental Health Services: Inmate Perceptions." *Psychiatric Services* 58(9):1181–1186.

Mueller-Johnson, Katrin U., and Mandeep K. Dhami. 2009. "Effects of Offenders' Age and Health on Sentencing Decisions." *Journal of Social Psychology* 150(1):77–97.

Mukherjee, Anita. 2016. *Does Prison Privatization Distort Justice? Evidence on Time Served and Recidivism.* Madison: University of Wisconsin. Available at SSRN: http://ssrn.com/abstract=2523238 or http://dx.doi.org/10.2139/ssrn.2523238.

Mumola, Christopher J. 2007. *Medical Causes of Death in State Prisons, 2001–2004.* Washington, DC: Bureau of Justice Statistics.

Muskegon Community Health Project. 2007. *Michigan Pathways Project Links Ex-Prisoners to Medical Services, Contributing to a Decline in Recidivism.* Rockville, MD: Agency for Healthcare Research and Quality, Innovations Exchange.

Nagin, Daniel S., Francis T. Cullen, and Cheryl Lero Jonson. 2009. "Imprisonment and Reoffending." *Crime and Justice* 38(1):115–200.

Najdowski, Cynthia J. 2011. "Stereotype Threat in Criminal Interrogations: Why Innocent Black Suspects Are at Risk for Confessing Falsely." *Psychology, Public Policy, and Law* 17(4):562–591.

National Drug Court Resource Center. 2014. *How Many Drug Courts Are There?* Alexandria, VA: National Drug Court Resource Center.

National Research Council. 2014. *The Growth of Incarceration in the United States: Exploring Causes and Consequences.* Washington, DC: National Academies.

Nellis, Ashley. 2021. *No End in Sight: America's Enduring Reliance on Life Imprisonment.* Washington, DC: Sentencing Project.

Neuhausen, Katherine, Anna C. Davis, Jack Needleman, Robert H. Brook, David Zingmond, and Dylan H. Roby. 2014. "Disproportionate-Share Hospital Payment Reductions May Threaten the Financial Stability of Safety-Net Hospitals." *Health Affairs* 33(6):988–996.

Noonan, Margaret E. 2010. *Mortality in Local Jails, 2000–2007.* Washington, DC: US Department of Justice, Office of Justice Programs, Bureau of Justice Statistics.

Noonan, Margaret E., and E. Ann Carson. 2011. *Prison and Jail Deaths in Custody, 2000–2009, Statistical Tables.* Washington, DC: US Department of Justice, Office of Justice Programs, Bureau of Justice Statistics.

Noonan, Margaret E., Harley Rohloff, and Scott Ginder. 2015. *Mortality in Local Jails and State Prisons, 2000–2013—Statistical Tables.* Washington, DC: US Department of Justice, Office of Justice Programs, Bureau of Justice Statistics.

O'Keefe, Maureen L., Kelli J. Klebe, Jeffrey Metzner, Joel Dvoskin, Jamie Fellner, and Alysha Stucker. 2013. "A Longitudinal Study of Administrative Segregation." *Journal of the American Academy of Psychiatry and the Law Online* 41(1):49–60.

Page, Joshua. 2011. *The Toughest Beat: Politics, Punishment, and the Prison Officers Union in California.* New York: Oxford University.

Pager, Devah. 2003. "The Mark of a Criminal Record." *American Journal of Sociology* 108:937–975.

Pager, Devah. 2008. "Marked: Race, Crime, and Finding Work in an Era of Mass Incarceration." Pp. 683–690 in *Social Stratification: Class, Race, and Gender in Sociological Perspective*, edited by D. B. Grusky. Boulder, CO: Westview Press.

Pastuszak, Alexander W., Evan P. Wenker, Peggy B. Smith, Allyssa Abacan, Dolores J. Lamb, Larry I. Lipshultz, and Ruth Buzi. 2016. "Comprehensive Assessment of Health Needs of Young Minority Males Attending a Family Planning Clinic." *American Journal of Men's Health* 11(3):542–551.

Patel, Kavita, Amy Boutwell, Bradley W. Brockmann, and Josiah D. Rich. 2014. "Integrating Correctional and Community Health Care for Formerly Incarcerated People Who Are Eligible for Medicaid." *Health Affairs* 33(3):468–473.

Paterline, Brent A., and David M. Petersen. 1999. "Structural and Social Psychological Determinants of Prisonization." *Journal of Criminal Justice* 27(5):427–441.

Patterson, Evelyn. 2010. "Incarcerating Death: Mortality in the U.S. State Correctional Facilities, 1985–1998." *Demography* 47:587–607.

Patterson, Evelyn J. 2013. "The Dose–Response of Time Served in Prison on Mortality: New York State, 1989–2003." *American Journal of Public Health* 103(3):523–528.

Patterson, Raymond F., and Kerry Hughes. 2008. "Review of Completed Suicides in the California Department of Corrections and Rehabilitation, 1999 to 2004." *Psychiatric Services* 59(6):676–682.

Pauly, Mark V., and José A. Pagán. 2007. "Spillovers and Vulnerability: The Case of Community Uninsurance." *Health Affairs* 26(5):1304–1314.

Paz, R. Samuel. 2007. "Accommodating Disabilities in Jails and Prisons." Pp. 42–55 in *Public Health Behind Bars: From Prisons to Communities*, edited by R. B. Greifinger. New York: Springer.

Pearlin, Leonard I., Carol S. Aneshensel, and Allen J. Leblanc. 1997. "The Forms and Mechanisms of Stress Proliferation: The Case of AIDS Caregivers." *Journal of Health and Social Behavior* 38(3):223–236.

Perrone, Dina, and Travis C. Pratt. 2003. "Comparing the Quality of Confinement and Cost-Effectiveness of Public versus Private Prisons: What We Know, Why We Do Not Know More, and Where to Go from Here." *Prison Journal* 83(3):301–322.

Petersilia, Joan. 2003. *When Prisoners Come Home: Parole and Prisoner Reentry*. New York: Oxford University.

Peterson, Jillian K., Jennifer Skeem, Patrick Kennealy, Beth Bray, and Andrea Zvonkovic. 2014. "How Often and How Consistently Do Symptoms Directly Precede Criminal Behavior among Offenders with Mental Illness?" *Law and Human Behavior* 38(5):439–449.

Pettit, Becky. 2012. *Invisible Men: Mass Incarceration and the Myth of Black Progress*. New York: Russell Sage Foundation.

Pettit, Becky, and Bruce Western. 2004. "Mass Imprisonment and the Life Course: Race and Class Inequality in U.S. Incarceration." *American Sociological Review* 69:151–169.

Pew Center on the States. 2010. *Prison Count 2010: State Population Declines for the First Time in 38 Years*. Philadelphia, PA: Pew Charitable Trusts.

Pew Charitable Trusts. 2013. *Managing Prison Health Care Spending*. Philadelphia, PA: Pew Charitable Trusts.

Pew Charitable Trusts. 2014. *State Prison Health Care Spending*. Philadelphia, PA: Pew Charitable Trusts.

Pew Charitable Trusts. 2017. *Prison Health Care: Costs and Quality*. Philadelphia, PA: Pew Charitable Trusts.

Pew Research Center. 2017. *Intermarriage in the U.S. 50 Years after Loving v. Virginia*. Washington, DC: Pew Research Center.

Pont, Jörg, Heino Stöver, and Hans Wolff. 2012. "Dual Loyalty in Prison Health Care." *American Journal of Public Health* 102(3):475–480.

Porter, Nicole D. 2016. *The State of Sentencing 2015: Developments in Policy and Practice*. Washington, DC: Sentencing Project.

Pouget, Enrique R., Trace S. Kershaw, Linda M. Niccolai, Jeannette R. Ickovics, and Kim M. Blankenship. 2010. "Associations of Sex Ratios and Male Incarceration Rates with Multiple Opposite-Sex Partners: Potential Social Determinants of HIV/ STI Transmission." *Public Health Reports* 125(Suppl 4):70–80.

Powers, Ráchael A., Catherine Kaukinen, and Michelle Jeanis. 2017. "An Examination of Recidivism among Inmates Released from a Private Reentry Center and Public Institutions in Colorado." *Prison Journal* 97(5):609–627.

Pratt, Daniel, Mary Piper, Louis Appleby, Roger Webb, and Jenny Shaw. 2006. "Suicide in Recently Release Prisoners: A Population-Based Cohort Study." *Lancet* 368:119–123.

Prins, Seth J. 2014. "Prevalence of Mental Illnesses in U.S. State Prisons: A Systematic Review." *Psychiatric Services* 65(7):862–872.

Prison Policy Initiative. 2021. "Responses to the Covid-19 Pandemic." Accessed March 19, 2021. https://www.prisonpolicy.org/virus/virusresponse.html#resources.

Raimer, Ben G., and John D. Stobo. 2004. "Health Care Delivery in the Texas Prison System: The Role of Academic Medicine." *Journal of the American Medical Association* 292(4):485–489.

Raphael, Steven, and Michael A. Stoll. 2013. *Why Are So Many Americans in Prison?* New York: Russell Sage Foundation.

Regenstein, Marsha, and Sara Rosenbaum. 2014. "What the Affordable Care Act Means for People with Jail Stays." *Health Affairs* 33(3):448–454.

Rehm, Jürgen, T. Bedirhan Üstün, Shekhar Saxena, Christopher B. Nelson, Somnath Chatterji, Frank Ivis, and E. D. Adlaf. 1999. "On the Development and Psychometric Testing of the WHO Screening Instrument to Assess Disablement in the General Population." *International Journal of Methods in Psychiatric Research* 8(2):110–122.

Reinhart, Eric, and Daniel L. Chen. 2020. "Incarceration and Its Disseminations: Covid-19 Pandemic Lessons from Chicago's Cook County Jail." *Health Affairs* 39(8):1412–1418.

Resnick, Heidi S., Ron Acierno, and Dean G. Kilpatrick. 1997. "Health Impact of Interpersonal Violence 2: Medical and Mental Health Outcomes." *Behavioral Medicine* 23(2):65–78.

Rhine, E. E., W. R. Smith, and R. W. Jackson. 1991. *Paroling Authorities: Recent History and Current Practice*. Alexandria, VA: American Correctional Association.

Rhodes, Lorna A. 2000. "Taxonomic Anxieties: Axis I and Axis II in Prison." *Medical Anthropology Quarterly* 14:346–373.

Rich, Josiah D., Michelle McKenzie, Sarah Larney, John B. Wong, Liem Tran, Jennifer Clarke, Amanda Noska, Manasa Reddy, and Nickolas Zaller. 2015. "Methadone Continuation Versus Forced Withdrawal on Incarceration in a Combined Use Prison and Jail: A Randomised, Open-Label Trial." *The Lancet* 386(9991):350–359.

Rifkin, Marjorie. 1994-1995. "Farmer v. Brennan: Spotlight on an Obvious Risk of Rape in a Hidden World." *Columbia Human Rights Law Review* 26:273–308.

Roeder, Oliver, Lauren-Brooke Eisen, and Julia Bowling. 2015. *What Caused the Crime Decline?* New York: Brennan Center for Justice, New York University School of Law.

Rold, William J. 2008. "Thirty Years after Estelle v. Gamble: A Legal Retrospective." *Journal of Correctional Health Care* 14(1):11–20.

Rose, Dina R., and Todd R. Clear. 1998. "Incarceration, Social Capital, and Crime: Implications for Social Disorganization Theory." *Criminology* 36:441–479.

Rosen, David L., Victor J. Schoenbach, and David A. Wohl. 2008. "All-Cause and Cause-Specific Mortality among Men Released from State Prison, 1980–2005." *American Journal of Public Health* 98(12):2278–2284.

Sabol, William J., Heather C. West, and Matthew Cooper. 2009. *Prisoners in 2008.* Washington, DC: US Department of Justice, Office of Justice Programs, Bureau of Justice Statistics.

Sampson, Robert J. 2011. "The Incarceration Ledger." *Criminology & Public Policy* 10(3):819–828.

Sampson, Robert J., and John H. Laub. 1993. *Crime in the Making: Pathways and Turning Points through Life.* Cambridge, MA: Harvard University Press.

Sandler, Lowenstein. January 14, 2020. "Pandemic Is Changing Compassionate Release Calculus." JD Supra. https://www.jdsupra.com/legalnews/pandemic-is-changing-compassionate-5368705/.

Sandoval, Elizabeth, Sandy Smith, James Walter, Sarah-Anne Henning Schuman, Mary Pat Olson, Rebecca Striefler, Stephen Brown, and John Hickner. 2010. "A Comparison of Frequent and Infrequent Visitors to an Urban Emergency Department." *Journal of Emergency Medicine* 38(2):115–121.

Schlanger, Margo. 2003. "Inmate Litigation." *Harvard Law Review* 116:1555–1706.

Schlanger, Margo. 2006. "Civil Rights Injunctions over Time: A Case Study of Jail and Prison Court Orders." *New York University Law Review* 81(2):550–630.

Schlenger, William E., Juesta M. Caddell, Lori Ebert, B. Kathleen Jordan, Kathryn M. Rourke, David Wilson, Lisa Thalji, J. Michael Dennis, John A. Fairbank, and Richard A. Kulka. 2002. "Psychological Reactions to Terrorist Attacks: Findings from the National Study of Americans' Reactions to September 11." *Journal of the American Medical Association* 288(5):581–588.

Schlesinger, Mark, and Tae-ku Lee. 1993. "Is Health Care Different? Popular Support of Federal Health and Social Policies." *Journal of Health Politics, Policy and Law* 18(3):551–628.

Schnittker, Jason, and Valerio Bacak. 2013. "A Mark of Disgrace or a Badge of Honor?: Subjective Status among Former Inmates." *Social Problems* 60(2):234–254.

Schnittker, Jason, Michael Massoglia, and Christopher Uggen. 2012. "Out and Down: Incarceration and Psychiatric Disorders." *Journal of Health and Social Behavior* 53:448–464.

Schnittker, Jason, Christopher Uggen, Sarah K. S. Shannon, and Suzy Maves McElrath. 2015. "The Institutional Effects of Incarceration: Spillovers from Criminal Justice to Health Care." *Milbank Quarterly* 93(3):516–560.

Schwartz, Martin A. 1995. "Supreme Court Defines Deliberate Indifference." *Supreme Court Preview* 1994–1995(159):159–162.

Schwartzapfel, Beth, Katie Park, and Andrew Demillo. 2020. *1-in-5 Prisoners in the U.S. Has Had Covid-19.* New York: Marshall Project.

Scott, Eugene. July 3, 2011. "Temperatures Rise to 145 inside Tent City." *Arizona Republic.*

Sexton, Lori, and Valerie Jenness. 2016. "'We're Like Community': Collective Identity and Collective Efficacy among Transgender Women in Prisons for Men." *Punishment & Society* 18(5):544–577.

Shames, Alison, Jessa Wilcox, and Ram Subramanian. 2015. *Solitary Confinement: Common Misconceptions and Emerging Safe Alternatives.* New York: Vera Institute of Justice.

Shannon, Sarah K. S., Christopher Uggen, Jason Schnittker, Melissa Thompson, Sara Wakefield, and Michael Massoglia. 2017. "The Growth, Scope, and Spatial Distribution of People with Felony Records in the United States, 1948–2010." *Demography* 54(5):1795–1818.

Shlafer, Rebecca J., Rachel R. Hardeman, and Elizabeth A. Carlson. 2019. "Reproductive Justice for Incarcerated Mothers and Advocacy for Their Infants and Young Children." *Infant Mental Health Journal* 40(5):725–741.

Silver, Eric, and Brent Teasdale. 2005. "Mental Disorder and Violence: An Examination of Stressful Life Events and Impaired Social Support." *Social Problems* 52(1):62–78.

Sirois, Catherine. 2020. "The Strain of Sons' Incarceration on Mothers' Health." *Social Science & Medicine* 264:113264.

Sloop, John M. 1996. *The Cultural Prison: Discourse, Prisoners, and Punishment.* Tuscaloosa, AL: University of Alabama.

Somers, Stephen A., Elena Nicolella, Allison Hamblin, Shannon M. McMahon, Christian Heiss, and Bradley W. Brockmann. 2014. "Medicaid Expansion: Considerations for States Regarding Newly Eligible Jail-Involved Individuals." *Health Affairs* 33(3):455–461.

Spaulding, Anne C., Ryan M. Seals, Victoria A. McCallum, Sebastian D. Perez, Amanda K. Brzozowski, and N. Kyle Steenland. 2011. "Prisoner Survival Inside and Outside of the Institution: Implications for Health-Care Planning." *American Journal of Epidemiology* 173(5):479–487.

Spaulding, Anne, Becky Stephenson, Grace Macalino, William Ruby, Jennifer G. Clarke, and Timothy P. Flanigan. 2002. "Human Immunodeficiency Virus in Correctional Facilities: A Review." *Clinical Infectious Diseases* 35(3):305–312.

Springer, Sandra A., Edward Pesanti, John Hodges, Thomas Macura, Gheorghe Doros, and Frederick L. Altice. 2004. "Effectiveness of Antiretroviral Therapy among HIV-Infected Prisoners: Reincarceration and the Lack of Sustained Benefit after Release to the Community." *Clinical Infectious Diseases* 38(12):1754–1760.

Stanko, Elizabeth A., and Kathy Hobdell. 1993. "Assault on Men: Masculinity and Male Victimization." *British Journal of Criminology* 33(3):400–415.

Steadman, Henry J., Allison Redlich, Lisa Callahan, Pamela Clark Robbins, and Roumen Vesselinov. 2011. "Effect of Mental Health Courts on Arrests and Jail Days: A Multisite Study." *Archives of General Psychiatry* 68(2):167–172.

Stewart, Robert, and Christopher Uggen. 2020. "Criminal Records and College Admissions: A Modified Experimental Audit." *Criminology* 58(1):156–188.

Sufrin, Carolyn, Lauren Beal, Jennifer Clarke, Rachel Jones, and William D. Mosher. 2019. "Pregnancy Outcomes in US Prisons, 2016–2017." *American Journal of Public Health* 109(5):799–805.

Swales, Vanessa. February 13, 2021. "Covid-19 Infects Half of Wisconsin Inmates, Five Times the Overall State Rate." *Wisconsin Watch*. https://madison.com/ct/news/local/health-med-fit/covid-19-infects-half-of-wisconsin-inmates-five-times-the-overall-state-rate/article_4301715d-5c9f-5dad-b023-ccbfa93d2534.html.

Swann, Christopher A., and Sylvester Michelle Sheran. 2006. "The Foster Care Crisis: What Caused Caseloads to Grow?" *Demography* 43(2):309–335.

Teplin, Linda A. 1990. "Detecting Disorder: The Treatment of Mental Illness among Jail Detainees." *Journal of Consulting and Clinical Psychology* 58(2):233–236.

Thomas, Charles W. 1977. "Theoretical Perspectives on Prisonization: A Comparison of the Importation and Deprivation Models." *Journal of Criminal Law and Criminology* 68:135–145.

Thomas, James C., Elizabeth A. Torrone, and Christopher R. Browning. 2010. "Neighborhood Factors Affecting Rates of Sexually Transmitted Diseases in Chicago." *Journal of Urban Health* 87(1):102–112.

Tonry, Michael. 2001. "Unthought Thoughts: The Influence of Changing Sensibilities on Penal Policies." *Punishment & Society* 3(1):167–181.

Torrey, E. Fuller, Mary T. Zdanowicz, Aaron D. Kennard, H. Richard Lamb, Donald F. Eslinger, Michael C. Biasotti, and Doris A. Fuller. 2014. *The Treatment of Persons with Mental Illness in Prisons and Jails: A State Survey*. Arlington, VA: Treatment Advocacy Center.

Travis, Jeremy. 2005. *But They All Come Back: Facing the Challenges of Prisoner Reentry*. Washington, DC: Urban Institute Press.

Travis, Jeremy, and Sarah Lawrence. 2002. *Beyond the Prison Gates: The State of Parole in America*. Washington, DC: Urban Institute Press.

Tuite, Helen, Katherine Browne, and Desmond O'Neill. 2006. "Prisoners in General Hospitals: Doctors' Attitudes and Practice." *BMJ* 332(7540):548–549.

Tumin, Dmitry. 2018. "Does Marriage Protect Health? A Birth Cohort Comparison." *Social Science Quarterly* 99(2):626–643.

Turney, Kristin. 2014. "Stress Proliferation across Generations? Examining the Relationship between Parental Incarceration and Childhood Health." *Journal of Health and Social Behavior* 55(3):302–319.

Turney, Kristin, Jason Schnittker, and Christopher Wildeman. 2012. "Those They Leave Behind: Paternal Incarceration and Maternal Instrumental Support." *Journal of Marriage and Family* 74(5):1149–1165.

Uggen, Christopher, and Lindsay Blahnik. 2016. "The Increasing Stickiness of Public Labels." Pp. 222–243 in *Global Perspectives on Desistance*, edited by J. Shapland, S. Farrall, and A. Bottoms. New York: Routledge.

Uggen, Christopher, and Ryan Larson. 2017. "Is the Public Getting Smarter on Crime?" *Contexts* 16(4):76–78.

Uggen, Christopher, Jeff Manza, and Melissa Thompson. 2006. "Citizenship, Democracy, and the Civic Reintegration of Criminal Offenders." *Annals of the American Academy of Political and Social Science* 605(1):281–310.

Uggen, Christopher, and Robert Stewart. 2015. "Piling On: Collateral Consequences and Community Supervision." *Minnesota Law Review* 99:1871–1910.

Uggen, Christopher, Robert Stewart, and Veronica Horowitz. 2018. "Why Not Minnesota? Norway, Justice Reform, and 50-Labs Federalism." *Federal Sentencing Reporter* 31(1):5–13.

Uggen, Christopher, and Melissa Thompson. 2003. "The Socioeconomic Determinants of Ill-Gotten Gains: Within-Person Changes in Drug Use and Illegal Earnings." *American Journal of Sociology* 109(1):146–185.

Uggen, Christopher, Mike Vuolo, Sarah Lageson, Ebony Ruhland, and Hilary K. Whitham. 2014. "The Edge of Stigma: An Experimental Audit of the Effects of Low-Level Criminal Records on Employment." *Criminology* 52(4):627–654.

US Department of Justice. 1996. "Program Statement 6070.05: Birth Control, Pregnancy, Child Placement, and Abortion." Accessed August 20, 2021. https://www.bop.gov/policy/progstat/6070_005.pdf.

US Department of Justice, Civil Rights Division. 2019. *Investigation of Alabama's State Prisons for Men*. Washington, DC: US Department of Justice.

Üstün, T. B., J. L. Ayuso-Mateos, S. Chatterji, C. Mathers, and C. J. L. Murray. 2004. "Global Burden of Depressive Disorders in the Year 2000." *British Journal of Psychiatry* 184(5):386–392.

Van Handel, Michelle, John F. Beltrami, Robin J. MacGowan, Craig B. Borkowf, and Andrew D. Margolis. 2012. "Newly Identified HIV Infections in Correctional Facilities, United States, 2007." *American Journal of Public Health* 102(S2):S201–S204.

VanderWeele, Tyler J. 2020. "Challenges Estimating Total Lives Lost in Covid-19 Decisions: Consideration of Mortality Related to Unemployment, Social Isolation, and Depression." *JAMA* 324(5):445–446.

Vera Institute of Justice. 2010. *The Continuing Fiscal Crisis in Corrections: Setting a New Course*. New York: Vera Institute of Justice.

Vuolo, Mike, Sarah Lageson, and Christopher Uggen. 2017. "Criminal Record Questions in the Era of 'Ban the Box.'" *Criminology & Public Policy* 16(1):139–165.

Wakefield, Sarah, and Christopher Wildeman. 2013. *Children of the Prison Boom: Mass Incarceration and the Future of American Inequality*. New York: Oxford University Press.

Wakeman, Sarah, Margaret McKinney, and Josiah Rich. 2009. "Filling the Gap: The Importance of Medicaid Continuity for Former Inmates." *Journal of General Internal Medicine* 24(7):860–862.

Wang, Emily A., Clemens S. Hong, Shira Shavit, Ronald Sanders, Eric Kessell, and Margot B. Kushel. 2012. "Engaging Individuals Recently Released from Prison into Primary Care: A Randomized Trial." *American Journal of Public Health* 102(9):e22–e29.

Wang, Emily A., Mary C. White, Ross Jamison, Joe Goldenson, Milton Estes, and Jacqueline P. Tulsky. 2008. "Discharge Planning and Continuity of Health Care: Findings from the San Francisco County Jail." *American Journal of Public Health* 98(12):2182–2184.

Warr, Mark. 1995. "Public Opinion on Crime and Punishment." *Public Opinion Quarterly* 59:296–310.

Warren, Jenifer, Adam Gelb, Jake Horowitz, and Jessica Riordan. 2008. *One in 100: Behind Bars in America 2008*. Washington, DC: Pew Center on the States, Pew Charitable Trusts.

Waters, Robin. December 11, 2020. "Federal Compassionate Release in the Era of Covid-19: Practice Tips." American Bar Association. https://www.americanbar.org/groups/litigation/committees/criminal/articles/2020/winter2021-federal-compassionate-release-in-the-era-of-covid-19-practice-tips/.

Weaver, Vesla M., and Amanda Geller. 2019. "De-Policing America's Youth: Disrupting Criminal Justice Policy Feedbacks That Distort Power and Derail Prospects." *Annals of the American Academy of Political and Social Science* 685(1):190–226.

Weiss, Dan. 2015. "Privatization and Its Discontents: The Troubling Record of Privatized Prison Health Care Casenotes and Comments." *University of Colorado Law Review* 86(2):725–788.

Western, Bruce. 2006. *Punishment and Inequality in America*. New York: Russell Sage Foundation.

Western, Bruce. 2018. *Homeward: Life in the Year after Prison*: New York: Russell Sage Foundation.

Western, Bruce, Anthony A. Braga, Jaclyn Davis, and Catherine Sirois. 2015. "Stress and Hardship after Prison." *American Journal of Sociology* 120(5):1512–1547.

Wiehe, Sarah E., Marc B. Rosenman, Matthew C. Aalsma, Michael L. Scanlon, and J. Dennis Fortenberry. 2015. "Epidemiology of Sexually Transmitted Infections among Offenders Following Arrest or Incarceration." *American Journal of Public Health* 105(12):e26–e32.

Wildeman, Christopher, and Christopher Muller. 2012. "Mass Imprisonment and Inequality in Health and Family Life." *Annual Review of Law and Social Science* 8(1):11–30.

Wildeman, Christopher, Jason Schnittker, and Kristin Turney. 2012. "Despair by Association? The Mental Health of Mothers with Children by Recently Incarcerated Fathers." *American Sociological Review* 77(2):216–243.

Williams, Brie A., Rebecca L. Sudore, Robert Greifinger, and R. Sean Morrison. 2011. "Balancing Punishment and Compassion for Seriously Ill Prisoners." *Annals of Internal Medicine* 155(2):122–126.

Wilper, Andrew P., Steffie Woolhandler, J. Wesley Boyd, Karen E. Lasser, Danny McCormick, David H. Bor, and David U. Himmelstein. 2009. "The Health and Health Care of US Prisoners: Results of a Nationwide Survey." *American Journal of Public Health* 99(4):666–672.

Winkelman, Tyler N. A., Virginia W. Chang, and Ingrid A. Binswanger. 2018. "Health, Polysubstance Use, and Criminal Justice Involvement among Adults with Varying Levels of Opioid Use." *JAMA Network Open* 1(3):e180558–e180558.

Wohl, David Alain, Carol Golin, David L. Rosen, Jeanine M. May, and Becky L. White. 2013. "Detection of Undiagnosed HIV among State Prison Entrants." *JAMA* 310(20):2198–2199.

Wool, Jon. 2007. "Litigating for Better Medical Care." Pp. 25–41 in *Public Health behind Bars: From Prisons to Communities*, edited by R. B. Greifinger. Dobbs Ferry, NY: Springer Science.

Zamble, Edward. 1992. "Behavior and Adaptation in Long-Term Prison Inmates: Descriptive Longitudinal Results." *Criminal Justice and Behavior* 19:409–425.

Zandbergen, Paul A., and Timothy C. Hart. 2006. "Reducing Housing Options for Convicted Sex Offenders: Investigating the Impact of Residency Restriction Laws Using GIs." *Justice Research and Policy* 8(2):1–24.

Zeng, Zhen. 2020. "Jail Inmates in 2018." Washington, DC: [NCJ 253044] US Department of Justice, Bureau of Justice Statistics.

Index

For the benefit of digital users, indexed terms that span two pages (e.g., 52–53) may, on occasion, appear on only one of those pages.

Note: Tables and figures are indicated by *t* and *f* following the page number

190 Index

Newman v. Alabama (US Court of Appeals, Fifth Circuit), 13–14, 15
New Mexico, 145–46
New York (state)
  compassionate release in, 46–47
  homelessness after release in, 73
  mortality and former prisoners in, 88
New York City jails, 145–46
  dual-loyalty in, mental health and, 53
  HIV in entrants, 37–38
  self-harm in, 49–50
normality, principle of, 154
North Carolina, 37–38
Norway, 154

Obama administration, 127–28
opioid dependence, 76, 88, 138–39
overcrowding, 62–63, 111, 128, 132–33
oversight, health care, 56–57

pains of imprisonment, 60–61
parity, for mental and physical health, 143
parole, 5–6, 94, 148–49, 158
  mental health and, 156–57
  realignment of, with law enforcement, 71–73
  violations of, 72–73
patients, prisoners as, 23
Patterson, Evelyn, 43–44
payment, for health care provision, 31
physicians, criminal justice system and, 122–23
PLRA. *See* Prison Litigation Reform Act
police violence, racialized, 106
policy challenges, of incarceration and health, 125–33
population health, incarceration and, 151
postrelease. *See* release
pregnant women, 24, 103
prevalence, of infectious diseases, 40, 41, 80–81
prevention, control, of infectious diseases, 38–39, 139, 152
prisonization, 62
Prison Litigation Reform Act (PLRA), 25–28
prisons. *See specific topics*
private prisons, 129
  accountability of, 130–31
  costs, reducing, and, 129
  health care in, 131–32
  public prisons compared with, 129, 132–33
  states and, 129–30
probation, 72–73, 158

Procunier v. Martinez (US Supreme Court), 14–15
protective custody, 1
provision, of medical care, 29–33
psychiatric disorders. *See* mental health
psychiatric hospitals, decline of, 32–33
public opinion, on criminals, 82–83, 155–56
public prisons, private compared with, 129, 132–33
punishment, 3, 157–58
  concision of, 156–57
  health care and, 12, 13–22, 153–54
  prison administration and, 13
punishment, cruel and unusual. *See* cruel and unusual punishment
punishment, digital, 71, 81–82

race, 106, 113, 151. *See also* African Americans
  COVID-19 and, 110–11
  in criminal justice system, disparities of, 7–8
  hospital care and, 119
  incarceration, reducing, and, 126
  incarceration rates and, 7–8
  marriage, sexual markets, and, 97–99
  mortality, after release, and, 88–89
  mortality and, 1–2, 43–45
  prisoners, portrayal of, and, 82–83
  residential mobility and, 73
rape. *See* sexual violence
recessions, 127–28
recidivism, 132–33
  mental health and, 57–58, 128, 154
  systems integration and, 148
re-entry, 3–4, 56, 72–73
rehabilitation, 3–4, 82–83
reintegration, 154
  challenges of, 73–81, 151
  health protections and successful, 92–95
  turning point in, 77–78
release, 68–69, 71, 94–95. *See also* parole; probation
  benefits, exclusion from, after, 77–78
  disability after, 92–94, 93t
  discrimination after, 78–79, 81, 85–86
  educational attainment after, 79
  employment after, 77–79, 81, 85–86
  health after, 80–81, 86–91, 89t, 92–95
  health care after, 74–76
  health insurance after, 74–75, 116–18
  home confinement, 41–42